Western Sexuality

Practice and Precept in Past and Present Times

Edited by
Philippe Ariès and André Béjin

Translated by
Anthony Forster

BARNES
&NOBLE
BOOKS
NEW YORK

English translation © Basil Blackwell Ltd 1985

First published as *Sexualités Occidentales* © Editions du Seuil/Communications 1982

This edition published by Barnes & Noble Books, Inc.
by arrangement with Blackwell Publishers

1997 Barnes & Noble Books

Printed and bound in the United States of America

ISBN 0-7607-0346-9

97 98 99 00 01 M 9 8 7 6 5 4 3 2 1

QF

Contents

Foreword

This book, *Western Sexuality*, arose from a seminar held by
Philippe Ariès at the headquarters of social science in France,
L'Ecole des Hautes Etudes en Sciences Sociales, in 1979/80.
It consists essentially of some of the papers read to that seminar,
and it is a tribute to the high interest and previous academic
neglect of the subject that the chapters read so well. That it should
also have a coherence as a whole is a tribute to Ariès himself,
as leader of the seminar. For he was certainly one of the most
remarkable men ever to have presided over such an occasion in
that black-framed, glass building on the Boulevard Raspail, crowded
as it always is with great talents from every quarter of France and
from many parts of the world.

When these meetings took place Ariès was in the final years of
his life: he was to die within less than three years. The series
continued for some time after these contributions were delivered,
and was still running in May 1982, when I myself attended on
two occasions. Eager students crowded the room and the corridor
outside it, thronging Philippe Ariès, whose crop of white hair
marked him out. I thought his face looked a little wizened, but
when he talked what he said was as sharp as ever — that affectionate,
tolerant, gifted, courteous, ever-smiling, often laughing, charis-
matic man, who never seemed sad or disappointed. Enough to
give the reader some idea of his flair and his insight, his extraordinary intellectual stance, comes out in this last of his books —
at least the last which he himself saw through the press. It would
not surprise me if there were posthumous works yet to come
among his papers. He was that sort of man.

I had been warned before I visited the seminar that Ariès was not quite so successful as a teacher as had been expected from his high standing amongst French intellectuals before his appointment to L'Ecole. This seemed to be quite untrue, from my experience of this class. But it would not in itself have been surprising, since he must have been well into his sixties before he joined the university as a teacher. He had spent his whole professional life up to that time as an expert, in due course a world expert, on the botany of fruit trees, and a historian only in his spare time.

Un historien de dimanche was the title he gave to his own book about himself. The formal reason for his having come into the academic theatre only for the last scene or two of the final act was that he had failed to get through the required exams at the right level at the outset — faint echos here of the career of A.E. Housman in England. But he once assured me that he had never wanted to be in the university system of his country: 'J'ai refusé l'université', he declared.

Yet by the late 1970s he had written a series of books which had become part of the curriculum of many teaching institutions, as well as popular with the reading public. One of them — translated into English as *Centuries of Childhood* — had spread his reputation from his native country all over the world, especially the Anglo-Saxon world. Written in the 1950s and published originally in 1960, this book is still influential, still being read, debated, refuted and its doctrines modified and developed. Its subject matter, entirely novel when it appeared, is still a revelation to anyone who takes it up by chance.

Ariès was a marvellous man and a great loss, even though he was of a respectable age when he died. This book which he and André Béjin have produced should establish itself inside and outside the university world. Enormous as is the literature which has been unleashed by what people delight to call the sexual revolution, few books are so detached, so soberly informative, so alive with the intellectual interest and importance of the western forms and traditions of sexuality. That it should have been in France that this important topic first developed is perhaps what one might expect, since France has been the place of origin of so much that is new in the social sciences, especially when applied to the past.

It is illustrative also of the high standing and great success of such subjects in that country that persons of worldwide standing, other than Ariès himself, talked to the seminar and appear here as authors. The name of Michel Foucault speaks for itself. Paul Veyne has the very highest standing as an authority on the manners of the Ancient World, and Jean Louis Flandrin is the universally acknowledged master of the interpretation of the teaching of the Catholic church of medieval times and after in the matter of sexual life.

The reader will find these short studies neither prurient nor sensational, though some of the practices and beliefs they describe are truly extraordinary. What he or she will discover in that world hidden until very recently under the clinging, stifling folds of the mantle of respectability is a variety which can only fascinate. One of the most valuable lessons we are taught is that Christian doctrine, never uniform in any case, failed almost entirely to control western sexual expression. To read back from clerical commands, adjuration and theoretical reflection to what actually went on between lover and lover, man and wife in the so-called Christian centuries is to get nowhere, as Jean-Louis Flandrin has always insisted.

It is typical of contemporary French social science that a prominent Anglo-Saxon expert, Robin Fox, should begin the book with an astonishingly informative, perceptive piece on sexual evolution from the sociobiological point of view. The discussion of biology and of what might be called regular or routine sexual behaviour ends at that point. Still, this is not a book which informs us about the extent of such practices as homosexuality or bestiality, nor does it attempt to calculate the times at which one or other grew more widespread, or more restricted, and where, and why. It records attitudinal materials only, with something to intrigue the reader on nearly every page. Béjin's final chapters on the psychoanalysts and the sexologists are typical of the approach. Heavily sententious, or slightly or wholly leering treatments of these themes are very common. Here you will find clear analysis, just judgements and a remarkable sense of proportion.

Sexual attitudes and sexual life affect large numbers of fields of enquiry from biology and medicine to demography, from literary and religious life to education, not to speak of psychology and psychiatry. It is scarcely to be doubted that this first work to be published in our new series, Family, Sexuality and Social Relations in Past Times, will be found as valuable in its English version as it has already proved itself to be in its French original.

Peter Laslett

1

The conditions of sexual evolution

Robin Fox

There are various levels of approach to the evolution of sexual behaviour, from that of all sexually reproducing organisms (including plants) to that of a particular species or sub-species. The problems of the latter cannot ignore the more general problems of sexual reproduction, in particular the problem of why there should be sexual reproduction at all. Theoretically, in any competitive situation, sexually reproducing organisms should lose in competition with asexual. Assuming the original situation to be asexual, it remains a constant theoretical problem how sexual reproduction can have arisen, since any favourable mutation in an asexually reproducing organism can be immediately and rapidly replicated, while its sexual competitor must dilute the next-generation effect through breeding. Even inbreeding will not help for sexual competitors, since it is bound to be slower than in the asexual, and also will produce lethal homozygotes.

The only conclusion is that the one advantage of sexual reproduction — increased genetic variation — must have been of such overwhelming advantage in some circumstances that it had a slight competitive edge and became the dominant partner in an evolutionarily stable strategy. This still raises theoretical difficulties, but it can be seen that recombination might just win out over simple mutation and mitosis under marginal conditions. A 'very rapidly changing environment' is often invoked (although this too is vague), as is sibling conflict in offspring.

However started, sexual reproduction, at whatever level, sets certain conditions. Some are minimal. The two sexes must have sufficient contact to exchange genetic material — this is perhaps the only basic requirement. The more complicated this exchange becomes, the more complicated the relations between the sexes. Hermaphroditic species solve the problem by having both sexes in the same organism. In some primitive organisms there is no definite sex distinction. The faster-moving organism of any two by definition becomes 'male' because its slightly greater speed implants material in the slower one. But it is relative. In higher organisms this becomes fixed. But the basics are not lost: sperm is faster than ovum.

Exchange not only has to take place, but it then becomes the responsibility of one 'sex' to undertake gestation. After that, one or both or neither undertake nurturance depending on the evolutionary path the organism has taken. Usually the 'female' undertakes gestation, and either the female alone, the female in consort with other females, the female and the inseminating male, or groups of males and females — and other combinations — undertake a variety of forms of gestation and nurturance. There is no need here to elaborate the many forms this can take throughout sexually reproducing species — this would simply stress their variety.

When we come to the mammals, we also find much variety, but this is constricted by the very characteristics of mammalian adaptation: warm blood, live birth, suckled young, internal gestation etc. A great deal that can be said about human sexuality can be disposed of as the sexual behaviour to be expected of a large-bodied, large-brained, slow-breeding, omnivorous mammal, with moderate sexual dimorphism and a lack of seasonal breeding. This does not mean that only one pattern of sexual behaviour is to be expected: it simply sets the limits within which variation will occur. We can best understand this variation by asking what the variables are, and this is difficult since it is all too easy to beg the question by the way it is posed. Rather than take cultural categories of dubious universality like 'nuclear family' and 'marriage', it is better to take as a starting point an objective unit that is, by definition, universal in the mammals and thus not contaminated by cultural categories. The obvious unit is the mother and her dependent offspring.

It is basic to the definition of a mammal that the young are born live and suckled by the mother. What varies is (a) the amount of investment the mother herself puts into the offspring beyond the necessary minimum, and (b) the degree and nature of the attachment of a male or males to this basic unit (and the relations of the units to each other).

One interesting result of the human development of culture is that we reproduce within our own species almost all the variation found across the mammalian orders — but we shall return to that. For the moment let us consider some mammalian extremes by way of illustration. The hamster lives in solitary burrows, and the contact of males and females is limited to a brief encounter during a brief mating season when a male enters a female's burrow and copulates. The female has a short gestation period; suckles the young for a few weeks, after which they disperse and make their own burrows. This is about the lower limit of mating organization in mammals. Consider then certain ungulates such as gazelles, zebra, deer, etc. They differ considerably in their herd organization, but basically the permanent herd is one of females and young. The males are either solitary for most of the year or rove in all-male bands. During the breeding season (autumn) the males compete, and the winners mate with the herds of females, then depart. The females give birth (in the spring) to precocial young who are soon able to follow and suckle. After one year the males disperse. Take then a band of hunting dogs, or hyenas. The males and females are together all year round whether or not there is a breeding season. There is a complex hierarchy of mating. The females give birth to slow-maturing young and both males and females care for the offspring in various ways, including the regurgitation of food from kills, etc.

Thus we move from virtually no male-female contact save for the necessary ninety seconds, through seasonal contact, to permanent year-round contact. We also move from absolutely minimal parental care, through care from the mother and the herd females, to care by all the males and females of a complexly organized pack. There are many variations on these themes including monogamous territorial pair-bonding (gibbons, for example) and large male-female troops (howler monkeys) — but the variables we are looking at are what are important. In each case, the crucial variables we have mentioned earlier are affected by circumstances of adaptation to involve the males more or less in the affairs of the females and young. Basically, the males are dispensable. If the female has no need of the male over and above his procreative function — then he is usually dispensed with. The more complex the life of the animal, however, the more likely it is that the male will serve some other function, largely that of defence, but in some carnivores also that of providing meat for the relatively slow-developing young, and even of 'teaching' them (if only through imitation) the arts of hunting. The females will also differ in the degree to which they need each other. Female hamsters are solitary, female gibbons live only with their mates, ungulate females congregate in herds, and so on.

One thing is relatively certain: when females congregate to their mutual advantage, they are likely to be related. The same *may* be true of males, but is less likely. To understand this, and consequently to understand the human variant which we call 'systems of kinship and marriage', it is necessary to look at the process Darwin christened 'sexual selection', and its subsidiary process which has recently found a name as 'kin selection'.

Basically, sexual selection is a variant of natural selection but one where the struggle is not so much against what Darwin called 'the hostile forces of nature', but is the struggle of the sexes for reproductive advantage. This involves the *competition* between animals of one sex — usually the males — for mates from the other, and the *choice* by the other sex — usually the females — of mates from the successful competitors.

We can see this arising from the adaptational exigencies discussed earlier: the females need the males for at least insemination, but also for protection and food perhaps, and therefore they select among them the most able as demonstrated by success in competition. This competition can take many forms, and Darwin was chiefly interested in it as a process which explained extraordinary anatomical developments such as the antlers of the stag, or the huge claw of the fiddler crab. But of course the developments can be purely behavioural and involve 'ritualized' fighting displays for example. What is demanded of the males will differ according to the species. In the ungulates and sea mammals for example, where the male-female association is purely seasonal and for breeding, displays of superior strength are sufficient. Where the males and females are permanently together, other qualities may be more important — the ability to rise in the male hierarchy, for example, which may involve far more than just strength.

The point about sexual selection however is that *whatever* criterion is used (strength, speed, territory, display, etc.) the result is that only a minority of the males get to breed, while all the females usually succeed in breeding at least once. The reason why it should be this way is easy to see: a male can breed successfully with a large number of females, while a female, once pregnant, is committed to the foetus for anything up to a year, and in many cases well beyond that in suckling and rearing the infant. The 'strategies' of the two sexes therefore are bound to differ markedly. It is to the male's reproductive advantage to mate with as many females as possible, while the female must try — since she has only one chance a year — to obtain the 'best' genes for herself. The point about 'kin selection' in this context is that she is often better off doing this in collaboration with related females — and we must explore why. But first we should note that the above 'strategies' will be severely restricted once it is in the male's reproductive interest to invest in his offspring. Where there is no such advantage — as with most ungulates and sea mammals — then the out-and-out competition we have discussed seems to prevail. Where the males must invest in their offspring to ensure their survival, then competition still exists but becomes more subtle and complicated, and the male must pay more attention to fewer females. This becomes more important with the primates, the social carnivores, and in particular with man. It results, for example, in much less extreme sexual dimorphism and a lack of those highly specialized anatomical features that first led Darwin to enquire into this mode of selection.

But we must return to the question of relatedness or kinship since this concerns genes and this is where selection is in fact at work. And here, if I speak of the 'strategies' of the genes, or of the animals, it should be needless to point out that conscious strategies are not implied. (Otherwise well-educated people, however, still seem to miss this point.) It is just sometimes easier to speak metaphorically of 'intentions' rather than to spell out the whole argument in correct 'selection' language. Strictly speaking, the only goal of the genes is to produce replicas of themselves. Organisms are their agents. However, identical genes are not confined to one organism, but are shared by related organisms in declining proportion as the degree of relatedness becomes more distant. There is always, therefore, a group of closely-related organisms sharing a large number of identical gene-replicas: a kind of small gene-pool. Parents and children are the closest in relatedness, together with groups of siblings. Now the 'groups of females' that we have been discussing above are almost always mother-daughter extended families; groups of female kin, closely related. If we view these, then, as a small pool of identical genes seeking to replicate themselves, we can see how, under certain evolutionary circumstances, they will do better if they act in concert than alone, and better still if they can choose 'superior' male genes to combine with their own to produce a new generation.

In earlier studies of sexual selection, the emphasis was heavily on the male competition and indeed selection does seem to work most spectacularly here. But it has more recently been seen that *female choice* may well be the ultimate determinant of the route selection will take. The males, as it were, exhaust themselves on competition, then the female groups pick out the winners as studs. Once it is realized that there can thus be considerable difference in reproductive success between the different female groups, the full dynamics of the system can be understood.

The females' strategy has to be to pick the 'best' male, whatever the criteria. If a group of females can become inseminated by superior male genes, not only do their female offspring get the immediate advantages, but the chance of their 'sons' inseminating many groups of females itself increases. Thus the genes of the original female kin-group will spread in the total population more successfully than those of rival groups. If we paraphrase Samuel Butler's famous statement (that a chicken is the egg's way of making another egg) and say that a male is the females' way of making more females (or that a male is the female kin-group's way of making another female kin-group) then we are getting close to the heart of the sexual selection process. But we have to see it, ultimately, as the strategy of the genes to produce replicas of themselves.

We cannot here go into all the conditions that produce such 'kin-coalition' behaviour and its consequent interesting mode of sexual selection — indeed they are not all known, although the most plausible candidate is advantages in foraging. It is enough that they *are* produced, and very important to us because the primates, our own order, show strong tendencies in this direction in many species including our own. The primates, however, unlike the ungulates we have been discussing, live in groups where there is year-round contact between males and females. This factor — shared for example by the social carnivores — exercises a profound influence. It does not stop the processes of either sexual selection or kin selection, but modifies them, and this modification is the first step on the road to human sexual behaviour.

It is as if the ungulate females, instead of meeting briefly with the successful males in the mating season, had decided to incorporate them permanently into the group, and what is more, to amalgamate several female kin-groups into a larger group. The reasons why this occurs in some species (like the primates) are variable, with foraging success, the need for the defence of the females, and, with the carnivores, the need for provisioning the relatively slow-maturing young by the males, as leading contenders. The higher primates are vegetarian (baboons and chimpanzees hunt only sporadically) and do *not* provision their young who must find their own food once weaned. Protection therefore seems the most likely reason. Now the number and combination of males incorporated, and the resulting modes of social organization are very varied across species, and we can only here give a highly summary sketch of some very general features. At one extreme, there will only be one male incorporated into one group of females: at the other there will be many males incorporated into an equally large number of female families. Monogamous pairs — as with the gibbon — can be seen as a limiting case where, for ecological reasons, a territory will only support one female and one male. With the orang-utan, females establish ranges, and males attempt to monopolize several of these females without staying permanently with any one. With chimpanzees, groups of males on the one hand, and groups of female families on the other, form a forest 'band', thus bringing the males more closely into the group — but still as a separate 'block' of the social system. With common baboons and macaques, female families, hierarchically arranged, are arrayed against a hierarchy of individual males. With hamadryas baboons and geladas, herds are composed of 'harems' each under the control of one male. Gorillas live in bands with one dominant male, some younger males and females with young.

The 'law of the dispensable male' operates here. Under extreme conditions, for example, macaque groups 'shed' males until there is only one, while under lush conditions there may be a large number. Those species characterized by 'one-male groups' or harems are most like the ungulates: males compete in various ways and only some get harems. In the 'multi-male groups' it is different: the competition between the males is there, but since they stay together, they must settle it by arranging themselves in a hierarchy. Similarly the female families are hierarchically organized, with the higher-ranking families tending to mate more frequently with high-ranked males. The 'sons' of these families in turn, are more likely than others to become high-ranking and thus perpetuate the process. Thus we can see how the ungulate 'seasonal' pattern has been, as it were, 'collapsed' here into a hierarchically organized year-round collaboration of males and female families.

The major modification this produces in the sexual selection process is in the criteria for 'best genes' in the male. The one-male group species are most like the ungulates, with, for example, greater sexual dimorphism and special anatomical features for the male (the mane and 'cape' of the hamadryas for example). The multi-male species show less sexual dimorphism and specialization, and capacities for group-living and organization are obviously being selected for rather than mere strength or endurance or display. High-ranking female groups, for example, will often not tolerate males who are too aggressive and competitive, and these leave the group and become solitaries.

Is there, however, a basic primate pattern in this wide range of breeding/social systems? It is important to establish if there is, since it would be the pattern that characterized our own ancestors before the 'transition to humanity' took place: it would be the raw material of hominid society: the breeding system that became the 'social system'. I think there is a pan-primate pattern in the group-living primates which involves the dynamics of relationship, or what we have called 'strategies', that exist between the three major 'blocks' or interest groups of the system: (a) the established males, (b) the females and young, and (c) the peripheral or aspirant males. The 'established' males are those who have access to the breeding females by virtue of having obtained harems, moved up in the hierarchy, maintained territories — or whatever is demanded. Against them are arranged the — usually younger — males who aspire to breeding status. The females are between these two groups 'supplying' young males to the peripheral groups, and seeking the 'best genes' from the mature males. The possible combinations are large, but the basic pattern is there. It is not all that different from the basic pattern of the other group-living mammals, with the exception that the males are permanently incorporated, and we have seen that this itself strongly influences the criteria for 'best male'.

If this then is the basic pattern of the vegetarian primate, we have next to ask ourselves what the crucial change was that produced the hominid line and finally ourselves. Our ancestors would have been vegetarian primates following some variant of the pattern — most likely, given the close genetic relationship with the chimpanzee and the similarity of ecological adaptation to the common baboon/macaque, some version of the 'multi-male group with female kin-group' system. What is incontestable now in view of the East African evidence is that somewhere between two and three million years ago this ancestor took up hunting and scavenging on a large scale. It was already bipedal, but the change from sporadic meat eating to a diet incorporating more than 50 per cent meat meant a radical change in the relations between the sexes and between the old and the young males. It is these changes that *created* man as we know him, for by the advent of *Homo erectus* the irreversible change had taken place — as measured by stature and brain size. And this is the crucial fact: the unprecedented rapidity of the evolution of the hominid brain (a threefold increase inside two million years) occurred exactly during the period when the scale of hunting increased — and increased in proportion. That is, exactly as the size and scale of prey increased, so did the size and complexity of the brain.

The causal factors are not too difficult to see here, but the consequences for the internal process of sexual selection are harder to spell out. Let us take it from the male point of view. In the 'winner-take-all' type of competition sheer strength is what counts; in the primate 'hierarchical' competition it is more control and timing; in the hunting situation it is obviously the ability to provide meat — to provision the females and children. But it is much more complex than this: strength, control and hunting ability cumulate in importance, but many other qualities must accrue to a successful dominant male in a co-operative hunting society. Leadership, organizational ability, and even such burgeoning talents as eloquence, shamanistic skills, etc. eventually come to characterize 'dominance' and hence breeding advantage. All this is of particular importance in hominid evolution since the evolving hominids did not have millions of years of carnivorous experience in their genes as do the social carnivores. They could not, for example, use their natural weapons in hunting but had to invent weapons; they could not regurgitate food for the young but had to carry it back to the home base — bipedalism and the freeing of the hands are of great importance here. But the major point for the males is that they had to develop intelligent solutions to the hunting challenge in all its facets; there was therefore a premium on intelligence over and above the other skills.

From the female point of view, the essential change lay in the division of labour forced on them by the new hunting way of life. Essentially, hominid females were the producers of vegetable food — for the omnivorous diet — for meat they depended on the males. Equally, the males depended on the females for two essential services that did not exist in the primate 'baseline' situation: gathering and preparation of vegetable food, and care and provision for the more slowly maturing young. (The young were maturing more slowly because of progressive neoteny that was a consequence of bipedalism, foetal birth, and the requirements of the larger brain to grow outside the mother's body.)

The requirement that the males 'invest' more heavily in their young is underlined here — as opposed to the primate situation where the weaned young fend for themselves. The strategy of the foraging female kin-groups therefore must have been not only to acquire the 'best genes' (which now meant 'best hunters'), but to hold on to the males in order to continue having the infants provisioned with the now necessary meat.

Overall what happened to the hominid breeding/social system in the period between two and a half and one million years ago, was that the relations between the three 'blocks' of the system were revolutionized, although building on the old base. We *must* understand that a new creature was being forged here in the crucible of natural and sexual selection: a hunting ape-man. And in evolutionary terms it was a rapid change. The tensions therefore between the basic pattern and the new demands made upon it by the new creature are at the heart of the current human condition. The three blocks still had to accommodate each other and make demands on each other, but this was under ever changing conditions. The major change, as we have seen, was in the origin of the division of labour between the sexes, which revolutionized not only the relations between the two sexes, but also the relations within the sexual groups.

The burden of this clearly fell — as is always the case in sexual selection — on the young or peripheral males. The conditions whereby they could rise in the hierarchy and become effective breeders were constantly made more complex. In turn, the older, established males found themselves faced by well-armed and capable youngsters. Thus the struggle within the male sex between established and aspirant males must have been intensified at the same time as the females were making demands for permanent provisioning from the males.

The revolutionary response to this, judging from the end product — that is, the social/breeding system of *Homo sapiens* — was the dual invention of initiation and alliance. There was no way, once the status of *Homo* was achieved, that the free-for-all competition of the males could continue. On the other hand, the rapidity of brain evolution could not have occurred without a highly assortative mating system in which only selected male genes were transferred to successive generations. The consequence was the evolution of a system geared to the control of the young males' access to the breeding system and the control of the allocation of mates by the older males.

The role of systems of initiation is easy to see in this. They are direct systems of constraint and selection, and have the psychological function of 'identification with the aggressor' (Freud) ensuring that the young males will identify with the older males. Since access to the breeding system is usually delayed until after initiation — and even service as a warrior — this ensures a 'pool' of young females for the old polygynists. The young males will of course try to circumvent this with illicit sexual liaisons. The higher the age of marriage of males is driven, and the younger the age at which females are betrothed, the greater the chances of polygyny flourishing. The most widespread marriage pattern in human society is 'the polygyny of the powerful' (75 per cent of human societies), and even in those either officially or 'ecologically' monogamous, the powerful usually enjoy extended sexual access to young females or at least a monopoly of them for marriage purposes.

What is not so easily seen is that human kinship systems — again building on the already existing kin-selection tendencies — are equally a response to the control of younger males by the older and/or more powerful males. (Originally this would have been a pure gerontocracy. With the advent of rank and class society, it was power rather than *simply* age that counted, although within classes the young-old clash continued.) It was obviously impossible for the old 'winner-take-all' system of mating to endure under the changed conditions of sexual division of labour and co-operative hunting. Freud's vision of a parricidal (and possibly fratricidal) primal horde is probably near the truth. Mitigation already existed in the selective influence of the female kin-groups, and this must have been further modified by the need of the males to form alliances both within and across bands, and of the females to enjoy some security of tenure with selected males. Among the primates both alliance, in the sense of permanent mating, and kinship, in the sense of groups based on common descent, existed — but not in the same system. The human innovation was to combine these in one system, by using the definition of relatedness to define the possibilities of alliance. (It was *not* the incest taboo. Humans, like most sexually reproducing species, avoid an excess of close inbreeding anyway. The taboo is simply confirmation of this, with certain uniquely human ingredients.)

Thus systems of 'kinship and marriage' arose to re-define the relationships and strategies between the three blocks. The major innovation was that kinship not only *linked* the members of the three blocks together, but it was used to define the mode of *allocation* of spouses: that is, effectively, the distribution of young females among the males. It is then exogamy — rightly seen by Lévi-Strauss as a positive system of exchange — that is the truly human innovation. What is not usually perceived is that kinship systems do not simply ensure the exchange of spouses, but that they are 'rigged' to ensure that the choice of mates open to the younger generation of males is made dependent on choices made by the older generation, thus controlling their access to the mating system through the rules themselves. The onus of control is therefore thrown on to the collectivity, and collective representations assume their role as 'constraints' on the behaviour of the young. Where the kinship system does not do this through its rules, the older (or more powerful) males have to intervene directly in the marriage choices and opportunities of the young. I have stressed the males, but of course the co-operative female kin-groups are not silent in this matter of with whom their members mate, and often exercise considerable influence — as the basic pattern would predict — although this is highly variable. Very rarely do the interests of these groups coincide, and the ensuing struggle is what lies behind the dynamics and high degree of variability of human mating and social systems. Many other factors — of ecology, economics, politics, class, power, ideology and technology (e.g. the pill) — intervene to present new challenges to the basic pattern. But as long as assortative mating must take place to ensure the production of future generations, the basic pattern must be respected and the new conditions have to come to terms with it. The much vaunted 'nuclear family', for example, is simply one possible kind of accommodation that occurs, predictably, in certain societies. It is certainly not the basic pattern itself, as has often been stated by social scientists.

In this evolutionary perspective, therefore, we are able to take a new look at historical developments in the relations between the sexes, and one of the most important lessons is that we must view this always as a triangular relationship: established males; females and young; aspirant males. Young females currently are exercising more free choice than ever before; the old, as a result of the pill, have lost considerable control. It will be interesting to see to what extent the basic pattern can reassert itself. I believe it shows signs of doing so and that many things — such as teenage pregnancy rates, growing divorce rates, female solidarity movements, etc. — are probable signs of a reassertion of the pattern rather than either pathologies or results of raised consciousness. They are only one or other of these if one takes the 'nuclear family' as a starting point, which it is not, but rather one possible outcome.

It will be interesting for historians and anthropologists to look again at their data which I believe can be reconciled in this framework. The work, for example, of Lévi-Strauss and Ariès makes good sense within this framework of analysis; both are dealing with aspects of the basic pattern. This is not to say that the basic scheme can never be sundered — but it is the cause of our present behaviour; it is what produced us and, as Freud saw, what we are fated to reproduce. Our brains, physiology, and behaviour are the living memory of its evolution; our societies the various outcomes of the possibilities it leaves open to us. We could depart totally from it — and we show great danger of so doing. But it would then be doubtful if what remained could still be considered 'human society' — or whether it would last.[1]

---

[1] Full references for all the evidence behind the summary assertions made here can be found in my book *The Red Lamp of Incest* (University of Notre Dame Press, 1983).

2

The battle for chastity

Michel Foucault

The following text is taken from the third volume of my Histoire de la sexualité. *After consulting Philippe Ariès I feel that its approach fits in with the general trend of the other papers. We both think that the prevailing notion of Christian ethics badly needs revision and that the highly significant question of masturbation goes back a lot further than the doctors of the eighteenth and nineteenth centuries.*

The battle for chastity is discussed in detail by Cassian in the sixth chapter of the *Institutiones*, 'Concerning the spirit of fornication', and in several of his *Conferences*: the fourth on 'the lusts of the flesh and of the spirit', the fifth on 'the eight principal vices', the twelfth on 'chastity' and the twenty-second on 'night visions'. It ranks second in a list of eight battles,[1] in the shape of a fight against the spirit of fornication. As for fornication itself it is subdivided into three categories.[2] On the face of it a very unjuridical list if one compares it with the catalogue of sins that are to be found when the medieval Church organizes the sacrament of penitence on the lines of a penal code. But Cassian's specifications obviously have a different meaning.

Let us first examine the place of fornication among the other sinful tendencies. Cassian arranges his eight sins in a particular order. He sets up pairs of vices that seem linked in some specifically close way:[3] pride and vainglory, sloth and accidie, avarice and wrath. Fornication is coupled with greed, for several reasons. They are two 'natural' vices, innate and hence very difficult to cure. They are also the two vices that involve the participation of the body,

---

1 The seven others are greed, avarice, wrath, sloth, accidie, vainglory and pride.
2 See below, p. 17.
3 *Conferences*, V, 10.

not only in their growth but also in achieving their object; and finally they also have a direct causal connection — over-indulgence in food and drink fuels the urge to commit fornication.[4] In addition, the spirit of fornication occupies a position of peculiar importance among the other vices, either because it is closely bound with greed, or simply by its very nature.

First the causal chain. Cassian emphasizes the fact that the vices do not exist in isolation, even though an individual may be particularly affected by one vice or another.[5] There is a causal link that binds them all together. It begins with greed, which arises in the body and inflames the spirit of fornication: these two engender avarice, understood as an attachment to worldly wealth, which in turn leads to rivalries, quarrelling and wrath. The result is despondency and sorrow, provoking the sin of accidie and total disgust with monastic life. Such a progression implies that one will never be able to conquer a vice unless one can conquer the one on which it leans: 'The defeat of the first weakens the one that depends on it; victory over the former leads to the collapse of the latter without further effort'. Like the others, the greed-fornication pair, like 'a huge tree whose shadow stretches afar', has to be uprooted. Hence the importance for the ascetic of fasting as a way of conquering greed and suppressing fornication. Therein lies the basis of the practice of asceticism, for it is the first link in the causal chain.

The spirit of fornication is seen as being in an odd relationship to the last vices on the list, and especially pride. In fact, for Cassian, pride and vainglory do not form part of the causal chain of other vices. Far from being generated by them they result from victory over them:[6] 'carnal pride', i.e. flaunting one's fasts, one's chastity, one's poverty etc. before other people, and 'spiritual pride', which makes one think that one's progress is all due to one's own merits.[7] One vice that springs from the defeat of another means a fall that is that much greater. And fornication, the most disgraceful of all the vices, the one that is most shameful, is the consequence of pride — a chastisement, but also a temptation, the proof that God sends to the presumptuous mortal to remind him that he is always threatened by the weakness of the flesh if the grace of God does not come to his help. 'Because someone has for long exulted in the pureness of his heart and his body, it

---

[4] *Institutions*, V and *Conferences*, V.
[5] *Conferences*, V, 13–14.
[6] *Conferences*, V, 10.
[7] *Institutions*, XII, 2.

naturally follows . . . that in the back of his mind he rather prides himself on it . . . so it is a good thing for the Lord to desert him, for his own good. The pureness which has been making him so self-assured begins to worry him, and in the midst of his spiritual well-being he finds himself faltering.[8] When the soul has only itself to combat, the wheel comes full circle, the battle begins again and the prickings of the flesh are felt anew, showing the inevitable continuance of the struggle and the threat of a perpetual recurrence.

Finally, fornication has, as compared with other vices, an ontological particularity which gives it a special ascetic importance. Like greed it is rooted in the body, and impossible to beat without chastisement. While wrath or despondency can be fought only in the mind, fornication cannot be eradicated without 'mortifying the flesh, by vigils, fasts and back-breaking labour'.[9] This still does not exclude the battle the mind has to wage against itself, since fornication may be born of thoughts, images and memories. 'When the Devil, with subtle cunning, has insinuated into our hearts the memory of a woman, beginning with our mother, our sisters, or certain pious women, we should as quickly as possible expel these memories for fear that, if we linger on them too long, the tempter may seize the opportunity to lead us unwittingly to think about other women.'[10] Nevertheless there is one fundamental difference between fornication and greed. The fight against the latter has to be carried on with a certain restraint, since one cannot give up all food: 'The requirements of life have to be provided for . . . for fear lest the body, deprived through our own error, may lose the strength to carry out the necessary spiritual exercises.'[11] This natural propensity for eating has to be kept at arm's length, treated unemotionally, but not abolished. It has its own legitimacy; to repudiate it totally, that is to say to the point of death, would be to burden one's soul with a crime. On the other hand there are no holds barred in the fight against the spirit of fornication; everything that can direct our steps to it must be eradicated and no call of nature can be allowed to justify the satisfaction of a need in this domain. This is an appetite whose suppression does not lead to our bodily death, and it has to be

[8] Conferences, XII, 6. For examples of lapses into pride and presumptuousness, see Conferences II, 13; and especially Institutions, XII, 20 and 21, where offences against humility are punished by the most humiliating temptation, that of a desire contra usum naturae.
[9] Conferences, V, 4.
[10] Institutions, VI, 13.
[11] Institutions, V, 8.

totally eradicated. Of the eight sins fornication is the only one which is at once innate, natural, physical in origin, and needing to be as totally destroyed as the vices of the soul, such as avarice and pride. There has to be severe mortification therefore, which lets us live in our bodies while releasing us from the flesh. 'Depart from this flesh while living in the body.'[12] It is into this region beyond nature, but in our earthly lives, that the fight against fornication leads us. It 'drags us from the slough of the earth'. It causes us to live in this world a life which is not of this world. Because this mortification is the harshest, it promises the most to us in this world below: 'rooted in the flesh', it offers 'the citizenship which the saints have the promise of possessing once they are delivered from the corruption of the flesh.'[13]

Thus one sees how fornication, although just one of the elements in the table of vices, has its own special position, heading the causal chain, and is the sin chiefly responsible for backsliding and spiritual turmoil, at one of the most difficult and decisive points in the struggle for an ascetic life.

In his fifth *Conference* Cassian divides fornication into three varieties. The first consists of the 'joining together of the two sexes' (*commixtio sexus utriusque*); the second takes place 'without contact with the woman' (*absque femineo tactu*) — the damnable sin of Onan; the third is 'conceived in the mind and the thoughts'.[14] Almost the same distinction is repeated in the twelfth *Conference*: 'carnal conjunction' (*carnalis commixtio*), which Cassian calls *fornicatio* in its restricted sense; next uncleanness, *immunditia*, which takes place without contact with a woman, while one is either sleeping or awake, and which is due to 'the negligence of an unwatchful mind'; finally there is *libido*, which develops in 'the dark corners of the soul' without 'physical passion' (*sine passione corporis*).[15] These distinctions are important, for they alone help one to understand what Cassian meant by the general term *fornicatio*, to which he gives no definition elsewhere. But they are particularly important for the way he uses these three categories — in a way that differs so much from what one finds in earlier texts.

There already existed a traditional trilogy of the sins of the flesh: adultery, fornication (meaning sexual relations outside marriage) and 'the corruption of children'. At least these are the three categories to be found in the *Didache*: 'Thou shalt not commit

[12] *Institutions*, VI, 6.
[13] *Institutions*, VI, 6.
[14] *Conferences*, V, 11.
[15] *Conferences*, XII, 2.

adultery; thou shalt not commit fornication; thou shalt not seduce young boys."[16] And these are what we find in the 'Epistle of St Barnabas': 'Do not commit fornication or adultery; do not corrupt the young.'[17] We often find later that only the first two precepts are imposed, fornication covering all sexual offences, and adultery covering those which infringe the marriage vows.[18] But in any case these were habitually accompanied by precepts about covetousness in thought or sight or anything that might lead one to commit a forbidden sexual act: 'Refrain from covetousness, for it leads to fornication; abstain from obscene talk and brazen looks, for all this sort of thing leads to adultery.'[19]

Cassian's analysis has two special features: one is that he does not deal separately with adultery but places it with fornication in its limited sense, and the other is that he devotes attention mostly to the other two categories. Nowhere in the various texts in which he speaks of the battle for chastity does he refer to actual sexual relations. Nowhere are the various sins set out dependent on actual sexual relations — the partner with whom it was committed, his or her age, or possible degree of consanguinity. Not one of the categories that in the Middle Ages were to be built up into a great code of sins is to be found here. Doubtless Cassian, who was addressing an audience of monks who had taken vows to renounce all sexual relations, felt he could skip these preliminaries. One notices, however, that on one very important aspect of celibacy, where Basil of Caesarea and Chrysostom had given explicit advice,[20] Cassian does make discreet allusion: 'Let no one, especially when among young folk, remain alone with another, even for a short time, or withdraw with him or take him by the hand.'[21] He carries on his discussion as if he is only interested in his last two categories (about what goes on without sexual

[16] Didache, II, 2.
[17] Epistle of St Barnabas, XIX, 4. Earlier on, dealing with forbidden foods, the same text interprets the ban on eating hyena flesh as forbidding adultery, of hare as forbidding the seduction of children, of weasel as forbidding oral sex.
[18] For instance St Augustine, Sermon, 56.
[19] Didache, III, 3.
[20] Basil of Caesarea, Exhortation to renounce the World, 5. 'Eschew all dealing, all relations with young men of your own age. Avoid them as you would fire. Many, alas, are those who through mixing with them, have been consigned by the Enemy to burn eternally in hell-fire.' Cf. the precautions laid down in The Great Precepts (34) and The Short Precepts (220). See also John Chrysostom, Adversus oppugnatores vitae monasticae.
[21] Institutions, II, 15. Those who infringe this rule commit a grave offence and are under suspicion (conjurationis pravique consilii). Are these words hinting at amorous behaviour, or are they simply aimed at the danger of members of the same community showing particular favour to one another? Similar recommendations are to be found in Institutions, IV, 16.

relationship or physical passion), as if he was passing over fornication as a physical union of two individuals and only devoting serious attention to behaviour which up till then had been severely censured only when leading up to real sexual acts.

But even though Cassian's analysis ignores physical sex, and its sphere of action is quite solitary and secluded, his reasoning is not purely negative. The whole essence of the fight for chastity is that it aims at a target which has nothing to do with actions or relationships; it concerns a different reality to that of a sexual connection between two individuals. A passage in the twelfth *Conference* reveals the nature of this reality. In it Cassian describes the six stages that mark the advance towards chastity. The object of the description is not to define chastity itself, but to pick out the negative signs by which one can trace progress towards it — the various signs of impurity which disappear one by one — and so get an idea of what one has to contend with in the fight for chastity.

First sign of progress: when the monk awakes he is not 'smitten by a carnal impulse' — *impugnatione carnali non eliditur*, i.e. the mind is no longer troubled by physical reactions over which the will has no control.

Second stage: if 'voluptuous thoughts' (*voluptariae cogitationes*) should arise in the monk's mind, he does not let it dwell on them. He can stop thinking about things that have arisen in his mind involuntarily and in spite of himself.[22]

Third stage: when a glimpse of the world outside can no longer arouse lustful feelings, and one can look upon a woman without any feeling of desire.

Fourth stage: one no longer on one's waking hours feels any, even the most innocent, movement of the flesh. Does Cassian mean that there *is* no movement of the flesh, and that therefore one has total control over one's own body? Probably not, since elsewhere he often insists on the persistence of involuntary bodily movements. The term he uses, *perferre*, signifies no doubt that such movements are not capable of affecting the mind, which thus does not suffer from them.

Fifth stage: 'If the subject of a discourse or the logical consequence of a reading involves the idea of human procreation, the mind does not allow itself to be touched by the remotest thought of sexual pleasure, but contemplates the act in a mood of calmness and purity, as a simple function, a necessary adjunct to the

[22] The word used by Cassian for dwelling on such thoughts is *immorari*. Later, *delectatio morosa* has an important place in the medieval sexual ethic.

prolongation of the human race, and departs no more affected by the recollection of it than if it had been thinking about brick-making or some other trade.'

Finally, the last stage is reached when our sleep is not troubled by the vision of a seductive woman. Even though we may not think it a sin to be subject to such illusions, it is however a sign that some lustful feeling still lurks in the depths of our being.[23]

Amid all this description of the different symptoms of fornication, gradually fading out as one approaches the state of chastity, there is no mention of relationships with others, no acts, not even any intention of committing one. In fact there is no fornication in the strict sense of the word. This microcosm of the solitary life lacks the two major elements on which are centred the sexual ethic not only of the philosophers of the ancient world, but also that of a Christian like Clement of Alexandria (at least in Epistle II of his *Pedagogus*), namely the sexual union of two individuals (*sunousia*) and the pleasure of the act (*aphrodisia*). Cassian is interested in the movements of the body and the mind, images, feelings, memories, faces in dreams, the spontaneous movements of thoughts, the consenting (or refusing) will, waking and sleeping. Now two opposing poles appear, not, one has to realize, those of mind versus body. They are, firstly, the involuntary pole, which consists either of physical movements or of feelings evoked by memories and images that survive from the past and ferment in the mind, besieging and enticing the will, and, secondly, the pole of the will itself, which accepts or repels, averts its eyes or allows itself to be ensnared, holds back or consents. On the one side then bodily and mental reflexes that bypass the mind and, becoming infected with impurity, may proceed to corruption, and on the other side an internal play of thoughts. Here we find the two kinds of 'fornication' as broadly defined by Cassian, to which he confines the whole of his analysis, leaving aside the question of physical sex. His theme is *immunditia*, something which catches the mind, waking or sleeping, off its guard and can lead to pollution, without any contact with another; and the *libido*, which develops in the dark corners of the mind. In this connection Cassian reminds us that *libido* has the same origin as *libet* (it pleases).[24]

The spiritual battle and the advance towards chastity, whose six stages are described by Cassian, can thus be seen as a task of dissociation. We are now far away from the rationing of pleasure

[23] *Conferences*, XII, 7.
[24] *Conferences*, V, 11, and XII, 2. Cf. above.

and its strict limitation to permissible actions; far away too from the idea of as drastic a separation as possible between mind and body. But what does concern us is a never-ending struggle over the movements of our thoughts (whether they extend or reflect those of our body, or whether they motivate them), over its simplest manifestations, over the factors that can activate it. The aim is that the subject should never be affected in his effort by the obscurest or the most seemingly 'unwilled' presence of will. The six stages that lead to chastity represent steps towards the disinvolvement of the will. The first step is to exclude its involvement in bodily reactions; then exclude it from the imagination (not to linger on what crops up in one's mind); then exclude it from the action of the senses (cease to be conscious of bodily movements); then exclude it from figurative involvement (cease to think of things as possible objects of desire); and finally oneiric involvement (the desires that may be stirred by images that appear, albeit spontaneously, in dreams). This sort of involvement, of which the wilful act or the explicit will to commit an act, are the most visible form, Cassian calls *concupiscence*. This is the enemy in the spiritual battle, and this is the effort of dissociation and disinvolvement that has to be made.

Here is the reason why, all through this battle against the spirit of fornication and for chastity, the sole fundamental problem is that of pollution — whether as something that is subservient to the will and a possible form of self-indulgence, or as something happening spontaneously and involuntarily in sleep or dreams. So important is this that Cassian makes the absence of erotic dreams and nocturnal pollution a sign that one has reached the pinnacle of chastity. He often returns to this topic: 'The proof that one has achieved this state of purity will be that no apparition will beguile us when resting or stretched out in sleep,'[25] or again 'This is the sum of integrity and the final proof: that we are not visited by voluptuous thoughts during sleep and that we should be unaware of the pollutions to which we are subjected by nature.'[26] The whole of the twenty-second *Conference* is devoted to the question of 'nocturnal pollutions' and 'the necessity of using all our strength to be delivered from them'. And on various occasions Cassian calls to mind holy characters like Serenus, who had attained such a high degree of virtue that they were never troubled by inconveniences of this kind.[27]

[25] *Institutions*, VI, 10.
[26] *Institutions*, VI, 20.
[27] *Conferences*, VII, 1; XII, 7. Other allusions to this theme in *Institutions*, II, 13.

Obviously, in a rule of life where renunciation of all sexual relations was absolutely basic, it was quite logical that this topic should assume such importance. One is reminded of the importance, in groups inspired by Pythagorean ideas, accorded to the phenomena of sleep and dreams for what they reveal about the quality of existence, and to the self-purification that was supposed to guarantee its serenity. Above all one must realize that nocturnal pollution raised problems where ritual purity was concerned, and it was precisely these problems which prompted the twenty-second *Conference*: can one draw near to the 'holy altars' and partake of the bread and wine when one has suffered nocturnal defilement?[28] But even if all these reasons can explain such preoccupations among the theoreticians of monastic life, they cannot account for the absolutely central position occupied by the question of voluntary/involuntary pollution in the whole discussion of the battle for chastity. Pollution was not simply the object of a stricter ban than anything else, or harder to control. It was a yardstick of concupiscence in that it helped to decide — in the light of what formed its background, initiated it and finally unleashed it — the part played by the will in forming these images, feelings and memories in the mind. The monk concentrates his whole energy on never letting his will be involved in this reaction, which goes from the body to the mind and from the mind to the body, and over which the will may have a hold, either to encourage it or halt it through mental activity. The first five stages of the advance towards chastity constitute increasingly subtle disengagements of the will from the increasingly restricted reactions that may bring on this pollution.

There remains the final stage, attainable by holiness: absence of 'absolutely' involuntary pollutions during sleep. Again Cassian points out that these pollutions are not necessarily all involuntary. Over-eating and impure thoughts during the day all show that one is willing, if not intending, to have them. He makes a distinction between the type of dream that accompanies them, and the degree of impurity of the images. Anyone who is taken by surprise would be wrong to blame his body or sleep: 'It is a sign of the corruption that festers within, and not just a product of the night. Buried in the depth of the soul, the corruption has come to the surface during sleep, revealing the hidden fever of passions with which we have become infected by glutting ourselves all day long on unhealthy emotions.'[29] Finally there is the

[28] *Conferences*, XXII, 5.
[29] *Institutions*, VI, 11.

pollution that is totally involuntary, devoid of the pleasure that implies consent, without even the slightest trace of a dream image. Doubtless this is the goal attainable by the ascetic who has practised with sufficient rigour; the pollution is only a 'residue', in which the person concerned plays no part. 'We have to repress the reactions of our minds and the emotions of our bodies until the flesh can satisfy the demands of nature without giving rise to any pleasurable feelings, getting rid of the excess of our bodily humours without any unhealthy urges and without having to plunge back into the battle for our chastity.'[30] Since this is a supra-natural phenomenon, only a supra-natural power can give us this freedom, spiritual grace. This is why non-pollution is the sign of holiness, the stamp of the highest chastity possible, a blessing one may hope for but not attain.

For his part man must do no less than keep ceaseless watch over his thoughts and bodily movements day and night — during the night for the benefit of the day and during the day in thinking of the approaching night. 'As purity and vigilance during the day dispose one to be chaste during the night, so too nocturnal vigilance replenishes the strength of the heart to observe chastity during the day.'[31] This vigilance means exerting the sort of 'discrimination' that lies at the heart of the self-analysis developed in active spirituality. The work of the miller sorting out his grain, the centurion picking his troops, the money-changer who weighs coins before accepting or refusing them — this is how the monk must unceasingly treat his own thoughts, so as to identify those that may bring temptation. Such an effort will allow him to sort out his thoughts according to their origin, to distinguish them by their quality and to separate the objects they represent from the pleasure they can evoke. This is an endless task of analysis that one has to apply to oneself and, by the duty of confession, to our relations with others.[32] Neither the idea of the inseparability of chastity and 'fornication' affirmed by Cassian, nor the way in which he analyses them, nor the different elements that, according to him, inhere in them, nor the connections he establishes between

[30] *Institutions*, VI, 22.

[31] *Institutions*, VI, 23.

[32] Cf. in the twenty-second *Conference* (6) the case of a consultation over a monk, who each time he was going to communion suffered a nocturnal visitation and dared not participate in the holy mysteries. The 'spiritual physicians' after an interrogation and discussions diagnosed that it was the Devil who sent these visitations so as to prevent the monk from attending the desired communion. To abstain was to fall into the Devil's trap; to communicate in spite of everything was to defeat him. Once this decision had been taken the Devil appeared no more.

them — pollution, libido, concupiscence — can be understood without reference to the techniques of self-analysis which characterize monastic life and the spiritual battle that is fought across it.

Do we find that, between Tertullian and Cassian, prohibitions have been intensified, an even greater importance attached to absolute continence, and the sexual act increasingly stigmatized? Whatever the answer, this is not the way the question should be framed. The organization of monasticism and the dimorphism that developed between monastic and secular life brought about important changes in the problem of sexual renunciation. They brought with them the development of very complex techniques of self-analysis. So, in the very manner in which sex was renounced there appeared a rule of life and a mode of analysis which, in spite of obvious continuities, showed important differences with the past. With Tertullian the state of virginity implied the external and internal posture of one who has renounced the world and has adopted the rules governing appearance, behaviour and general conduct that this renunciation involves. In the mystique of virginity which developed after the thirteenth century the rigour of this renunciation (in line with the theme, already found in Tertullian, of union with Christ) transforms the negative aspect of continence into the promise of spiritual marriage. With Cassian, who describes rather than innovates, there occurs a sort of double action, a withdrawal that also reveals hidden depths within.

This has nothing to do with the internalization of a whole list of forbidden things, merely substituting the prohibition of the intention for that of the act itself. It is rather the opening up of an area (whose importance has already been stressed by the writings of Gregory of Nyssa and, especially, of Basil of Ancyra) which is that of thought, operating erratically and spontaneously, with its images, memories and perceptions, with movements and impressions transmitted from the body to the mind and the mind to the body. This has nothing to do with a code of permitted or forbidden actions, but is a whole technique for analysing and diagnosing thought, its origins, its qualities, its dangers, its potential for temptation and all the dark forces that can lurk behind the mask it may assume. Given the objective of expelling for good everything impure or conducive to impurity, this can only be achieved by eternal vigilance, a suspiciousness directed every moment against one's every thought, an endless self-questioning to flush out any secret fornication lurking in the inmost recesses of the mind.

In this chastity-oriented asceticism one can see a process of 'subjectivization' which has nothing to do with a sexual ethic based on physical self-control. But two things stand out. This subjectivization is linked with a process of self-knowledge which makes the obligation to seek and state the truth about oneself an indispensable and permanent condition of this asceticism; and if there is subjectivization, it also involves an indeterminate objectivization of the self by the self-indeterminate in the sense that one must be forever extending as far as possible the range of one's thoughts, however insignificant and innocent they may appear to be. Morever, this subjectivization, in its quest for the truth about oneself, functions through complex relations with others, and in many ways. One has to rid oneself of the power of the Other, the Enemy, who hides behind seeming likenesses of oneself, and eternal warfare has to be waged against this Other, which one cannot win without the help of the Almighty, who is mightier than he. Finally, confession to others, submission to their advice and permanent obedience to one's superiors is essential in this battle.

These new fashions in monastic sexual mores, the build-up of a new relationship between the subject and the truth, and the establishment of complex relations of obedience to the other self all form part of a whole whose coherence is well illustrated in Cassian's text. No new point of departure is involved. Going back in time before Christianity, one may find many of these elements in embryonic form and sometimes fully shaped in ancient philosophy — Stoic or Neo-Platonic, for instance. Moreover Cassian himself presents in a systematic way (how far he makes his own contribution is another question which need not concern us here) a sum of experience which he asserts to be that of eastern monasticism. In any case study of a text of this kind shows that it hardly makes sense to talk about a 'Christian sexual ethic', still less about a 'Judaeo-Christian' one. So far as consideration of sexual behaviour was concerned, some fairly involved thinking went on between the Hellenistic period and St Augustine. Certain important events stand out such as the guidelines for conscience laid down by the Stoics and the Cynics, the organization of monasticism, and many others. On the other hand the coming of Christianity, considered as a massive rupture with earlier moralities and the dominant introduction of a quite different one, is barely noticeable. As P. Brown says, in speaking of Christianity as part of our reading of the giant mass of antiquity, the topography of the parting of the waters is hard to pin down.

3

Homosexuality in ancient Rome

Paul Veyne

Towards the end of pagan antiquity the ascetic and mystical philosopher Plotinus expressed the wish that real thinkers should 'scorn the beauty of boys and women'.[1] The love of boys and women, as applied to men, is referred to scores of times in ancient literature: the one was the same as the other, and what one thought of one went for the other as well. It is incorrect to say that the ancients took an indulgent view of homosexuality. The truth is that they did not see it as a separate problem; they either tolerated or condemned the passion of love, whose legitimacy they questioned, as well as moral laxity.

If they censured homosexuality, they censured it as they did love, courtesans or extra-marital affairs — at least as far as active homosexuality was concerned. They had three standards which were quite distinct from ours: free love or exclusive marriage, sexual activity or sexual passivity, freedom or slavery. To seduce one's slave was a venial offence, and even severe moralists hardly bothered about such a trifling matter;[2] on the other hand it was disgraceful for a Roman citizen to act as the passive instrument of another's pleasure.

Apuleius defines as unnatural certain revolting practices indulged in among men,[3] not because they are homosexual but because they involve servility and excessive sophistication. For when an ancient says that something is unnatural, he does not mean that it is disgraceful, but that it does not conform with the rules of society, or that it is perverted and artificial. Nature meant either society or a sort of ecological ideal, directing people

---

[1] Plotinus, *Enneads*, ii, 9, 17.
[2] But see Musonius, xii, 6—7; cf. Quintilian, v, 11, 34.
[3] Apuleius, *Metamorphoses*, viii, 29.

to self-mastery and self-sufficiency. One had to learn to be satisfied with nature's fairly small requirements. Hence there were two attitudes towards homosexuality: the lenient majority found it normal, while the moralists found it sometimes artificial, just as they did all the pleasures of love.

Artemidorus,[4] who is a fair representative of the indulgent majority, singles out 'relations that conform with normal behaviour' (his own words), i.e. with one's wife, with a mistress or with a 'male or female slave': but 'to let onself be buggered by one's own slave is not right. It is an assault on one's person and leads to one being despised by one's slave.' Abnormal relations are incestuous. Relations that conflict with nature include bestiality, necrophily and intercourse with divine personages.

Political thinkers arrived at puritanical conclusions because they felt that all forms of love or lust, homosexual or not, were uncontrollable and enervated the citizen-soldier. Their ideal was victory over pleasure, of whatever kind.[5] Plato drew up the laws of a utopian city from which he banished pederasty, which he said was against nature, since animals (he thought) never copulated with their own sex. But re-reading his works[6] one finds that pederasty is not so much against nature as in excess of what nature demands of us. Sodomy is an excessively licentious and unnatural practice. Plato is opposed to slackness and the distractions of love, nature being to him simply an additional factor. His plan is not to lead passion back to strictly natural habits by only allowing love for women, but to suppress it altogether, only allowing sexual activity for the purpose of reproduction. It does not seem to have crossed his mind that one could be in love with a woman! With a similar line of reasoning he might have denounced gastronomy as enervating: nature, he would say, shows us, through the example of animals, that one should eat to live, not live to eat. What is unnatural about pederasty is not so much the use of the wrong sex, as the complicated pleasure it gives. Plato does not see it as a capital offence, but rather as an improper act — by reason of its 'positions'. It is forbidden, but for the same reason that associating with a woman who is not one's wife is forbidden.

It is not enough simply to find the expression 'against nature' in the texts. One has to understand what it meant to antiquity. For Plato it was not the homosexual who was unnatural, but only

---

[4] *Onirocritica*, pp. 88–9.
[5] Cf. Plato, *Laws*, 840C.
[6] *Laws*, 636B–D, and 836Bff.; *Symposium*, 211B, 291CD; *Phaedrus*, 249A; *Republic*, 403B.

the act he committed. It was a question of degree. A pederast was not a monster, a member of some alien race with incomprehensible impulses, but simply a libertine impelled by the universal desire for pleasure, who went so far as to perform an act — sodomy — that was unknown among animals. There was no ritual taboo on pederasty.

Greek and Roman texts are full of homosexuality in action. Catullus boasts of his prowess, and Cicero celebrates the kisses he plucks from the lips of his slave-secretary.[7] According to taste some chose women, some boys, some both. Virgil preferred boys only,[8] the Emperor Claudius women. Horace repeatedly tells us he adores both. Poets glorified the favourite of the formidable Emperor Domitian as freely as the writers of the eighteenth century were to celebrate *la Pompadour*, and it is notorious that Antinous, Hadrian's catamite, was honoured by an official cult after his early death.[9] So as to please every reader, the Latin poets, whatever their own personal tastes, made a point of hymning both sorts of love. A favourite theme of light literature was to describe and compare the pleasures of the two.[10] In a society where the most straight-laced critics regarded sodomy as merely licentious, no concealment was necessary and lovers of boys were just as numerous as lovers of women: all of which says much for the 'un-natural' character of human sexuality.

Classical authors allow themselves just as many allusions to homosexuality as they do to any other ribald topic. There is no difference between Greek and Latin writers, and the love that tends to be called Greek might equally be called Roman. Should we believe that the Romans learnt it from the Greeks, who taught them so much else? If the answer is yes, one might infer that homosexuality is such a rare perversion that one people can only have picked it up through another's bad example. If, on the other hand, it appears that pederasty was indigenous in Rome, the astonishing thing is not that a society should practise pederasty, but that it should not practise it. What needs explanation is not Roman tolerance but contemporary intolerance.

The second answer is correct. Rome did not have to wait for hellenization to allow various forms of love between males. One of the earliest relics of Latin literature, the plays of Plautus, which pre-date the craze for things Greek, are full of homosexual

---

[7] Cicero, quoted by the younger Pliny, vii, 4, 3—6.
[8] From *Vitae Vergilianae*.
[9] From Suetonius, *Lives of the Caesars*.
[10] See the astonishing *Comparisons of Love* by Lucian or the pseudo-Lucian.

allusions of a very native character. A much repeated way of teasing a slave is to remind him of what his master expects of him, i.e. to get down on all fours. The *Fasti Praenestini*, the 25 April in the Roman calendar, was the festival of the male prostitutes, the day after that of the courtesans, and Plautus describes them waiting for their customers on the Tuscany road.[11] The poems of Catullus are full of stock juvenile insults in which the poet threatens to ravish his enemies to show his superiority. This is the world of heroic bravado, with a very Mediterranean flavour, where the important thing is to be the ravisher, never mind the sex of the victim. The same principles ruled in Greece; but, going one better, they tolerated, even admired a romantic habit that scandalized the Romans. This was the supposedly Platonic love of adults for *epheboi*, the free-born youths who frequented the gymnasium, where their admirers went to watch them exercising naked. In Rome the place of the free-born *ephebos* was taken by the favourite male slave. If the master was so oversexed that his girl slaves were not enough, he had to ravish the boys;[12] rather in excess of what nature allowed, but still smiled on by ordinary folk.

The important thing was to respect married women, virgins and youths of free birth. Legislation allegedly suppressing homosexuality was in fact meant to stop free-born citizens from being ravished like slaves. The *Lex Scantinia* of 149 BC was confirmed by proper Augustan legislation on the same subject. This protected free-born youths and girls alike. Sex had nothing to do with the question. What mattered was being free and not being a passive agent. The lawgiver was not trying to ban homosexuality; he simply wanted to protect the young citizen against infringement of his or her person.

It was a world in which marriage contracts specified that the future husband would take 'neither concubine nor catamite', and where Marcus Aurelius congratulates himself in his journal for having resisted the attraction he felt for his male and female slaves, Theodotus and Benedicta; a world in which one's behaviour was judged not by one's preference for girls or boys, but by whether one played an active or a passive role. To be active was to be male, whatever the sex of the compliant partner. To take one's pleasure was virile, to accept it servile — that was the whole

---

[11] Plautus, *Curculio*, 482; for slaves' passivity (*puerile officium*) cf. *Cistellaria*, 657, and many other texts. On servile sexuality, see the important study by R. Martin, '*La Vie sexuelle des esclaves*' in J. Collard et al., *Varron, Grammaire antique et stylistique latine*, Paris, 1978, p. 113ff.

[12] Seneca, *Naturales Quaestiones*, i, 16; Petronius, xliii, 8.

story. Woman was passive by definition, unless she was the sort of freak we are not concerned with here. Problems were looked at from the masculine viewpoint. Children were of no great importance, as long as adults did not allow themselves to be used for their pleasure and confined themselves to taking it from them. In Rome these children were slaves and counted for nothing, while in Greece the *epheboi*, being not yet citizens, could still play the passive role without dishonour.

Utter scorn was heaped on the free-born adult male who was a homosexual of the passive variety — *impudicus* or *diatithemenos.* Some of the Stoics were maliciously suspected of secret effeminacy, which they concealed under an affectation of exaggerated virility. They probably had in mind the philosopher Seneca who preferred athletes to boys.[13] Passive homosexuals were thrown out of the army, and at a time of mass executions[14] the Emperor Claudius is recorded as sparing the life of one *impudicus* who had 'female inclinations'. The blood of such a one would have soiled the executioner's sword.

The passive homosexual was not rejected for his homosexuality but for his passivity, a very serious moral, or rather political infirmity. The passive individual's effeminacy was not the result of his perversion, far from it: it was simply one of the results of his lack of virility, and this was still a vice, even where no homosexuality was present. Roman society never bothered to ask if people were homosexual or not, but it devoted an excessive scrutiny to tiny details of dress, speech, gesture, and deportment in furthering its contempt for those who showed a lack of virility, whatever their sexual tastes. On several occasions musical shows (for which the name 'pantomime' was invented) were banned by the state as being enervating — unlike gladiatorial performances.

This all helps to explain another, unexpected obsession. There was one type of sexual behaviour which was absolutely disgraceful, such that people would pass the time asking who was 'one of them'. This behaviour, which among scandalmongers was on the same lines as contemporary references to 'queers', was fellatio. The historian needs no excuse for bringing it up since Greek and Roman texts refer constantly to it, and it is our business to give our own society a sense of the relativity of values. Fellatio was a very dirty word, and we read about cases[15] where disgraceful

---

[13] Dio Cassius, lxi, 10, 3—4. For the concealed softness of the Stoics, beside Martial and Juvenal, see Quintilian, i, *praef*, 15.

[14] From Tacitus, at the time of the trials of Messalina's lovers.

[15] From Martial.

fellators try to hide their infamy under the lesser shame of pretending to be passive homosexuals! There is an appalling scene in Tacitus where Nero is having the slave of his wife Octavia put to torture to make her confess that the Empress has been guilty of adultery. She endures every torment to save her mistress's honour and replies to her torturer 'Octavia's vagina is purer than your mouth'. We might think she meant that nothing could be more unclean than the mouth of a slanderer. Not so. She means that the torturer is a monster of vice, and signifies her meaning by a single gesture — fellatio. This perversion was depicted as something fantastically depraved, similar to the present-day insults of racism. Apuleius describes bandits, and Suetonius even Nero, who abandon themselves to fellatio, as people who indulge in vices whose pleasure lies in their very viciousness. Was not fellatio the basest form of self-humiliation? It gets a kick out of supinely giving pleasure to another, and servilely offers up any part of the body for another's enjoyment; sex has nothing to do with it. For there was a second practice, no less vile, which obsessed people just as much — cunnilingus. How remote from Japanese culture, where the libertine Samurai boasted of the variegated pleasure he could lavish on his women.

Whence comes this extraordinary balance sheet of pleasure and vices? There are at least three causes, which must not be confused with one another. Rome was a 'macho' society like many others, some slave-owning, some not. Women were there to serve men, to satisfy their desires at need, to get pleasure from them if they could; and even that pleasure was suspect, for, against all probability, prostitutes were thought to be women who were looking for sensual enjoyment. Secondly, the cult of virility was the hidden part of the iceberg in ancient societies. As a brief analogy, consider the hatred of effeminacy in militaristic groups or in pioneer communities that feel themselves in a hostile environment. Finally, Rome was a slave-owning society in which the master had sexual dominance, so that slaves made a virtue of necessity in the saying 'There is nothing shameful in doing whatever the master orders.'

In this slave-owning society — before the days when Stoics and Christians preached equal sexual morality for all (more to make the masters chaste than to protect their slaves) — moral standards varied with social status: 'To be *impudicus* (that is passive) is disgraceful for a free man' wrote the elder Seneca, 'but it is the slave's absolute obligation towards his master, and the freedman owes a moral duty of compliance.'

Thus the sort of homosexuality which was completely tolerated consisted in active relations between a master and a young slave, his catamite. A typical Roman aristocrat had a wife (whom he treated with some consideration, for she could divorce him and take back her dowry), female slaves who were concubines if he so desired, and his offspring (of whom he saw little for fear of displaying weakness, for they were the future masters who had a harsh upbringing at the hands of servants or a grandfather). He also had a slave boy, an *alumnus*, on whom he lavished his paternal instincts, if he had any, and who was often a child he had had by a slave (though it was absolutely forbidden for anybody, even the father, to suggest such a thing). Finally he had his favourite, or a whole army of favourites. Madam was jealous of them; the master protested that he did nothing wrong with them; nobody was taken in, but nobody was allowed to cast aspersions. Madam was not happy till the day the favourite grew a moustache, for this was the moment when the master ceased to subject him to indignities that were unsuitable for a grown man. Some, more lecherous, preferred not to cease: then the overgrown favourite was known as an *exoletus*, meaning that he was no longer *adolescens*, and decent people found him repellent. Seneca, who thought that nature should always be left alone, was disgusted that some dissipated characters had their beards removed from favourites, even when they had outgrown the age of compliance.

We would be wrong to look on antiquity as a paradise of permissiveness and to imagine a total lack of moral principles. It is simply that the principles seem shocking to us: something which might make us suspect that our own most strongly held convictions are not much better. Did homosexuality have to be concealed? Was it allowed? A distinction has to be made. Liaisons existed, illicit but tolerated, like adultery in high places today, or free cohabitation. As such they are mentioned in literature without censure; but the interested parties would be discreet enough to admit nothing, and pretend to know nothing. This was how the Romans treated affairs with favourites, and the Greeks with *epheboi*.

There were many other relationships that were regarded as immoral as well as illicit. Most homosexual behaviour was disapproved of, though not for present-day reasons. Relationships with *exoleti* were considered particularly repugnant; so were all-male ménages; so was the homosexual behaviour tolerated in the closed world of the army (we have to wait for Salvian and the period of the great invasions for details of this), and finally the prostitution of adolescent youths from good families. Prostitution in this sense is rather a big word, for in Rome the sexual objectives — boys and girls — were regarded as such passive agents that money was unhesitatingly offered to the little creatures. The result was that, even if a virtuous matron or an upright young man were offered money for their favours, they did not have to look upon themselves as venal. In Rome, paying court meant naming a figure. So much so that for parents it was a problem to find a school where their sons' morals would be shielded from temptation. To reassure his clientele the schoolmaster Quintilian in his writings expressed great horror of love for *epheboi*.

Finally, there were relationships that were illicit, immoral and, above all, loathsome. These were more than blameworthy actions committed in an unguarded moment, but acts the awfulness of which recoiled on the author and showed that simply to be capable of such an act proved that he or she must be beyond the pale. This was to pass from moral condemnation to something like racial apartheid today. Of such a kind were passivity in free men, excessive compliance in women, cunnilingus, finally lesbianism, especially in the active partner. A woman who behaved like a man was simply a wrecker of the natural order — a monster, as bad as a woman who mounts her lover, said Seneca.

So in the end we are left with a picture of homosexuality which was just as idealized as our own, but in a different way. Every variety was reduced to one supposedly typical model: the relationship of an adult with an adolescent who derived no pleasure from it. The Romans liked to think that this was typical, because such a relationship, that was active and called for no display of tender feeling, was soothing, unruffled by the storms and enslavements of passion: 'May my enemies all fall in love with women and my friends with boys' wrote the poet Propertius in a moment of bitterness, for pederasty 'is a gently flowing river, marked by no shipwrecks.What harm can one come to in such a narrow channel?'[16] Roman homosexuality, with all its oddities and disconcerting limitations, derived from a politically motivated puritanism. Praise for women had to come from someone as carefree as the poet Ovid, who explained that the charm of heterosexuality lay in the shared pleasure, something that boys never felt.

In conclusion, one might ask how homosexuality came to be so widely practised. Was the number of homosexuals perhaps artificially increased by just one particular idiosyncrasy of the ancient world — contempt for women? Or is homosexuality

[16] Propertius, ii, 4.

a normal condition of human sexuality, which in this case was given a chance to reveal itself through a different sort of repression? The second answer is no doubt the correct one. We have to be clear about this, surprising though it may be. Living with a man, preferring boys to girls, are facts of life: it is a question of character, of the Oedipus complex, of what you will. It may not be a majority taste, but it is not that of a very small minority. Moreover almost anybody can have physical relations with his own sex, and what is more, get as much pleasure as he does with the opposite sex. So a heterosexual who tries it as an experiment finds to his intense surprise that it is really no different, and that the trip was hardly worth while. Some useful evidence on this subject emerged during the international congress of the homosexual movement 'Arcadia'. It should be emphasized that heterosexuals who made this sort of statement had never considered having relations with boys, had never suffered from any repressed desire to do so, and had hardly thought about it at all. They imagined that, if they 'had a go', they would merely be disgusted. Everything went well and they were not disgusted. But that was all: they did not try again, because women in the long term were more interesting and to their taste, and in present day society, more accessible.

All this is enlightening. Imagine a society in which homosexuality is tolerated, where boys are not under surveillance and lovers can woo them without fuss. Let us suppose that in this society marriage is not the central institution that it is in ours, and that fleeting emotional relationships may be kept on one side and serious things like marital relationships on the other. Rome yesterday, Japan today, are examples of this. In such societies there will undoubtedly be a constant minority interested in boys only; but the majority too will occasionally enjoy a homosexual affair, since these brief indulgences will be tolerated and no one need be inhibited by social disapproval. Men are not animals and physical love is not dominated by the sex difference. As Elisabeth Mathiot-Ravel used to say — sexual behaviour is not sex-bound.

Bibliography

Michel Foucault's *magnum opus* on the *Aphrodisia* will appear shortly. Meanwhile the first chapter of John Boswell's *Christianity, Social Tolerance and Homosexuality*, Chicago, 1980, should be read. The essential work on Greek homosexuality is K.J. Dover, *Greek Homosexuality*, London, 1978. F. Buffière has made a useful and interesting collection of texts in *La*

Pédérastie dans la Grèce antique, Paris, 1980. I have not read F. Gonfroy's thesis, *Un Fait de civilisation méconnu: l'homosexualité à Rome*, Poitiers, 1972, mentioned by Georges Fabre in *Libertus: patrons et affranchis à Rome*, 1981, pp. 258ff.

4

St Paul and the flesh

Philippe Ariès

On two separate occasions (I Cor. 6, 9—10; I Tim. 1, 9—10) St Paul gives us a list of sins which seem to be organized in some definite order of seriousness. It displays a concept of evil that is a mixture of contemporary Jewish and Greek ideas from which Christian morality was to arise, but which was already a pagan body of ethics in embryo. The place occupied by sex is interesting.

In these two texts sins are divided into five main categories: sins against God, against human life, against the human body, against property and objects, and finally lying and perjury. First, those who sin against God: obviously the worshippers of idols, then the lawless and unruly, those who disobey the commandments, the impious and irreligious. Next, those who sin against human life — parricides, matricides and all kinds of murderers. Then come those who sin against their bodies, defined by St Paul as shrines of the Holy Spirit, and thus sacred places, not to be misused; what yesterday we should have called sins of the flesh, but today — sexual offences! Those who sin against the flesh are in turn divided into four sub-groups, and here we must pay strict attention to the meaning of the words, even if some are used in a rather general and vague sense, e.g. fornication. We appear to move from one group to the next on an ascending curve of sinfulness. The first group consists of those who prostitute themselves, *fornicarii* (Greek, *pornoi*). The second group is that of adulterers, that is those who seduce another's wife, and women who allow themselves to be seduced. The etymology of the word *adulteratio* suggests 'debasement' rather than the sexual act. The third group is that of the *molles* (*malakoi*) and is of particular interest, for it reveals something important and new (this is also Michel Foucault's opinion, which he clearly expounded in our seminar). What is *mollities?* It is remarkable that the expressions used to describe sexual activities such as fornication and adultery mention neither parts of the body nor actions. This is not from a sense of decency, for neither Greek nor Latin was afraid of being frank, and a little further on St Paul allows himself a kind of joke about the foreskin of the circumcised. Personally I see in this omission a survival from a linguistic period in which sexual behaviour was not discussed and categorized. The only distinctions in use were between prostitution and marriage in general, and there were no details of what exactly went on in the prostitute's den (*fornix*) or the marital bed, it always being understood that one never had the right to go to bed with the wife of *another*. At a time when contemporary culture devotes a large proportion of its vocabulary to sexual matters, one cannot help being struck by the apparent discretion of the Latins, whose most telling phrases were chosen by criteria other than those of biology, or even pleasure!

With the appearance of *mollities* a change takes place. The word is derogatory, rather like passivity, which, according to Dover and Paul Veyne, the Romans considered a shameful and blameworthy posture, leading to dishonour and degradation. The Roman citizen – and the Japanese, adds Paul Veyne — must never play a passive role in love, whether homosexual or heterosexual. This disapprobation was also reserved for certain other sexual practices, because they were passive. Michel Foucault should enlighten us on the various forms of *mollities* — which in later Roman times included masturbation. *Mollities* is an ambiguous sort of word, not necessarily sexual by implication, since there are other forms of effeminacy than the merely sexual. It included eroticism, that is a repertoire of diversions for delaying coition, or even avoiding it altogether, with the aim of having a better and longer climax. In fact, acting just for pleasure. This was something that St Paul naturally frowned on, seeing it as a sin against the body. *Mollities* was probably one of the great inventions of the Stoic-Christian era.

After the *fornicarii*, the *adulteri* and the *molles*, St Paul adds the *masculorum concubitores*, the men who go to bed together. It is curious that St Paul says nothing about women who do this; among crimes of violence he lists matricides beside parricides, though in this the woman is the victim not the author of the crime! One feels that men are the real sinners, since both power and responsibility are theirs. This seems contrary to contemporary opinion that the Church looked on woman as the devil's instrument. Elsewhere St Paul states that sin came into the world through woman, not man. All the same, it is curious that the apostle's *machismo* does not appear in this particular text, which is more ethical than theological. It may be that in the Middle Ages mistrust of women among men, and especially among clerics, increased as a kind of defence mechanism against women's growing influence. There is a connection between Abelard's castration and the fame of Heloise. In any case it is male homosexuality that is denounced by St Paul.

So much for sexual behaviour. Next in St Paul's list of sinners come those who sell freemen into slavery, thieves, those who are too covetous of the things of this world (*avari*), or who gain them by brutal means (*rapaces*), or who over-indulge (drunkards). The list ends with those who sin with their tongues, a serious matter in a society where oral culture still counted in spite of the progress of literacy: the slanderers, swindlers, liars and perjurers.

Sexual sins rate fairly high on the list, after homicide and before offences against property, always assuming, as seems fairly likely, that the arrangement was deliberate. Henceforward we have a code of sexual morals: sins against the body arising from the use or abuse of sexual urges — lust, in fact. Then there are wicked and forbidden forms of sexual behaviour, almost as bad as homicide. These are always described in terms foreign to the physiology of sex, but *mollities* introduces a completely new idea. Furthermore homosexuality, widely practised throughout the Hellenistic world and considered normal, becomes an abominable and forbidden act. Of all the sexual offences it is the only one whose name frankly conjures up a physical scene — *masculorum concubitores*.

While this code of forbidden practices is being sharpened up, a new ideal appears — virginity both for men and women, challenging the received and legitimate custom of sexuality in marriage: 'It is a good thing for a man to have nothing to do with women.' The Epicurean idea that the body must yield to lust as the stomach does to hunger is repudiated. Hunger is admissible, but lust is suspect and rigorously controlled.

From now on there was a settled ideology. All that was necessary was to go on developing it. But it needs to be made clear that this is a pre-Christian ethic. All the changes in sexual behaviour, as Paul Veyne has shown in his brilliant article on love in Rome, are pre-Christian. The two principal changes mark the transition from a man's freedom to ravish slaves of either sex (such being the claim to an active role, the opposite of *mollities*) to a heterosexuality aimed at procreation, and from a society, where marriage is in no way an institution, to a society where it is taken for granted that marriage is a fundamental institution for all societies, as well as for society as a whole. St Paul certainly did not put procreation first; he was too convinced that the end of the world was at hand to bother about that. Marriage to him was a lawful means, though one rather to be avoided, of satisfying desires that one was unable to control: 'Better be married than burn with vain desires.' In spite of this, procreation soon became in Christian society what it was already in Stoic ethics, one of the two reasons for sexuality.

So Paul Veyne and probably Michel Foucault end up by defining the three pillars on which western societies from the second century AD onwards were to found their new sexual system, i.e. their attitudes towards homosexuality, marriage and *mollities*. The change began in the first centuries of our era, a time of crucial importance in the establishment of the fundamental character of our cultural background.

5

Male homosexuality – or happiness in the ghetto

Michael Pollak

'Not all boys dream of being a marine!'
Poster carried by a transvestite at the
'Gay Pride Parade' in New York, 1979

One of the most spectacular results of the sexual emancipation of
the last twenty years has been the emergence of homosexuality
from the clouds of silence in which it was shrouded. We have come
a long way since the days when Dr Tardieu could write 'If only I
could avoid soiling my pen with the loathsome vileness of the
pederasts!'[1] In the last fifteen years especially we have seen an
absolute flood of discussion on this subject and a complete reshaping
of the image of homosexuality.

Any attempt to look at homosexuality 'scientifically' gives
rise to problems. The very definition of homosexuality and the
dissensions it has provoked have resulted in some diametrically
opposed theories. Broadly speaking they can be divided into theories
that set up heterosexuality as the absolute norm, and others that
treat all manifestations of sex on the same level. The former see
non-heterosexual practices as deviations — even perversions —
while the latter see them as different ways of achieving orgasm,
without any discrimination between them.

In the prevailing psychiatric view of the time, the classification
of homosexuality as a form of perversion, established by R. von
Krafft-Ebing and A. von Schrenk-Notzing at the end of the last
century, retained all its power up to the 1960s.[2] The decision,

---

[1] Quoted in J.P. Aron and R. Kempf, *Le Pénis et la démoralisation de l'Occident*,
Paris, 1978, p. 51.

in 1974, of the American Psychiatric Association to abandon the idea of homosexuality as a mental disease was a symbolic act which upset the balance of power between different theories of sexual behaviour. But this upset worked in favour of a view which made homosexuality a natural phenomenon. Caught up in the vicious circle of condemnation/justification, those writers who were opposed to the classification of homosexuality as a perversion were displaying political courage rather than a spirit of innovation. Thus the theory of 'constitutional homosexuality'[3] of I. Bloch, elaborated about 1900, and the works of H.M. Hirschfeld are only understandable if one realizes their function as political weapons in the fight against a penal code that banned homosexuality as an unnatural act. The argument of homosexuality's inherently constitutional character seemed the only possible one to use against its official inclusion among the perversions that had to be dealt with and stamped out.[4]

Entrapped in this view of homosexuality as a natural phenomenon, these writers could only either assert that the homosexual was no different from the heterosexual apart from his choice of object, or talk about a totally different homosexual character type, a sort of 'third sex'. A.C. Kinsey and H. Giese, following I. Bloch, fall in with the former line of thought. In a political sense, to support this as a scientific fact meant adopting a 'liberal' attitude which reduced social discrimination against homosexuals merely to its juridical aspect. Those writers who propounded an entirely separate homosexual type of human being were often simply providing a scientific cloak for current views of the homosexual fact. Thus C.H. Ulrich, constantly quoted by Hirschfeld, wrote about 1860 that the homosexual nature contained feminine characteristics, clearly shown by a partiality for virile men. This analysis was systematized in his concept of a 'third sex'. H.M. Hirschfeld takes this concept even further by specifying particular physiological traits visible in homosexuals, which reveal the biological basis of a different psychological type. As a natural phenomenon was in question, he also asserted that the proportion

[2] R. von Krafft-Ebing, *Psychopathia sexualis, mit besonderer Berücksichtigung der conträren Sexualempfindung; eine klinisch forensische Studie*, 3rd ed., Stuttgart, 1888; R. von Krafft-Ebing, *Der Conträrsexuale vor dem Strafrichter*, 2nd ed., Leipzig, 1895; A. von Schrenck-Notzing, *Die Suggestionstherapie bei krankhaften Erscheinungen des Geschlechtssinnes mit besonderer Berücksichtigung der conträren Sexualempfindung*, Stuttgart, 1892.

[3] I. Bloch, *Das Sexualleben unserer Zeit in seinen Beziehungen zur modernen Kultur*, Berlin, 1908, pp. 534ff.

[4] See M. Dannecker, *Der Homosexuelle und die Homosexualität*, Frankfurt, pp. 42ff.

of homosexuals in the world's population was constant in space and time.[5]

Conceived as part of a struggle against the German penal code, Hirschfeld's theory contained all the elements that enabled it to be used in a way totally opposed to the author's intentions. Any attention drawn to the specific qualities he describes makes it possible to drag out all the clichés, stereotypes and figures of caricature that occur in all social talk about homosexuality. What is novel in the view of homosexuality to be found in the works of the last fifteen years is not that they give a new explanation, but that they abandon all classification and explanation and restate the problem as 'How do homosexuals live?'[6] Many authors make a point of saying that their objective is to improve the social condition of homosexuals. The two biggest pieces of research on homosexuality in Germany and the United States have each been carried out by two authors of whom one in each case is a confessed homosexual.[7]

In this chapter I shall try to show that this interest in the life styles of homosexuals and this changed approach to homosexuality may — partly at least — be explicable by the pattern that homosexuality tends to assume at a time of general liberalization of sexual behaviour. This liberalization amounts to a twofold movement towards relative autonomization and rationalization of sexual behaviour. Its conditions involve the disjunction of sexual appetite and the desire to procreate, and the fact that independent

[5] H.M. Hirschfeld, 'Ursachen und Wesen des Uranismus', in *Jahrbuch für sexuelle Zwischenstufen*, 5, 1903.

[6] See the excellent critical biography in M.S. Weinberg and A.P. Bell, *Homosexuality, An annotated Bibliography*, New York, 1972.

[7] M. Dannecker and R. Reiche, *Der gewöhnliche Homosexuelle*, Frankfurt, 1974; A.P. Bell and M.S. Weinberg, *Homosexualities, A Study of Diversity Among Men and Women*, New York, 1978. A comparative study of the homosexual situation in three countries, the United States, Holland and Denmark, shows that, in spite of numerous differences in legislation and public opinion, the homosexual milieus are remarkably similar and the sexual markets function in just the same way. M.S. Weinberg and C.J. Williams, *Male Homosexuals*, New York, 1974, attempts to describe the typical features of the homosexual milieu in western Europe and north America, without stressing the differences in the quantitative distribution of the phenomena which vary from one country to another. A French work, similar in aim, lacks experimental rigour: J. Corraze, *Dimensions de l'homosexualité*, Toulouse, 1969. A large-scale piece of research carried out in France on behalf of the Association Arcadie, reaches conclusions similar to those of Dannecker and Reiche, Bell and Weinberg: M. Bon and A. d'Arc, *Rapport sur l'homosexualité de l'homme*, Paris, 1974; a conceptual structure borrowed from psycho-analysis and an excessive regard for the social respectability of the subsidizing body considerably limit the interest of this study. Moreover no statistical material is included.

sexual practices may be rendered measurable i.e. they may be susceptible to finite calculability, depending on an assessment of pleasure that has the orgasm as its unit of measurement.[8]

The first condition, the separation of sexual interest from procreation, is fulfilled by the very definition of homosexuality. Furthermore, the outlawing of homosexuality certainly increased the separation of affective tendencies from this form of sexuality. It also helped in forcing homosexual life to be worked out carefully. All forms of clandestine activity are constricted to a system that minimizes risks and optimizes effectiveness. In the case of homosexuality this resulted in the isolation of the sexual act in time and space, and limited it to a minimum of ritual leading up to the act and to the termination of the relationship immediately afterwards. In addition, a system of communication developed which made for the minimization of emotional involvement with the maximization of orgasmic yield. It is hardly surprising that a sexual market free of 'non-sexual' inhibitions should be developed initially among such fringe sexual activities as are relegated to quasi-secrecy, beginning with homosexuality. But it is not merely this avant-garde role of homosexuality in the whole process of the rationalization of sexual behaviour that explains the growing interest in it today. The 'homosexual way of life' forms structures that allow for an affective and social life to be carried on without the constraints imposed by stable and lasting relationships. In studying the homosexual milieu it is fascinating to see the development of life styles that are very diversified as a result of increasingly specialized sexual and affective desires. It is because it seems to provide practical answers to wider questions that the homosexual milieu has so much attention paid to it today by those who create and spread social habits. How is one to combine the satisfaction of sexual and affective needs without having to pay for it by incurring the constraints often inherent in a pair relationship? An analysis of how the homosexual milieu functions, in so far as it can be reconstructed from social research, should allow a more precise enquiry into the phenomenon of homosexuality raised to the status of a cultural mode. Are we dealing with a desire to imitate new life styles, and with a hitherto unheard-of tolerance or — quite simply — with one big mistake?

---

[8] This line of thought is developed in A. Béjin and M. Pollak, 'La Rationalisation de la sexualité' in *Cahiers internationaux de Sociologie*, LXVII, 1977, pp. 105ff.

The sexual vocation and its market

Homosexuality is not innate but learned. The homosexual's career begins with his recognition of specific sexual desires and familiarizing himself with places and means of meeting partners This 'coming out' stage takes place most frequently between the ages of 16 and 30 (see table A1 in the appendix to this chapter). Most homosexuals are convinced of their sexual inclination long before indulging in the act. The time-scale from the first homosexual feeling to the first contact, and to the moment when the homosexual is finally committed, stretches nearly always over several years and lasts in many cases up to the age of 30.[9]

Once he has accepted his sexual difference, the homosexual enters the sexual market. Of all the different types of masculine sexual behaviour, homosexuality is undoubtedly the one whose functioning is most strongly suggestive of a market, in which in the last analysis one orgasm is bartered for another. The key institutions of homosexual life are initially the 'pick-up' spots: bars, saunas, cinemas, specialized restaurants and public parks. With an average several dozen partners a year (see table A2), and some hundreds in a lifetime (see table A3) the sexual life of the 'average homosexual' is very active between the ages of 28 and 38 or 40, marked by a very high frequency of sexual relations. There is tremendous promiscuity, and a wide diversification as well as specialization of practices. Diversification goes hand in hand with specialization. The disposition of pick-up spots and the ingenuity of the various signals, by means of which the taste of the moment may be indicated, all help in the forward planning of the sexual act. The individual, too, may change both locality and his personal 'presentation'.

The homosexual pick-up system is the product of a search for efficiency and economy in attaining the maximization of 'yield' (in numbers of partners and orgasms) and the minimization of 'cost' (waste of time and risk of one's advances being rejected). Certain places are known for a particular clientele and immediate consummation: such are 'leather' bars, which often have a backroom specially reserved for the purpose, saunas and public parks. Such places often afford the simultaneous satisfaction of a variety of desires, for example, exhibitionism, voyeurism, at the same time as all kinds of pair or group activities. But even

---

[9] Dannecker and Reiche, *Der gewöhnliche Homosexuelle*, pp. 23ff.

in less specialized places, where consummation on the spot is not possible, one may study the search for effectiveness. The more an individual is sexually set in his ways, the less he will take the risk of making a mistake, or approaching a 'normal' person. This shows the crucial importance of distinguishing marks and choice of background. The finesse of communication during the pick-up is a sign less of the search for quantity than extreme choosiness and fear of a painful rejection.[10] Lack of response to a furtive glance or hidden smile often brings an attempted approach to an abrupt end.

External signs indicate the sexual taste of the moment. For example there is the key ploy: keys worn above the left hip pocket of jeans indicate a preference for an active role, on the right for the passive. The same with a handkerchief sticking out of a hip pocket: the side chosen indicates an active or a passive role, the colour of the handkerchief the form of activity required. Light blue jeans means oral practices; dark blue, buggery; bright red, manual penetration, and so on.[11] The more homosexuality comes out into the open and the techniques of self-advertisement become publicized, like fashions, outside the milieu, the more the signs become overstated, and they often lose their initial significance. One example is the little gold earring in the left ear which has become an everyday ornament.

The sectors that are most liberated from all external constraints observe two rules in their performance on the sexual market. First there is the exact indication of the type of sex required in physical terms (anus, mouth, etc.) and of the desired form of activity (active, passive, SM or sado-masochist). The sexual preference must be clearly indicated, without imposture, without any by-play, without hesitation, without enticement. Quite unequivocally, the name of the game is the sexual act. Secondly, anonymity: silence is a strictly observed rule in meeting-places that in themselves are without identity — parks, saunas, public lavatories — secluded, isolated enough for two or more to gather without too much risk of being surprised by the police or hooligans. Often the forename muttered after the act is the only word exchanged before the partners separate.

The mere indication of desire provides no visual evidence of a

---

[10] W. Sage, 'Inside the colossal closet', in M.P. Levine, *Gay Men, The sociology of male Homosexuality*, New York, 1979, p. 159.

[11] Further examples of such ploys are given in M. Emory, *The Gay Picturebook*, Chicago, 1979.

homosexual's specialization. On the contrary, there appears to be a relative lack of differentiation between active and passive roles played by one individual. Homosexual behaviour seems to conform with a twofold pattern; specialization, where one gets to know more and more certainly what one wants at a given moment; and differentiation, where one seeks out more and more variegated practices. It is a fact that homosexuals who have the greatest number of sexual relations also have the largest repertoire of practices and meeting places. Obviously even the homosexual market is not 'purely' single-minded, i.e. it is affected by external influences. For instance there are aesthetic influences, and the myth of youth brings about a sharp fall in sexual activity after the age of 38/42 (see table A4). The sexual market is also shaped by racial criteria. Thus in the United States there are radically mixed centres of homosexuality, but also others frequented exclusively by either blacks or whites only. In American slang those who make love only with whites are called 'snow queens', while those who prefer blacks are 'chocolate queens'.[12] Other external influences that affect the homosexual market are financial interest (in prostitution) and emotional security (the search for a partner).

The extent to which its members participate in the sexual market and submit to its rules — which are, after all, fairly restrictive — divides the milieu into sub-groups, who live out their homosexual destiny in very different ways. There are very few who suceed in freeing themselves totally from the socializing influence imprinted on them in childhood, an influence totally oriented towards a life of heterosexuality. This gives rise to guilt complexes and self-hatred. And even when they have managed to shake off the heterosexual modes of life instilled in childhood, few homosexuals readily accept the demands of sexual productivism that prevail in the milieu. In short the conditions of 'coming out' are seldom totally fulfilled, such conditions being integration into the homosexual milieu and a cheerful and unworried public admission of one's proclivities. Most homosexuals remain tied to a schizophrenic existence, and the conduct of their homosexual career is the outcome of the kind of socialization experienced prior to 'coming out', and the extent to which they have internalized the rules of the milieu. Bell and Weinberg have postulated four types of homosexual who vary according to these two influences (see table 1). This classification depicts the homosexual milieu as a world that varies widely in the ways the individual relates

---

[12] J.V. Soares, 'Black and Gay' in Levine, *Gay Men*, pp. 263ff.

Table 1 Categories of homosexuals (after Bell and Weinberg)

		closed coupled (quasi-marriage)	open coupled (free marriage)	functionals (adapted to the rules of the sexual market)	dysfunctionals (following the rules but disapproving)	asexuals
A	number of partners	few	many	many	many	few
	frequency of sexual activity	great	great	great	great	small
	pick-ups	little	much	much	much	little
B	sexual problems	no	yes	no	many	many
	regrets at being homosexual	no	no	no	yes	yes

A: indicators of acceptance and internalization of the rules of the homosexual milieu
B: indicators of the extent of socialization prior to 'coming out'

to all the rules governing socio-sexual relations. But it has all the drawbacks of an approach that is characteristic of behaviouristic sexology, which is at the same time empirical and very normative. This kind of analysis takes no account of the pressures imposed by the rules of the homosexual milieu. Psychic and sexual equilibrium is simply thought of as 'adaptation' to social norms, in this case to those of the milieu, and this is shown by the terms used in the analysis, such as 'functional' and 'dysfunctional'. The origins and legitimacy of the norms are never questioned; hence the deep-seated ties which bind this new sexual order to the old repressiveness are underestimated. Born of simple negation and an assertion of contrariness, this new order is still saturated with the mentality of the old one. By imprisoning the minority that it claims to be liberating in a new vicious circle of 'adaptation', this time to the norms of the milieu, sexological empiricism is reinforcing the tendencies towards social autosegregation of a group which has barely emerged from the shadows, and in the end is simply opening already open doors.

Homosexuality and social class

Although the collective character of homosexual 'life tends to blunt social distinctions, class origin and membership affect the ease with which an individual succeeds in integrating with the milieu and in leading a double life. The German enquiry has shown that class origin has a different effect on sexual behaviour on the one hand, and on the guilt feelings caused by homosexuality on the other. The higher one climbs in the social hierarchy, the fewer become one's sexual contacts; and with increasing age they diminish more rapidly in the higher classes than in the world of the working class and junior employees.[13] In contrast, it seems that the differentiation of sexual practices does not follow the same pattern. But the sample used in the Germans' research was not large enough for any very significant conclusions to be drawn. Much stronger feelings of guilt, however, seem to be experienced by the working classes, minor employees and officials than by the higher executive class and members of the liberal professions.[14] According to Reiche and Dannecker the explanation of this paradox is to be found in the way techniques of socialization

---

[13] Dannecker and Reiche, *Der gewöhnliche Homosexuelle*, pp. 198ff.
[14] Ibid., pp. 42ff.

and attitudes towards homosexuality vary from one class to another. Socialization in the lower classes is very rigid and clearly defined in terms of restrictions and demands. At the same time the techniques of inculcation are less insidious than in the higher classes, and children are not so endlessly supervised. The result is that the strict norms peculiar to lower class socialization are often followed without being internalized, hence the lower degree of inhibition among youths of this class, which enables them to launch out early into a fairly intense sexual career. The rules of the milieu are also less internalized, and the myth of youth that produces a diminution of sexual activity towards the age of 40 affects them much less; their sex life in its full intensity lasts a good deal beyond that age.

According to Reiche and Dannecker guilt feelings are much more persistent among the lower classes — in spite of a more satisfactory sex life — because of the much greater hostility to homosexuality in their own class; this obliges homosexuals to keep the two sides of their lives much more strictly apart, and to feign a heterosexual life style at their place of work.

The American studies of Bell and Weinberg show no significant correlation between sexual behaviour and social class. On the other hand their analysis throws up differences between blacks and whites, and these correspond to the differences between classes in Germany. Given the correlation between racial origin and social status, one may regard these two studies as almost identical in their findings. The American study shows that blacks start their sex life before whites, that it is more intense, and lasts longer.[15] The reason given in the German case, differences in socialization, applies also to the Americans, but only in part. One must not forget the great cultural difference. Thus homosexuality is traditionally accepted in poor black circles, which are remote from the influences of 'Middle America'. In these circles a homosexual relationship fits in quite comfortably with the extended family, and homosexuals tend not to accept the detachment of sex from affection, and the anonymity that prevails in the homosexual market.[16] They do, however, suffer from the confined character of the homosexual milieu, which prevents them from benefitting from the toleration afforded them in their own racial milieu.

The extent to which homosexuals are tolerated in different professional milieus gives rise to special social strategies. Homo-

---

[15] Bell and Weinberg, *Homosexualities*, p. 124.
[16] Ibid., p. 77; Soares, 'Black and Gay' p. 264.

sexuals of modest origins often aim for an above average educational level to try and escape from a hostile environment. Thus one may see a marked disparity between social origin, i.e. the father's socio-professional category, and social position. While the social origin of homosexuals corresponds more or less with the general distribution of the total population in social classes, one does see an over-representation of homosexuals in the new *petite bourgeoisie*, in service jobs (hairdressing, waiters) and particularly in occupations that set a premium on the kind of social graces and diplomatic skills that homosexuals, leading a double life and playing different parts before different audiences, may well have had to acquire from childhood. Public relations, selling and personnel management constitute a few of these professions. On the other hand there are relatively few homosexuals among manual and farm workers.

Higher up in the social hierarchy the reverse is true. Homosexuality seems rather to impede advancement in a career. Obliged to combine their homosexual predilections with a fairly conspicuous social life not easy to fit in with fringe sex, and having to cope with the risk of blackmail or the necessity of accepting a *mariage de convenance*, the sons of the upper classes often prefer to turn their attention to intellectual and artistic careers rather than business or politics. They often content themselves with achieving rather less than their social origin may have promised.

To sum up, the concentration of homosexuals in particular socio-professional categories has nothing to do with myths about their natural sensitiveness, their innate artistic gifts, or a special sort of intelligence or brilliance. The logical compulsions of social life and the milieu dictate the encroachment of sexual strategies on professional careers. The sensitivity specially attributed to homosexuals is nothing but a form of clear-sightedness derived from continuous role playing, a distancing from themselves, in reaction to an ever-present, though unstated, feeling of being excluded. The extent of the exclusion is known only to the victim who, without either the will or the power to rebel against this discrimination, learns to adapt himself to the situation and his own manoeuvres.

The yearning for a partner

Most of the pangs and problems of the homosexual condition come from the great divide between affectivity and sexuality, caused by the lack of social and material cement that tends to make heterosexual relationships last. Often based only on the sexual act, a pair relationship rarely stands up to the test of time (see table A5). Seldom lasting more than two years, it is often bedevilled from the start by dramas, anguish and infidelities. Faced with the example of the heterosexual norm and without any real life pattern of its own, the pair relationship still remains the deep-felt ideal in spite of successive and almost inevitable setbacks. How can sexual impulses stimulated by the existence of a highly accessible and almost inexhaustible market be reconciled with the sentimental ideal of a stable relationship? This is the commonest problem that homosexuals who contact sexual and psychological consultants hope to solve.[17]

The antithesis between the loving couple ideal and the turbulence of the sexual market occasionally erupts into a highly dramatized, almost hysterical way of life. Partings, even after quite a short relationship (a few months), are often accompanied by passionate explosions with devastating, long-drawn-out scenes. It is obvious that real drama underlies this kind of play acting.

There are plenty of psychological problems, especially during the 'coming out' period. Many homosexuals suffer from depression, claim they need treatment, or are tempted to commit suicide. In the German research report, 13 per cent said they would certainly like to have treatment, and an additional 22 per cent said they would provided there was a genuinely validated method of sexual reorientation (see table A6). This rate of attempted suicides is twice that for the population as a whole; 13 per cent said they had made one or more attempts to commit suicide. Nearly all homosexual suicide attempts take place between the ages of 16 and 18; after 21 they almost cease. Paradoxically, suicide attempts in the whole population are uniformly distributed between the ages of 19 and 40. This seems to show that homosexuals have greater psychological stability and more capacity for putting up with their own inner contradictions, once they have cleared the 'coming out' fence. Bell and Weinberg's research shows the same tendencies in the United States. Although the homosexual rate of attempted suicide is higher than the national average, it falls well below it among fully confirmed homosexuals.[18]

The sufferings homosexuals endure in pursuit of an almost unattainable ideal get dramatized; and this gives rise to a particular

---

[17] R. Reece, 'Coping with Couplehood', in Levine, *Gay Men*, pp. 211ff.

[18] Dannecker and Reiche, *Der gewöhnliche Homosexuelle*, pp. 359–360, Bell and Weinberg, *Homosexualities*, pp. 123ff and 195ff.

sort of humour which wryly 'sends up' its own milieu. Like the humour of every other minority group, such as the Jews or the American blacks, it is only totally comprehensible to members of the group. It borrows many cult figures from sentimental Hollywood comedies, and the milieu's heroines are often stars who personify femininity or the essence of womanhood, prized and sought after for its sexual attributes, while wanting to be understood as a human, fragile creature. One can well understand why Marilyn Monroe should be one of the stars most beloved of homosexuals. Hence too their liking for theatrical shows in which sexual intrigue and sentimental 'kitsch' run riot.[19] Most homosexuals secretly long for an audience they can entertain with a clownish and extravagant version of their own character.

Furthermore, this humour and by-play seems universally accepted. A broken relationship rarely leads to enmity or total separation. Basically one can interpret all the drama surrounding a rupture between homosexuals as part of the rites of passage from love to a friendship that signifies the stability of a relationship. A stabilization of this kind often involves a renunciation of sex and its replacement by a bond of mutual trust. Out of this a whole network of friendly relationships may grow, providing an emotional security which is almost impossible to achieve in a pair relationship. Little groups of friends, often former lovers who in the past have all had sexual relations with each other, form a sort of 'extended homosexual family'. Moreover a kind of incest taboo frequently inhibits casual sexual contacts in these groups that are bound by fraternal feelings. 'Brother' or 'little brother' is often the special name for those former lovers with whom the ups and downs of life together, as well as a common vocation, have been shared.

From culture to ghetto

Secrecy is responsible for the two outstanding features of homosexual culture — its language and its humour. The two are closely connected. The dictionary of homosexual slang produced in the United States[20] gives hundreds of examples of a vocabulary that is full of variations on the theme of love, pick ups, timidity, grief

---

[19] V. Russo, 'Camp', in Levine, Gay Men, pp. 208ff.

[20] B. Rodgers, Gay Talk. The Queens Vernacular, A (sometimes outrageous) dictionary of gay slang, New York, 1979.

and joy, aggressive cynicism. The use of female christian names and epithets and affectedly precious diminutives expresses, often in the same breath, the game of social hide-and-seek and the irony that many homosexuals cultivate in the persona that they present to the world. The 'crazy old queen' figure, which is the typical version of homosexuality as seen by heterosexuals, and the actual pose adopted by some homosexuals, combines all the elements of anti-homosexual prejudice as well as being an 'in' joke of the milieu. The 'crazy old queen', the figure that constantly crops up in jokes and music hall acts, is the extreme case of the homosexual who has resigned himself to behave like the caricature his oppressors make of him. By such behaviour he hopes to mitigate the aggression he anticipates from his heterosexual companions by making them laugh, and by fulfilling all the expectations expressed in the heterosexual view of homosexuality. Morever the fact that homosexual behaviour does actually correspond to some extent with the mental picture that heterosexuals have of homosexuality reflects the need for homosexuals to maintain a group identity in a situation of social oppression. At a time when homosexuals are openly under duress, and when it seems impossible for them to formulate any consistent view of homosexuality as such, the only way to preserve a group identity is to accept the burlesque image that the majority imposes on the minority. Out of this humiliating version of group identity there develops the solidarity that eventually achieves emancipation.

It is understandable that, once social pressure was relaxed, the militant homosexuals at once tried to reshape the homosexual image, dissociating it from the conventional view which saw the homosexual as at best an effeminate man, at worst a second-rate woman. The reaction against such distortions has caused the 'super-virile', the 'macho' man to become the homosexual pin-up type: crew cut, moustache or beard, and muscular body. And while the topic of heterosexual freedom is often seen in terms of a lack of differentiation between male and female roles, homosexual emancipation is today passing through a phase in which sexual identity is sharply defined. The myth types depicted in the homosexual press and the specialized pornographic magazines are cowboys, lorry drivers and athletes. The 'macho' style predominates.[21] There is a certain uneasiness over pederasty and

---

[21] L. Humphreys, 'Exodus and identity: the emerging gay culture', in Levine, *Gay Men*, pp. 141ff. See equally M. Walter, *The nude Male. A new perspective*, Harmondsworth, 1979, pp. 296–370.

bisexuality, often felt as attempts to conceal homosexuality. This move of the homosexual milieu towards a style that stresses virility is often accused of being sexist, and tends to exclude such homosexuals as do not conform to this new definition of the homosexual identity. While admitting the existence of these manifestations of exclusiveness, one must emphasize that the quest for such a very strict sexual identity occurs at a moment when, for the first time, the opportunity is offered to homosexuals to form their own social image and to stress their masculine rather than their feminine traits. If in the near future society were to become more tolerant of homosexuality, one might find a slight weakening of this will to construct a 'macho' image.

In the sixties emancipation began by provoking an explosion of sexual commercialization. Besides a great increase in the number of bars, cinemas and saunas, there came the development of a homosexual press, pornographic literature and a whole industry of gadgets and sex aids, from leather toys, sex rings and creams to 'poppers' (vaso-dilators used as aphrodisiacs). As the earliest militants of *Gay Lib* remarked 'Have we brought about our revolution merely to have the right to open another seven hundred leather bars?'[22]

The tourist industry was equally quick to exploit the homosexual milieu. The propensity for promiscuity rapidly exhausts the local market in small and medium sized towns; hence travel and weekends away. Homosexual geography ramifies in all large urban centres. Certain cities have well-established reputations for being particularly 'gay': in Europe, Amsterdam, Berlin, Paris, Hamburg and Munich; in the United States, New York and San Francisco. During the holiday season various *plages* are well known for their specialized *habitués*: the island of Sylt in the North Sea, Mykonos in Greece, Le Touquet and L'Espiguette in France, Key West and Cape Cod in the United States, and so on. These holiday resorts sometimes provide 'unique happenings' like the Carnival of Rio. This commercialization, which has come with emancipation, is beginning to underline class differences which, though always present in the milieu, used hardly to come to the surface on account of the very strong sense of unity which linked its members in support of their shared addiction. Today homosexuals accept this commercialization and see it as liberating to the extent that it promotes greater tolerance for them.

---

[22] R. von Praunheim, *Armee der Liebenden oder Aufstand der Perversen*, Munich, 1979, p. 27.

The emergence from the heart of the homosexual milieu of an image of virility to set up against the effeminate one depicted by heterosexuals has brought about the formation of a homosexual community that demands rights and organizes itself to achieve them. For this strategy to succeed homosexuals see as essential the 'coming out' of the greatest possible number and a public proclamation of their homosexuality. The development of places of resort, the organization of collective activities, and material and psychological supports (emergency telephone services, radio and television stations, medical services for the discreet treatment of venereal disease, sympathetic therapists, and legal help in cases of loss of employment or broken leases, etc.), have as their function the assistance of all homosexuals in their daily life and the encouragement of the 'coming out' move.

The homosexual identity and its community have only just emerged from the shadows into broad daylight, but this has already led to economic, political and topographical organization. One consequence, in the big American conurbations, has been the growth of 'ghettos', i.e. in the classic sense of the word, urban districts inhabited by groups segregated from the rest of society, leading a relatively autonomous life and developing their own culture.[23] This 'ghettoization' is particularly marked in West Village in Manhattan, the Castro district in San Francisco, South End in Boston, round Dupont Circle in Washington, and in certain parts of Chicago and Los Angeles. In these districts homosexuals constitute a large proportion of the population, control much of the trade, especially the bars, the housing and the labour market. Occasionally they have even managed to organize significant pressure groups at elections. This tendency towards ghettoization may also be seen in Europe, but to a much lesser extent.

The formation of a campaigning body of this kind can lead to difficulties with local society. Creating almost official systems of mutual help in the labour and housing market is likely to cause problems of competition such as affect any social group acting as an aggressive minority in pursuit of social advancement. Such problems have already appeared in the American ghettos where homosexuals, who want to establish themselves in particular districts, often come up against ethnic minorities with less economic muscle.[24] The ideology of the united front shared by all

[23] M.P. Levine, 'Gay Ghetto', in Levine, *Gay Men*, pp. 182ff.
[24] See the article by M. Singer, 'Gay-Black ties fray in post-Milk era', in *In these Times*, 13—19 June, 1979, p.7.

oppressed people risks being eroded by the realities of competition when minorities in society attempt to turn it to their own advantage.

In addition to all this the solidarity begotten of enforced secrecy will be harder to maintain in a group that has won a certain social acceptance. Initially the commercialism that surrounded homosexuality brought it much more sharply into the public eye, indirectly enhancing group cohesiveness. But in the long run it exposes the social divisions that cut across the milieu: for instance, pick-up haunts and leisure resorts come to be differentiated by social and economic status. The sense of shared destiny which unites homosexuals across the barriers that separate social classes will tend to disappear.

Sexual identity and social classification

A large number of recent works on homosexuality, and especially those of sociological inspiration, describe 'coming out' — the double process of joining the homosexual club and asserting one's homosexual character before the outside world — as not only an initiation and acceptance of homosexuality, but also a quest for a life style. In putting forward this process as a solution to the problems of homosexuals in a social context that continues to be hostile, this sort of literature furthers the realization of what it is describing — a homosexual community and culture that form part of a rather wider liberalization of morals. Implicitly, the advice given in this literature — and it concerns not only homosexuals — is 'Shape your surroundings and your own way of life to accord with your sexual desires!'

What is written about homosexuality follows, and at the same time helps to shape, the various definitions attached by society to the homosexual identity. At the end of the nineteenth century and at the beginning of the twentieth it was a question either of justifying or opposing scientifically the stigma attached to a social group labelled 'homosexuals' by elaborating a sexual geography with territories classified according to their relation to nature. The concern of contemporary writing is to try and transform the stigma into an actual criterion for belonging to a social group on its way to emancipation. To encourage 'coming out', seen as the individual's admission of his homosexual identity, but also as his membership of a social movement enabling many people to identify themselves most positively, is to help create a situation in which sexual orientation impinges on the way things are seen or defined in every kind of social relation.[25]

It is clear that sexologists have one eye on the objectives aimed at by the militants, who tend to reduce all interpretation of social reality to the criterion of sexual identity, as witness the discovery of a specifically homosexual literary sensibility, art and even history. To some extent 'scientific' pronouncements about homosexuality are subordinated to practical ends and directed to the achievement of social objectives. But this sort of scientific discourse about homosexuality cannot in practice be confined to being a mere travelling companion in the movement towards homosexual emancipation. It belongs, in a wider sense, to the whole body of serious literature on sexuality, and, while it contributes to the social definition of homosexuality, it has the effect of emphasizing the importance of 'sexuality' in the multi-dimensional classification of us all.

In socio-sexological literature the homosexual milieu seems to foreshadow a social life in which sexuality becomes progressively freed from all traditional inhibitions and fitted into the complex web of all social interactions. According to this interpretation the homosexual milieu is seen as a model which demonstrates that one can indulge in the appetites of the flesh in all sorts of ways and at the same time overcome a sense of isolation, and that it is perfectly possible to keep the satisfaction of one's sexual and affective needs in separate compartments. The increase in the number of young people who choose to live alone shows that a large part of the population wants to experiment in ways of life that combine fleeting sexual relations with a social and affective life based on a variety of relationships, not necessarily destined to last long.

The latest book by Masters and Johnson, which compares homosexual and heterosexual behaviour, serves to reinforce this picture.[26] Much of what they say is addressed to heterosexuals. They reproach them for not devoting enough time to preliminary love-play, for being ignorant of all the pleasures of having a lover, and for remaining incapable of making known their specific sexual needs. According to them these problems are less felt in a homosexual relationship. Homosexuality built up into an ideal pattern? Will homosexuals soon find themselves living in a society

[25] P. Bourdieu, 'L'Identité et la représentation' in *Actes de la recherche en sciences sociales*, 35, 1980, p. 69.

[26] W.H. Masters and V.E. Johnson, *Homosexuality in Perspective*, Boston, 1979.

which not merely tolerates them, but actually finds qualities in them worth imitating?

One comes across similar phenomena in other sectors in which the homosexual image is an energizing force in the transformation of life styles. The 'disco' phenomenon symbolizes the trendsetting influence that the homosexual milieu has on certain sectors of society. All self-respecting discos try to make themselves equally attractive to a homosexual clientele and to create an ambivalent atmosphere in which all sorts of tastes can mingle. Very many disco hits — perhaps a majority — coming from the United States allude to homosexuality. One of the most successful groups, 'The Village People', addresses its songs directly to homosexuals: 'Macho Man', 'In the Navy' and 'YMCA' are stuffed with homo-erotic fantasies and allusions to places of homosexual initiation.

This unambiguous boost for homosexuality is not aimed either exclusively or principally at the betterment of the homosexual's lot. By treating all manifestations of sex on the same level and being concerned only with their efficacity in an exclusively sexual way, the Masters and Johnson approach tends to re-unite the territories of a sexual landscape that the literature about perversions had kept separate. The result of this is to eliminate the stigmas which earlier classifications had attached to certain sexual practices. In its initial stage, which is where we are today, this change in the scientific portrayal of sexuality, apart from abolishing the borders between different expressions of sexuality, prefers to differentiate between such portrayals in terms of separate sexual identities. Every one of these may give rise to a 'group' or a 'movement' that claims a place of its own and freedom (at the cost of segregation) to indulge unrestrainedly in its own form of sexual behaviour. Such a system of differentiation and segregation tends to diminish the violent enmity between heterosexuals and homo-sexuals. It could start up many realignments in the affiliations and viewpoints of those who take part in controversies about acceptable or inacceptable sexual practices.

Statistical appendix to chapter 5

These tables, taken from the American research of A.P. Bell and M.S. Weinberg (*Homosexualities. A Study of Diversity among Men and Women*, New York 1978, Statistical Appendix pp. 269–475) and from the German research of M. Dannecker and R. Reiche (*Der gerwöhnliche Homosexuelle*, Frankfurt, 1974) serve more to illustrate our text than show up the differences in homosexual life in two national environments. The likelihood of statistical inaccuracy in a field of research which is so new, so liable to change and so difficult to approach as homosexuality, is very great. Both research groups used the 'snowball' method: a limited number of homosexual acquaintances are asked to pass on questionnaires to their friends, asking them to pass on to theirs, and so on. But the sampling techniques were totally different in the two research groups. In the United States, San Francisco and its suburbs were deliberately chosen for their avant-garde character and tolerant and generous attitude toward homosexuality: 'San Francisco's sexual permissiveness foreshadows what could well happen elsewhere in the country. That was an important reason for choosing San Francisco for our research' (p. 28). In order to depict every variety of homosexual life Bell and Weinberg approached homosexuals in all kinds of places of resort, bars, saunas, restaurants, cafés, etc. Dannecker and Reiche, on the other hand, tried to arrive at balanced samples, based on size of towns, social origin and age of those questioned.

Table A1 Age at the time of first sexual act

Age group	USA whites % (N = 574)	blacks % (N = 111)	Age group	West Germany % (N = 789)
up to 19	13	43	up to 20	80
20–23	33	40	21–25	14
over 23	36	17	over 25	6

Table A2 Number of sexual partners in the twelve months prior to survey

number of partners	USA whites %	blacks %	number of partners	West Germany %
0	3	—	0	—
1–2	8	10	1	6
3–5	10	12	2–5	19
6–10	12	14	6–10	16
11–19	12	5	11–19	22
20–50	27	28	20–50	20
over 50	28	32	over 50	17

Table A3 Total number of sexual partners

number of partners	USA		West Germany %
	whites %	blacks %	
1–99	25	41	56
100–499	32	26	29
over 499	43	33	15

Table A4 Frequency of sexual activity per year and per person
at different ages (W. Germany only)

	18–20 (N=32)	21–25 (N=153)	26–30 (N=250)	31–35 (N=141)	36–40 (N=76)	41–50 (N=59)	over 50 (N=57)
Heterosexual activity	6	3	1	3	0	2	3
Homosexual activity	99	104	116	113	108	78	43
Masturbation	153	145	144	117	132	108	70
Total sexual frequency per year and per person	258	252	261	233	240	118	116

Table A5 Duration of stable relationships at time of interview

	USA		West Germany % (N=459)
	Whites % (N=249)	Blacks % (N=49)	
No stable relationship	57	53	42
Stable relationship	43	47	58
Durations of stable relationships:			
under 3 months	11	6	27*
under 1 year	18	45	8
1–3 years	28	35	16**
3–5 years	12	6	26***
over 5 years	31	8	23

* less than 6 months ** 1–2 years *** 2–5 years

Table A6 Desire to undergo treatment for homosexuality (if success assured)

	USA				
	Whites %		Blacks %		
	now*	initially*	now*	initially*	West Germany %
yes	14	28	13	23	13
perhaps**	–	–	–	–	22
no	86	72	87	77	65

* Question asked in USA
** Answer not catered for in US questionnaire

6

Thoughts on the history
of homosexuality

Philippe Ariès

As Michael Pollak has shown, one of the most striking features of contemporary western morality is the weakening of the ban on homosexuality. Today homosexuals form a compact group, still on the fringes of society but increasingly conscious of a group identity. It is a group which demands rights from a dominant society which is not yet ready to accept it, and in fact in France penalizes it with laws that double the punishment for sexual offences committed by members of the same sex. The long held dogmas of society are, however, beginning to show cracks. Signs of toleration, and even concession, unthinkable thirty years ago, are now appearing. Recently the newspapers reported a 'paramatrimonial' celebration in which a Protestant pastor (disavowed by his Church) tied two lesbians — not for life, of course, but for the longest time possible. The Pope has felt obliged to remind us of St Paul's denunciations of homosexuality, something which would hardly have been necessary were there not already signs of leniency within the Church itself. It is well known that in San Francisco the 'gays' have built up a formidable pressure group. In short, homosexuals are on the way to gaining recognition, and there are plenty of diehard moralists who fume over their brashness and the feebleness of their opponents. Michael Pollak, however, has certain reservations. He feels that this situation may not last, may even be reversed, and Gabriel Matzneff echoes these thoughts in an article in Le Monde (5 January 1980) under the title of 'Le Paradis clandestin'. Paradise has been reached, but it is still clandestine. 'We shall see the return and triumph of moral order (don't worry: it won't be tomorrow!) and we shall need to conceal ourselves more than ever. The future lies in the shadows.'

There are still a few worries. There is certainly a kind of tightening up going on, at the moment more for the sake of national security than public morality.[1] A beginning? But the normalization of sexuality and homosexuality has gone too far to be forced to yield to pressure from the police and the courts. It has to be admitted that the positions gained — or won — by homosexuality are not just because of tolerance or indifference or 'Anything goes, nothing matters.' There is something more deeply interfused, structural and permanent, or at least likely to be long lasting. Henceforward society as a whole is tending, with some resistance here and there, more and more to adapt itself to the homosexual pattern. This was one of Michael Pollak's propositions that I found particularly striking, namely that models of society as a whole tend to approximate to portrayals of themselves by homosexuals, an approximation due to a distortion of images and roles.

Let us pursue this line of thought. The generally accepted model of a homosexual, beginning with the time when he first felt and recognized his peculiar character, usually as a disease or perversion, i.e. from the beginning of the eighteenth to the beginning of the nineteenth century, was an effeminate type, a transvestite with a very high pitched voice. In this we see the homosexual conforming to the prevailing pattern: the men he loved looked like women, and this, in a sense, was reassuring for society. He could also love children or young folk (pederasty), an ancient relationship that we can call classical, since it goes back to Greco-Roman antiquity and survives today in the Moslem world, in spite of Ayatollah Khomeini and the executioner. It was tied up with traditional forms of education or initiation which could become degraded and furtive, while special friendships bordered on homosexuality without being conscious or recognized as such.

According to Michael Pollak, today's homosexual credo often totally rejects these two earlier types, the effeminate and the pederast, and replaces them with a macho, athletic, super-virile type, though still with a slim and youthful figure, unlike the muscular toughs of Mexican and Soviet art of the twenties and thirties. It is the hell's angel type, with a tight-fitting leather jacket and an earring, copied by an entire age group, without distinction of sex, an adolescent model that even girls adopt, so that often one hardly knows with whom one is dealing — him or her?

---

[1] These lines were written during the years 1979 and 1980 in an atmosphere of moral restrictiveness and obsession about state security.

Is not the obliteration, among adolescents, of the visible differences between men and women one of the most noteworthy and quite original features of our society, a *unisex society*? Roles are interchangeable, father and mother, husband and wife, lover and mistress. What is odd is the single idea of *virility*. Girls' figures start looking like boys'. They have lost that well-covered look so dear to painters from the sixteenth to the nineteenth century, still sought after in the Moslem world, perhaps because of the suggestion of potential maternity. Nobody today would make fun of a thin girl like this nineteenth-century poet who wrote:

I do not mind your scragginess, my dear;
A skinny bosom brings the heart more near.

Going back a little further in time one may find occasional hints of another faintly unisex society in fifteenth-century Italy, but without the ideal of virility and rather more androgynous.

The fact that the young everywhere aspire to an ideal physical type of obviously homosexual origin, perhaps explains their often sympathetic curiosity about homosexuality and their assumption of homosexual mannerisms at parties and pleasure spots generally. The 'homo' has indeed become a leading character in today's human comedy.

If my diagnosis is correct, the unisex fashion is a clear indication of a general change in society. Tolerance of homosexuality is the result of changes in the way the sexes present themselves to the world, in their actions, in their professional lives, in their families, but especially in their function as symbolic figures.

We have to make an effort to grasp what is going on before our eyes; but how can we get any idea of the moral postures of past ages except by studying the Church's interdictions? There a huge territory lies unexplored, and for the moment we have to content ourselves with a few impressions which could lead to avenues of research.

In the last few years books have appeared suggesting that homosexuality is an invention of the nineteenth century. In the discussion that followed his paper Michael Pollak expressed his doubts about this. Nevertheless the question is an interesting one. Obviously it does not mean that before then there were no homosexuals — an absurd idea. All we know is that there was homosexual behaviour, connected with certain periods of human life and special circumstances, which does not seem to have prevented those who indulged in it from behaving heterosexually at the same time. As Paul

Veyne has pointed out, our knowledge of classical antiquity indicates not homosexuality on one side and heterosexuality on the other, but a bisexuality whose manifestations *seem* to have been dependent on chance encounters rather than biological determinism.

Of course the appearance of a rigorous code of sexual morals based on a world philosophy that Christianity has built up and preserved to this day has favoured a stricter definition of 'sodomy'. But this term, derived from the habits of the men of Sodom in the Bible, denoted not only a form of copulation that was against nature but also men going to bed together, which was just as unnatural. Homosexuality was thus separated from heterosexuality, the only normal and permitted practice, but its rejection was so total that it was lumped in with every form of perversion. The *ars erotica* of the west is a catalogue of perversions that are all deadly sins. Hence arose a category of perverts, the so-called *luxuriosi*, from which it was hard for homosexuality to detach itself. The facts are, of course, a good deal more complex than this rather crude summary suggests. Later we shall see in Dante an example of this complexity turning into ambiguity. We have to admit that the homosexual of the Middle Ages and the *ancien régime* was a pervert.

By the end of the eighteenth and the beginning of the nineteenth century he has become a monster, a freak. This is an evolutionary process which incidentally makes one wonder about the link between the monster of the Middle Ages and the Renaissance and the biological sport of the age of the Enlightenment and the dawn of modern science (see J. Ceard). The freak, the dwarf, the old crone who gets suspected of witchcraft are affronts to God's creation and are accused of being creatures of the Devil. At the beginning of the nineteenth century the homosexual lived under this hereditary curse. He was at the same time a freak and a pervert. The Church was prepared to recognize the physical anomaly which made the homosexual a man-woman, an abnormal and always effeminate man; for we must not forget that this first stage towards the creation of an autonomous condition of homosexuality was under the label of effeminacy. The person who suffered from this anomaly certainly could not help it, but that did not save him from suspicion; for, being by his very nature more exposed to temptation, he was more liable to lead his neighbour astray. So he had to be shut up like a woman or watched over like a child, mistrusted by society. Merely by reason of his oddity he was suspected of becoming a pervert, a delinquent.

At the end of the eighteenth century the medical world adopted the Church's view of homosexuality, and it became an illness, or at least a disability, which could be diagnosed by clinical examination. Several recently published books have given us a recapitulation of these amazing doctors' views, which have caused much amusement. Within that murky world of prostitutes, wantons and debauchees a single *species* was emerging — consistent, homogeneous and with unique physical characteristics. The doctors had discovered how to track down the clandestine homosexual. Examination of anus and penis was enough to unmask them, for they displayed abnormalities, as did a circumcised Jew. They formed a sort of ethnic group, even though their characteristics had been acquired by use rather than inherited. Medical diagnosis was in fact caught between two forms of evidence. The physical evidence, the marks and blemishes of vice, could easily be found elsewhere among drunks and debauchees, whereas the moral evidence was an almost hereditary disposition for vice, which apparently threatened to corrupt their healthy-minded fellow beings. Faced with this wholesale denunciation as a race, homosexuals defended themselves, some by concealment, others by confessions. The latter were pathetic and pitiable, and occasionally cynical, but always displayed a distressing insistence, sometimes shamefaced, sometimes defiant, on their insurmountable separateness. Such confessions were not intended to be flaunted or made public, though one was sent to Zola, which so embarrassed him that he passed it on to someone else. These shamefaced avowals did not lead to special claims. Once the homosexual was declared as such, nothing was left for him but to retreat into the fringe society of perverts where he had languished till the doctors had brought him out to put him on show in their chamber of horrors. The anomaly condemned was one of sexual ambiguity, the effeminate man, the woman with male organs, the hermaphrodite.

In the next stage homosexuals threw off their clandestinity and the taint of perversion to claim their right to be openly what they were, and to assert their normality. As we have already seen, this change was accompanied by a change of pattern, with virility ousting effeminacy and boyishness. But this did not signify a return to the kind of classical bisexuality that still survived in college rags and school initiation ceremonies. The new type of homosexuality had no truck with heterosexuality, either from deliberate choice or through impotence. Now it was the homosexuals themselves — not the doctors and priests — who proclaimed their separateness, demanding, in the face of society, their own place in the sun.

I admit that Freud rejected the claim. 'Psycho-analysis absolutely refuses to admit that homosexuals constitute a group which has special characteristics distinguishable from those of other individuals.' In spite of this, the wider understanding of psychoanalysis has led not only to the emancipation of homosexuality, but also to its classification as a species, following in the path of the nineteenth-century doctors.

I have been tempted to argue that prior to the eighteenth century there was no such identifiable group as 'youth' or 'adolescence' — meaning an adolescence whose history might have been more or less the same (allowing for the difference in time-scale) as that of homosexuality: first the effeminate, Cherubino, then the virile, Siegfried. But, in contradiction, N.Z. Davis has rightly pointed to groups such as the *abbayes de la jeunesse* or the subculture of the London apprentices, which shows that there were social activities peculiar to adolescence and solidarity among young people.

All this is true. Youth did have its own status and functions, both in community life and in leisure activities, or in its working life and its relations with masters and mistresses. In other words there was a difference in status between unmarried adolescents and adults. *But this difference, even if it caused friction between them, did not divide them into two separate non-communicating worlds.* Although adolescents had their own special jobs to do, there was no separate category of adolescence, and so hardly any stereotype of adolescent. There were exceptions. For instance, in fifteenth-century Italy and in Elizabethan literature, adolescence does seem to be personified in a slim, elegant youthfulness, with a faintly ambivalent touch of homosexuality. In the eighteenth century, on the other hand, the male figure is virile, the female fecund. The seventeenth-century type is a youthful man, not a youth. It is the youthful man, and his wife, not the youth, who sit on the top of the age pyramid. Effeminacy, boyishness, even the slender youthfulness of the Quattrocento play no part in the dream fantasies of that age.

On the other hand, at the end of the eighteenth and especially in the nineteenth century, adolescence begins to acquire substance, though in contrast it gradually loses its status in society as a whole and ceases to be an organic part of it, becoming merely the threshold. This compartmentalization was restricted at the beginning of the nineteenth century (the Romantic period) to middle-class schoolboys. After the Second World War, for all manner of reasons, it was extended and generalized, so that now adolescence has swollen into a huge, unstructured age group that people enter early and leave, with some difficulty, rather late, after getting married. It has become a sort of dream state. It started by being a masculine affair, with girls continuing to share the life and activities of grown-up women. Later, when, as today, adolescence became unisex, girls and boys conformed to a common, rather masculine pattern.

It is interesting to compare the histories of the two myths — youth or adolescence and homosexuality. There are significant parallels.

The history of homosexuality raises another question linked with the history of sexuality in general. Up to the eighteenth century, and for long after, sex simply meant procreation and the functions of the sexual organs among the vast numbers of common folk in town and country. Poetry and high art bridged the gap between desire and love; but the world of feeling and the world of genesis were kept firmly apart. Popular songs and pictures and bawdy stories never strayed far from the genital. So there was a whole-heartedly sexy side facing a rather refined asexual side. Today, enlightened by Dostoevsky as well as Freud, and by our greater open-mindedness, we know this is not a true picture. The people of the *ancien régime* and the Middle Ages were deceiving themselves. We know that the asexual was soaked in sex, though in a diffused and unconscious way. This was as true of the mystics as it was of Bernini and the Baroque. Not but what contemporaries were quite unconscious of the fact and, protected by their ignorance, walked serenely beside the abyss without losing their balance.

After the eighteenth century the two worlds overlapped, the sexual infiltrating the asexual. The recent popularization of psycho-analysis (an effect rather than a cause of this) has demolished the last barriers. We now think we can attach a label to all those desires and hidden urges which were once invisible and anonymous. We go too far, and splashing around in all directions we see sex in everything. Every cylinder is a phallus. Sex no longer sticks to its own domain; leaving the purely genital it has invaded man, the child, the whole of social life. We are in the habit of explaining the pansexuality of our age by the weakened hold of religious morality and the search for happiness derived from a defiance of social inhibitions. It is also a phenomenon of sensuous awareness, one of the strongest traits of modernity. The same eye can find beauty in a Gothic church, a Baroque palace and an African mask, whereas formerly appreciation of one would have excluded the others. Likewise, just as arts of very contrasting kinds may be invested with beauty, so sex, which has its own kind of beauty, suffuses every sector of life, of individuals and of societies, where earlier it had passed unnoticed. Now its image, once hidden or undeveloped, emerges from the unconscious like a photographic plate in developing fluid. This is not a totally new phenomenon; in fact it goes back to the days of de Sade, but in the last twenty years we have seen it frenziedly speeded up.

One of the most striking aspects of this pansexuality has been the awareness and recognition of homosexuality. I wonder if there is not some connection between the spread of a conventionalized form of homosexuality and the diminishing role of personal friendship in contemporary society. Friendship once bulked large in people's lives, as is shown by the evidence of wills, and curiously enough the word *amitié* was used in a wider sense than today, including love, or at least the love between engaged and married couples. It seems to me that a history of friendship would show its decline during the nineteenth and twentieth centuries among adults, in favour of close family ties, and a return to it among adolescents. It has become a trait of adolescence, disappearing later.

In recent decades friendship has carried sexual overtones that make it rather sheepishly equivocal or shamefaced. Society looks askance on friendship between men of widely different ages. Today Hemingway's Old Man returning with the boy from their trip to sea would arouse the suspicions of the vice squad and mothers of families. Advance of homosexuality, decline of friendship, prolongation of adolescence, now ensconced at the centre of today's society: such are the nodal characteristics of our time, and who can tell how or why they are interrelated?

Thirty years — that is a generation ago — thoughts on homosexuality would have devoted a lot of attention to the equivocal friendship, the love which attracted a man irresistibly towards another man, a woman towards another woman — tragic passions which sometimes ended in death or suicide. For archetypes we would have chosen Achilles and Patroclus (comrades in arms), Harmodius and Aristogeiton (man and *ephebos*), the epicene and mysterious friendships of Michelangelo, Shakespeare and Marlowe, and nearer our own times the officer in Julien Green's play *Sud*. We see nothing like this in Michael Pollak's analysis and his picture of homosexuality. Here we find a total rejection of the heart's emotion and romantic love, and nothing but exclusively sexual goods for sale in the market-place for orgasms.

In actual fact the homosexual society he describes is not totally devoid of sentiment, but this is deferred until after the rather brief period of sexual activity. Homosexuals, like contemporary heterosexuals, cannot endure prolonged attachments. Their love is not lifelong but lasts only for an unrepeatable moment that leaves no room for tender feelings. Sentiment is left to the veterans. Former lovers, Michael Pollak tells us, when they meet again, do so on a level of pure brotherly affection; anything else would be considered incestuous. This, of course, is after, not during the affair.

Earlier we spoke of pansexuality and its intrusion into every aspect of life today. That is only one aspect of it; another, which seems at first totally inconsistent, is the way it gets concentrated, canalized as it were. Sex now has nothing to do with procreation or love in the old sense, which in their turn were akin to friendship. It is quite uncontaminated by such sentimental considerations. It is a consummation of the deepest urges, allowing man and woman to experience total fulfilment during the moment, lived like an eternity, of the orgasm. The orgasm has in fact become an object of veneration. This is why homosexuality, having by its nature nothing to do with procreation, is independent, free to disregard tradition and the rules of society, and able to exploit to the utmost the sexual dichotomy involved in the orgasm. It becomes sexuality in its purest state, a sexuality that makes its own way.

In earlier communities sex was indulged in either for procreation, hence legitimately, or for perversion, which was condemned. Beyond these restrictions sentiment might find a place. Today sentiment has been taken over by the family, which earlier had no such monopoly. That is why friendship played such an important role. But sentiment between men went beyond friendship, even in its widest sense: it acted as a lubricant in many service relationships that today are governed by contracts. Social life was organized round personal ties, dependence, patronage, mutual help. Relations at work were man-to-man relationships which could evolve from friendship or mutual confidence into exploitation and hatred — a hatred that was close to love; but they never settled down into indifference or impersonality. To relationships with dependents were added those with clients, fellow citizens, clan members, one's own circle. One existed in the middle of a web of sentiment which was at once vague and haphazard, only partially arising from birth or locality, quickly affected by chance encounters or *coups de foudre*.

This sort of sentiment had nothing to do with the sexuality that later intruded on it. Nevertheless we may guess that sexual feelings were not entirely absent from the bands of young men in the Middle Ages described by Georges Duby, nor from the epic friendships of the *Gestes* and the *Romans*, all of which involved the very young. Were they *amitiés particulières*? This by the way was the title of a novel by Roger Peyrefitte — a masterpiece — in which the 'friendships' are shrouded in ambiguity, a vagueness which totally disappears in later works by the same author, where homosexuality is flaunted by quite unambiguous characters as a mode of behaviour with clear-cut outlines. I think that in certain cultures, e.g. the Italian Quattrocento and Elizabethan England, there developed, out of an apparently asexual form of sentiment, a particular kind of manly love that verged on homosexuality; but it was a homosexuality that was undeclared and unadmitted, that remained a mystery, less through fear of prohibition than from a distaste for labelling oneself in the eyes of contemporary society as non-sexual or sexual. One hovered in a mixed zone that belonged to neither.

It is not always easy to tell who was really homosexual and who was not, the criteria being mostly anachronistic (i.e. of our own time) or merely polemical, like Agrippa d'Aubigné's accusations against Henry III and his *mignons*, or else simply vague. The attitude of ancient communities towards homosexuality — about which we know very little and which we should study with fresh eyes and a disregard for the anachronisms of psycho-analysis — seems more complex than the very strict and detailed codes of religious morality would lead us to believe. There were plenty of signs of vigorous repression. Take, for instance, the following extract from Barbier's *Journal*, dated 6 July 1750: 'Today, Monday the 6th, two workmen were publicly burnt at the stake in the Place de la Grève at 5 o'clock in the evening. They were a young carpenter and a pork butcher, aged 18 and 25, whom the watch had caught in the act of committing sodomy. It was felt that the judges had been a bit heavy-handed. Apparently a drop too much wine had led them to this degree of shamelessness' (meaning degree of unconcealment). If only they had been a bit more careful! But it was a period when the police were getting craftier, in order to catch more people by surprise, and punishments were heavier. 'I learnt on this occasion that a man dressed in dark clothes, who spies on what is going on in the streets without anyone suspecting him, walks ahead of the watch, and then calls it up.[2] The execution was to make an example, especially as this crime is said to be becoming very common, and there are many people being locked up for it in Bicêtre.' They preferred to shut 'public sinners' up in the General Hospital there.

So homosexuality seems to have been irrevocably damned. But when did this start? It is far from obvious. Perhaps in Barbier's time the guardians of public morality were tightening things up and sharpening their definition of the crimes they wanted to stamp on. We also have a view from much earlier times − the end of the thirteenth century − which we might expect to be much stricter, namely that of Dante. The way he classifies the damned, like the way St Paul classifies the sins, gives one an idea of how seriously or otherwise these sins were rated.

In St Paul the lustful come after homicides. Dante places them at the gates of Hell, just after Limbo, a 'noble castle' where 'on a green lawn' dwell in an attentuated form 'the great', who suffer only from being deprived of God, having lived before Christ − Homer and Horace, Aristotle and Plato. The patriarchs of the Old Testament sojourned there until the risen Christ withdrew them. The others, pagans like Virgil, remained, staying in the first circle of Hell. The second circle is more sinister. Here Minos sits in judgement; but the punishments are still mild compared with those of the seven other circles. They are the storm, the storm of lusts which continually whirls around the souls of those who have yielded to them on earth − 'a place deprived of every glimmer of light, which bellows like the sea battered in a gale by contrary winds'; 'I understand that into this torment carnal sinners were cast who abandoned reason to the onslaughts of lust.' Some are actual perverts, like Queen Semiramis: 'She was so broken to lascivious vice that she licensed lust by law in order to cover up her own guilt.' But these lascivious characters, lascivious even by our standards, were plucked, like Semiramis and Cleopatra, from the distant mists of antiquity. The confession of the beautiful Francesca da Rimini, Dante's own contemporary, is very different. Today, after de Musset and Tolstoy, we would never dare exclude her from the joy of God, so light was her fault, so poignant her suffering and so deep her love: 'Love, that inflames so soon a noble heart, seized him (her lover who is with her in Hell) for the

---

[2] Philippe Rey, in a master's dissertation (supervised by Jean-Louis Flandrin) on homosexuality in the eighteenth century, did some detailed research among police dossiers. He moved on from listing homosexual acts to defining a 'breed' of homosexuals.

lovely body that has been torn from me . . . Love, that to no loving heart can refuse love, took me with such great joy of him that, as you see, he is still with me.' Make no mistake, Dante had to put the couple among the damned, but he feels like us today, and his soul revolts against it. Here one senses the tension between the priest-made law and the instinctive resistance even of the devout.

At the sound of the lamentation of the two damned lovers 'I swooned for pity, as if I were dying, and fell like a dead man.' There is nothing repellent about these two damned souls, and they are on the very border of the realms of punishment, only to be lightly punished. Yet, though Dante pities and sympathizes with these sad lovers, he places them alongside genuine perverts like Semiramis and Cleopatra.

The circle of the lustful does not include 'sodomites' whom St Paul associates with *adulteri, molles* (effeminate) and *fornicarii*. Dante moves them away, taking them from the company of sinners 'through incontinence',[3] but far away among the *violent*, the sinners through *malizia* in the seventh circle. This is already fairly low, but not so low as the ninth, which harbours Cain and Judas, traitors and murderers, the very bottom of Hell where Satan lurks.

Let Dante himself explain (XI, 28) 'The Circle is full of violent men, but as they may have three kinds of victim it is divided into three rings. One may do violence to God, to oneself, to one's neighbour.'

1   Violence against one's neighbour: murder, robbery, banditry.
2   Violence against oneself and against one's own goods (note this association of being and having which seems an essential characteristic of the later Middle Ages): suicides and spend-thrifts.
3   Violence against God, which is the most serious.

One can do violence to God by denying Him one's heart and blaspheming against Him. The first sort are not unbelievers or idolaters, but blasphemers. The second are the people of Sodom and Cahors, that is sodomites and userers. They are more or less on the same level: each has dishonoured God and nature, but the crime of the sodomites is considered to be less serious than that of the usurers.

---

[3] Incontinence is a lesser offence against God and incurs less blame.

Dante mingles with the sodomites without any feeling of disgust; moreover among them he meets his beloved teacher Brunetto Latini. He addresses him in terms of respect, gratitude and affection, which to us in the twentieth century could not possibly be directed towards someone who had committed an awful crime, to which incidentally he makes no reference in the brief talk he has with him.[4] 'I still have with me engraved on my mind your dear and benign paternal image from the time when on earth you taught me how men may make themselves immortal; and as long as I live people shall learn from my words how deep is my gratitude.' That is how a man of the fourteenth century talked to an avowed sodomite: one, morever, among many, for the practice seems to have been widespread: 'Time is too short to mention the clerks and famous men of letters all defiled by the same taint on earth' says Master Brunetto. There were also husbands whose wives disgusted them: 'My shrewish wife certainly did me more wrong than anybody else.' Was that not an extenuating circumstance?

Dante does not feel the same outrage and scorn against the sodomites that he displays against the rest of the 'fraudulent', and nothing remotely like the outbursts of Dr Ambroise Tardieu in the 1870s! Yet he is under no illusions about the seriousness of their offence, though the seriousness does not attach to its incontinence, or the act of *concubitus*, but to *malizia*, the crime against God through His creation, nature. This makes the offence more serious, more metaphysical. What is interesting about Dante's testimony is that it comes from someone who was at the same time a scholastic philosopher, a Latin writer who was imbued with twelfth-century cosmology and theology, and an ordinary man who shared the views of ordinary men of his time. 'The theologian condemns, the ordinary man admits to leniency.' Sodomy is the sin of the clerks, of educators, perhaps of young folk. Dante does not go into details, but through the mouth of Master Brunetto he makes it clear how frequent these nameless practices are.

We are told elsewhere how the prostitutes of the Latin Quarter used to solicit students in the street, and cursed them for sodomites if they rebuffed them.

The ecclesiastical authorities of the fifteenth and sixteenth centuries tried to take a hard line with college feasts that were just

---

[4] This has given rise to several suggestions that the text has been misinterpreted and that Brunetto Latini was there for reasons other than sodomy.

initiation ceremonies, rites of passage with lots of drinking and some fairly crude horseplay. No doubt whores would be present. But what the censorious objected to in general was a rather less obvious perversion than the resort to prostitutes, more likely a traditional bisexuality, which lasted some time among adolescents. This amorphous sexuality also figured in the great junketings that took place at the end of the year, between Christmas and Twelfth Night, a time of masks and fancy dress, of mirror games and Lords of Misrule, a sexual ambiguity. As François Laroque has said, 'In this misty world where the old merges into the new . . . doubts about sexual differences arise. But thanks to the festive magic of disguise the figure of Viola-Cesario is able to cross the frontier between the sexes at will: *bissexus* rather than *bifrons*.'

This is not real homosexuality, but only a ritualized, disturbing reversal of roles when annual feast days are an excuse for throwing social taboos to the winds, just for the moment. Relics of this ambiguity are still with us today in spite of the determined efforts of homosexuals to achieve a genuine identity. At least this is what is suggested by a remark of Laurent Dispot in *Le Matin* of 6 November 1979: 'Who says there are men who don't love each other? What about the scenes footballers make when someone has scored a goal? They certainly aren't homosexuals. Yet, if real homosexuals behaved like that in a crowded street, passers-by would be very shocked. Must we conclude from this that sports grounds and sport provide a safety valve for normal male homosexuality?'

7

Prostitution, sex and society in French towns in the fifteenth century

Jacques Rossiaud

Today we know that in the fair cities of the fifteenth century prostitution was not merely tolerated or hidden away, but that even in quite small places there were *prostibula publica*, belonging to the community, or under seignorial control in towns with no communal governing body. Sometimes, as in Avignon or Paris, instead of the *grande maison*, there would be one or several precincts officially reserved for public prostitution. Whatever form they took — a big building, a courtyard with rooms all round, or a particular neighbourhood of streets lined with bawdy houses and taverns — the essential purpose was the same: they were all officially protected places dedicated to the practice of fornication. Some towns built or maintained a *prostibulum* in the shape of an enormous building, even when their public obligations were almost non-existent, and the local councillors took no interest in building schools. Normally the brothel would be farmed out to a tenant, the *abbesse*, who theoretically had a local monopoly in prostitution, and whose duty it was to recruit girls and keep an eye on them, stick to certain rules, and report to the local authorities anything said by customers who were not known locally. Not only did the *abbesse* earn money for the municipality but she was also a very valuable source of information.

In most places of any size there were, in addition to the public brothel, a number of bath-houses in which there were generally a good many more rooms than baths. There would be bath-houses in every district, some humble, some rather comfortable. Their public rooms were settings for cheerful gatherings, their kitchens were well stocked with pâtés and wine, and their rooms with young servant girls. In spite of all regulations these bath-houses were used as places of resort, permanent centres of prostitution, real *maisons de tolérance* of their day.

Over and above these institutions, and not to be found everywhere in a town, there arose what contemporaries called *bordelages privés*, little private brothels, each managed by a madam, a hostess or procuress, who would have at her disposal one, two or three girls, either under her own roof or at her beck and call. In Dijon, in 1485, there were eighteen such establishments, tolerated by the locals and far from shunned by society, since thirteen of them were managed by widows or wives of craftsmen who carried on their own trade, e.g. ploughmen, bakers, carpenters and coopers. They were far from being at the bottom of the social scale. For their trade these madams would employ 'loose women' who would also work on their own account, soliciting in lodging-houses and taverns, in markets or on the streets, when they were not on offer at their place of employment. This fluctuating group of secret and occasional prostitutes was periodically swollen by an influx of stray outsiders attracted by agricultural gatherings, fairs, holidays and royal occasions.

What is surprising is not the ubiquity of the prostitute, for long a familiar feature of the medieval street, but rather the co-existence of concentric circles, occasional prostitutes, first tolerated, then admitted, finally official, with the *grande maison* set up at a key junction of the urban scene. Did the authorities want to purify urban morals by restricting the girls to a municipal ghetto, and were they incapable of enforcing the law? Councils did take steps to make sure certain sanitary rules were observed. During outbreaks of the plague the *prostibula* and bath-houses were closed, just as trade gatherings and public dancing were forbidden. As time went on, restrictions at particular seasons were discontinued. It is significant that the leases of some *prostibula* fell in at the beginning of Lent, which shows that the Lenten ban had once been respected. After the departure of the former tenant the new one would have time to settle in and recruit girls before reopening after Easter. That did not last. In Arles and Dijon the only times the girls went into retreat, and the tenant was compensated for loss of earnings, were at Christmas and during Holy Week. For the rest of the time the house was open even on Sundays, though the *abbesse* had to make sure nothing unseemly went on while mass was being celebrated. In Dijon nobody thought it scandalous to go to the *prostibulum* on Whit Sunday.

The restrictions on prostitutes seem to have been harsh and yet frequently ignored. The signs of shame marking out the prostitute as 'untouchable' which one had to recognize at once to keep clear of her, fell into disuse. Admittedly, in the Avignon by-laws of 1441, the *meretrices* were obliged to buy any food they had touched with their hands in the market. However, these laws were mainly just repeating those of the thirteenth century, and one doubts whether they were very rigorously applied when one reads that in nearby towns of the Languedoc, Nîmes in particular, the prostitutes kneaded the dough on Ascension Day for the cakes given to the councillors to offer to the poor. In the same way, prostitutes were supposed to carry a distinguishing mark, an *aiguillette*, to go about bareheaded and to abstain from wearing costly furs or girdles; but these regulations about clothes were part of a whole catalogue of sumptuary rules whose aim was so wide that it limited their effect, while their constant reiteration showed how ineffective they were.

They seem to have been free to go almost where they liked: they were not confined to their *prostibula* or red light districts. Public prostitutes got their pick-ups in the streets, the taverns, the public squares or at the church door. Clearly the authorities made no attempt to shut them off, and were equally permissive in their dealings with the *maisons tolérés* (in St Flour, just as in Dijon, Lyons and Avignon). So much so that occasionally the girls from the *grande maison*, worried by unfair competition, would apply to the authorities to get a private brothel closed down.

Not surprisingly, from time to time, after a sudden rise in the death rate, a poor harvest, or the arrival of a great preacher, there were vague efforts to clean things up. Concubines and unofficial harlots were ordered to leave the town, and all sorts of crimes and villainies were imputed to the madams and the bath-house keepers. But between 1440 and 1490 these sanctimonious outbursts were rare, and when they happened denunciations of lechery were just one preliminary to a general moral clean up. Had the year been a disastrous one? Immediately the paupers, the vagabonds, the bawds and the whores were driven out. Had there been some prophecy of doom? All at once fornication, gambling, blasphemy and swearing had to be stamped out, traders had to be banned from graveyards, and markets on feast days discontinued; clerics must lead pure lives and citizens devout ones. The influence of a great sermon was totally counterproductive. The moment the saintly man departed, life went on as before.

Every now and then legal action was taken against private and sometimes even official prostitution. Occasionally the inhabitants of a 'decent' street would complain of scandal and bad behaviour, and the council would intervene, rather mildly. Even if it came to a trial, the brothels would still survive several years without closing. If the authorities did take action against a brothel keeper who had been openly in business for some time, it would be because more serious accusations than just prostitution had been levelled. There would have been brawling, or neighbours and important citizens would have been threatened.

There was nothing discreditable in frequenting bath-houses or *prostibula*. People went to them quite openly: all levels of society were to be found there, the better off in the bath-houses rather than the brothels; and the latter were not for paupers and tramps, since one had to pay for both girls and wine. Three-quarters of the *habitués* would be local inhabitants. Doubtless the authorities kept an eye on unfamiliar faces and were worried if a stranger or a very young lad spent too much time there. As to the rest — young men, apprentices and servants — they had their fun there like anyone else, tolerated by their betters, who preferred to see them there rather than in some illicit dive. It was cheaper and less risky. There was no worry about the girls, who were well known.

The girls were neither strays nor foreigners. Two-thirds of the prostitutes in Dijon were either born in the town or came from the Burgundy countryside. They had the same background as the other inhabitants, and only 15 per cent of them were just passing through or accompanying a boy friend. Four-fifths of them were either daughters or widows of craftsmen or casual labourers. Poverty or the break up of their families when they were quite young had left them unprotected: most of them had joined the 'profession' when they were about 17, and nearly half of them had been introduced by force. They had started with occasional prostituition, combining daytime work and cohabitation with one of several partners, whose temporary concubines or bound servants they were. Bought or recruited by procuresses they became servant girls in the public baths, then sooner or later ended up in the *grande maison*, either because the keepers of the bath-houses had no further use for them, or because they were taken there by their ponces, by the municipal authorities, or by the other public prostitutes.

Although there were plenty of whoremasters, and many of the municipal or princely officers were well-known pimps, procuring was basically a woman's trade. Indictments, trial records, and the very jargon used all bear witness to this. Of course rogues, vagabonds and beggars occasionally protected loose women, who lived off their 'chaps' as well as their bodies. Sometimes small groups of men pimped for and exploited girls from the city outskirts, but they formed no part of a criminal underworld. Most of the public or private whores had a 'friend' or 'fiancé' who took a share of their earnings, but these were not simply idle fellows, neither organized in gangs, nor living solely by pimping. It seems to me very significant that there were no cant terms for prostitution or pimping, which were such public activities that no private language or alternative groups were needed to conceal them. The language of the *fabliaux*, although extremely coarse, is very vague in this connection, the same word being used in several different senses; and the only ponce portrayed, the son of a procuress and rather a feeble creature, takes no particular part in the action except to be tumbled by his own mother . J. Favier has given us a vivid picture of prostitution in Paris at the end of the fourteenth century. He tells us of an occasion when the girls reproved one of their fellow tarts for the behaviour they considered scandalous: she was 'keeping' a man. They urged her to take him in honourable matrimony. It was the woman who was doing the 'keeping', not the man, and the usual practice among the Parisian girls (and those of Dijon and Lyons, who kept themselves by public or private prostitution) was the married state. There would be no doubt about the legality of this state, since in many of the suburbs and poorer parts of towns it was recognition by the neighbourhood that legalized matrimony, as we shall see later.

There certainly were men who lived off prostitutes, but they do not seem to have been much in evidence, probably because the girls who had taken the step of going public had a certain status, were protected by the community, and, at least between the years 1440 and 1490 when times were prosperous, had nothing to gain from paying a protector. Also, obviously, they had strong feelings of solidarity. United by their poverty and their identical way of life, they occasionally felt strong enough to act as a group, especially when times were bad and they wanted to drive out the private whores. Newcomers had to go through fellowship ceremonies, undergo a 'welcome', drink together a *vin du métier* and call their manageress *mère*, just as itinerant journeymen did their landladies. The material constraints, the traditions handed down by the oldest of them, the regulations imposed by their town, all helped to inculcate a sort of 'corporatist' mentality. They were bound by their oath to the authorities, every week they gave a few pence to the night watch which was supposed to give them protection; they shared expenses, ate together either in the house or in nearby taverns, and had to observe certain professional rules which were either taught them by the *abbesse* or developed out of their working habits. They could not receive at the same time two people related to one another; they must not, in theory, give themselves to married men of their own town or to boys of tender age; nor undoubtedly were they prepared to submit their bodies to clients in any but a totally orthodox manner. For in the *prostibula* and the most notoriously brothel-like bath-houses the goings on were quite uncomplicated. When the neighbours were 'scandalized' by the 'disgraceful' things that were going on practically on their doorsteps and ventured to describe them, what did they reveal? Everybody was larking about naked! When these same neighbours denounced Jeanne Saignant, a brothel keeper in Dijon, as the personification of lasciviousness and perversion, what was so shocking about her behaviour? One day they had seen her making love standing up, and at other times watching what was going on in the rooms of her house. But these goings on were only those of passing couples, who were consummating their affair in a totally natural way in the relative privacy of a room. Public brothels do not seem to have been haunts of depravity or abnormal sexual practices. The literature of the *fabliaux* depicts the realities of everyday life in the little Provençal towns studied by R. Lavoye. This is confirmed by the Dijon court records which give the impression of a gentle sexuality closely corresponding to the restrained eroticism of the Burgundian collections of obscene riddles of the middle of the fifteenth century. Men who went to *prostibula* in order to satisfy their natural urge towards fornication seem to have behaved no differently from married couples or lovers operating in the privacy of their own houses.

Sexual behaviour in the brothel or the bath-house seems in no way to have departed from the norms of married life. So, on this level, the prostitute did not conflict with or subvert the institution of matrimony. In literature she was even shown as rushing to the help of a family in distress. A pillar of family life? That at any rate was how the authorities saw her.

In fifteenth-century towns the family ideal was omnipresent — in public monuments, centres of worship, gatherings of neighbours. The puppets revolving on a clock tower advertised the hierarchy within a family; the retables in guild chapels told the story of a Holy Family whose faces were drawn from contemporary models. All the local feasts were organized round families, and in the middle of the top table were enthroned an ephemeral king and queen, a make-believe married couple surrounded by their children. The community as a whole saw itself as a vast gathering of householders or 'owners of hearths': hearths were the social nucleus around which everything revolved. People who saw themselves as urban also saw themselves primarily as family people, and every great demographic cataclysm reinforced this characteristic. If family images recur so insistently, it is not only because the family stands for sharing and interdependence, but also because it is a visible symbol of roots and success, a pattern of invincible steadfastness constantly threatened by plague and disruption.

Marriage was always, despite a certain relaxing of standards, whose extent has yet to be measured, a 'social victory' (P. Toubert). As far as we can tell from spot research in Rheims and Dijon, even when the population was at its lowest, between 1420 and 1450, men were marrying relatively late, between 24 and 25, in the middle and lower strata of urban society. At their first marriage husbands seem to have been not much older than their wives, few families being sufficiently well off to give their daughter a dowry at the age then considered ideal for marriage, that is about 15. However, marriages were often ended by disease and the higher mortality among women, and second and third marriages were very frequent. These led to considerable differences of age, and it was not unusual to find married couples 10, 15 or 20 years apart. In the complex negotiations that marriage involved, quite apart from considerations of wealth, family and professional background, especially when the man was well established (and for other rather obvious reasons), the woman's youthful charm was a most important aspect. Conversely, young widows, assuming they had any real freedom of choice, might choose the older of two candidates for greater immediate security and better prospects in the more distant future.

The records show that 30 per cent of the male population of Dijon between the ages of 30 to 39 had a wife 8 to 16 years younger, and 15 per cent of those aged 40 to 50 had a wife 20 to 30 years younger. So they had chosen wives from an age group in which they were competing with much younger men; and more than a third of the women available for marriage or remarriage had been taken by men who were established or elderly. Such was the pattern of marriage depicted in stone and on canvas, and which conformed with the way in which a family was traditionally ruled, with the reverence due from a young woman to marital authority, to the importance of offspring and to the preoccupations of a husband seeking to ensure his comfort in old age.

This establishment of men of substance naturally suffered a fair amount of disruption, firstly at the hands of those young men who, after lethal outbreaks of plague, woke up to an awareness of their own vulnerability. Chroniclers and doctors have all observed that adolescents were more open to infection than others, and one knew that it was the men of property who reaped the benefit of other people's deaths. It would be an exaggeration to represent the communities of this period as consisting predominantly of young people, as P. Desportes has demonstrated. Nevertheless, even at a period when the ranks of the young had been decimated by earlier deaths, in Rheims in 1422 the young males aged 15 to 25 in the, after all, well-to-do parish of St Pierre amounted to 60 per cent of the adults, either married or of an age to remarry (25 to 45 years old), not to mention the 67 boys of 12 to 15 whose behaviour gave householders cause for concern. But it would be wrong to speak of 'youth' as a single group. The sons of bourgeois or tolerably well-to-do families were not faced with the same problems as apprentices or young wage-earners. Nevertheless they all faced tough restrictions which they bore with little patience. Apprenticeship gave access to a family milieu without any real integration into the family. It meant a harsh tutelage, subjection to a strict discipline, even outside the hours of work, at the hands of the master, and also sometimes even of the master's wife, who was often scarcely older than the apprentices and journeymen she bossed about in her own household. Young sons submitted to paternal authority, but relatively late marriages meant that fathers had crossed the threshold of old age when sons were emerging from adolescence. Often too they had to knuckle under to a stepfather or stepmother and live with the offspring of an earlier marriage.

From time to time numbers of them found it impossible to put up with the trials of family life, their exclusion from municipal affairs, from responsibility and power. Many of them were young mechanics, apprentices and in search of jobs, who had recently arrived in town and sought to join up with locals of their own type. Some wanted to escape ties and go in search of adventure; they wanted to get around, see the world and other towns; others, more numerous, were looking for diversion in their own town. After nightfall, when householders were putting up the shutters, and taverns and dives were closing down, and only the night watch had the right to patrol the streets, the young fellows, escaping from the suffocating atmosphere of an unlit room in which parents, children and servants all slept together, shook off their isolation and boredom and joined their companions outside. They would go off together in a band, to drink, play dice, settle accounts with a rival gang, flout the authorities, dispense their own justice, put the wind up the bourgeois, meet a girl friend and torment another one.

Eventually the evening expedition would end up with a brawl or, more commonly, an assault on a woman. Probably about 20 'public rapes' (the name given to rapes committed away from private houses or brothels) were committed annually in Dijon. Four-fifths of these were group rapes, and we know what sort of people were guilty of them: they were the sons and manservants of permanent inhabitants of the town, and only about one in ten could be imputed to workmen or drop outs. These rapist groups consisted of upwards of ten or fifteen members, but more usually five or six − bachelor journeymen between the ages of 18 and 25, all from the same or related callings, led by one or two more mature individuals. One or two of them might have been up before the courts, but the rest would not have been hardened rapists. These nocturnal gallivanters were not like criminal gangs, but just an extension of daily friendships. Their victims were not social drop outs either, but maidservants, daughters of the impoverished working classes, or widows, or women living by themselves: the former about 16 to 20 years of age, the latter seldom over 25.

These assaults nearly always followed the same pattern. They rarely happened out of doors, for women dared not go outside after dark, even with a companion. The young men would nearly always force open the door of a house, while their accomplices hurled stones at the neighbours' shutters as a warning not to interfere. Then they would burst into the room and with a mixture of obscenities and blows either rape their victim on the spot or drag her off, cowed and terrified, to another house where they knew they would not be disturbed. Sometimes on previous nights they would come banging on the door and make a lot of noise, a good way of making the neighbours think the girl was no better than she should be, and hence easing the way for their assault.

Sometimes there was a pretext of 'lawfulness' in such actions. Raping a prostitute was not regarded as a crime, and certainly some of the women of Dijon who were carried off in this way had already been rather free with their favours, practised occasional prostitution, or had been concubines to priests. The gangs were glad to make use of them without payment; fallen women ought to be common to all. The 'game' could be very cruel when the victim was a girl who earlier, and out of poverty, had had to sell herself for money, but since then had done her best to earn her living by hard work, and so win her way back to 'respectability'. The same violence might be inflicted on women who had done nothing to their discredit except leave their family home. Their only crime was the infringement of a fundamental rule – the necessity of a settled way of life. Young women whose conduct was looked on as irregular were thus attacked, some because they had run away from a cruel or spendthrift husband, others simply because they lived alone or shared a room with a workmate. These *chasses joyeuses* preyed on girls who worked by day labour, going from house to house, staying from three days to several weeks, so laying themselves open to all sorts of suspicions.

The gangs would smear their victims in advance by calling them whores, so that they could present themselves as dispensers of justice, acting on behalf of some moral code. There was a strong moral element in these acts of violence. It came from a highly arbitrary form of social discrimination according to which all girls were either pure or public. It may also be that participation in these raids provided the nocturnal gangs with a chance of asserting themselves, of proving their manliness. But for the poorer members of the gang deeper feelings were involved: there was social protest. They liked to say that certain young servant girls were 'kept' by their masters, that priests' and, occasionally, lawyers' chambermaids were 'bawds', and finally that women whose husbands were away should 'give the lads some fun'. Rape set a mark of shame on the young widow or girl of marriageable age; with her reputation tarnished she lost her value on the marriage market; even when innocent she could feel that the gap separating her from the 'abandoned women' was dangerously narrowed. If she stayed in town she ran a grave risk of falling once more into the hands of the gangs, thence to end up in the bath-house or brothels. If she left for another town she exposed herself to all the dangers of a roving life.

A threat to the institution of marriage? On the whole these assaults were confined within narrow social limits. Attacks on the wives of well-to-do craftsmen or merchants were very unusual. This is why the municipal authorities did not worry unduly about acts of violence that mostly affected only the humbler folk. They could at a pinch be considered quite a good thing in maintaining barriers between classes – so long as they were not allowed to stray outside their usual terrain. In coping with these outbreaks the leaders of the town councils adopted a triple strategy.

1   Local justice made no attempt to be coercive; rather, it urged people to accept arbitration, and only intervened when there were complaints. Most of these rows about moral misbehaviour never reached the courts, and when they did they rarely ended with the imposition of a penalty. The exception was when the victim was a woman of some social standing, or a child. Otherwise the *procureur* pressed for conciliation and left it to the community feeling of the parish, the neighbourhood or the trade guild to settle the question of compensation. It was for them to punish the guilty, keep the peace and supervise public morals. The members of the trade associations bound themselves, under pain of expulsion, to render mutual help and accept the mediation of their officials.

2   With the twofold aim of containing violence and yet at the same time giving the young a chance to play their pranks and give vent freely but harmlessly to their grudges against society, the town authorities encouraged, but supervised, the merry companies known as *abbayes de jeunesse.* These were deeply imbued with team spirit and comprised a mixture of bachelors, young widowers, adolescents and adults, but no boys or middle-aged men. They made it their business to keep an eye on the behaviour of husbands and daughters, saw to it that their leaders went banging on the doors of a girl whose virtue was under suspicion, and decided what sort of rough music might be called for. They also discussed marriage problems and organized carnival processions. These various activities were carried out under the approving eye of the authorities and could be counted on not to end in violence. The *abbayes* ran the leisure activities of the young, calmed down any rebellious feelings by giving them a chance to blow off steam, and above all eased the ideological pressures of a hierarchic and patriarchal society. The public 'happenings' and the controlled horseplay gave full rein to spontaneity and enjoyment. The *abbayes* helped to foster a community spirit, set standards of behaviour, and in particular, in order to prevent violence and adultery, encouraged municipalized fornication in the *grande maison*.

3   It is in this last context that one must see the *prostibulum publicum*. It was no coincidence that wherever the 'merry companies' called themselves 'abbeys', the local madam was called 'the abbess'. In Toulouse the public brothel was commonly called the *grande abbaye*. The 'merry girls' were the counterpart of the 'merry fellows', and the 'abbot' would lead his 'monks' to the girls of the 'cloister' in the *grande maison*. This explains why the attitude of the authorities went beyond mere toleration: their relations with the tenants were on exactly the same footing as with all other

tenants of public properties. In Alès they were urged to seek out 'beautiful and pleasing prostitutes, lovely and tasty wantons', while in Romans and St Flour the girls were described as being 'for community use'. All this accounts for the sort of names applied to the *prostibulum* − *grande maison, maison commune,* or even *maison de la ville*; and it explains why on almsgiving days the girls would all be trooped out to the town centre to watch the 'abbess' giving the leader of the council a cake and receiving a kiss in exchange.

This was also the reason why the municipal brothel was open in the evenings, on the eve of feast days, and even on Sundays. It had to make itself available to the journeymen and craftsmen, to give them a chance to go there outside their hours of work. Even the poor and younger journeymen could afford the fornication that was on offer. The leading citizens recognized that the place was frequented by the most respectable and well-behaved young men; and its protagonists claimed that the presence of the girls went far to defend the honour of the virtuous ladies of the town. They stood in the way of worse things than mere fornication, as did the girls in the bath-house who entertained married men and even the clergy without a breath of scandal.

What all this amounts to is the fact that in fifteenth-century towns the main householders, faced with the problem of youthful violence and brutishness, used the municipal brothel as a form of tranquillizing agency. The *bonne maison,* the not-so-disorderly house, was one instrument in the maintenance of a *bonne policie,* a well-ordered society. They tried, not very energetically, to stop sexual assaults on women who were 'of humble estate' and hence of dubious morals, and who were not properly protected by the professional or parochial organizations in their neighbourhood. Finally they encouraged the *confrèries de jeunesse,* inclined as they were to carnal indulgence and the high-spirited pursuit of 'chicks', and applauded the satisfaction of Dame Nature's needs kindly provided by the *bonnes dames.*

Such was their aim. But the efficient functioning of this kind of moral system needed social and cultural conditions to help it protect and not corrupt society. Public, municipally encouraged prostitution flourished for only a short while, the briefly golden age of high wages.

Prostibula had long existed in the cities of Languedoc and the Rhône basin. Nevertheless it seems that the transition from merely tolerated prostitution to prostitution openly taken over by the municipalities came relatively late in the fifteenth century. This change was also, of course, connected with the increase of the city councils' powers, at least in those towns that had acquired greater autonomy as a result of the crises of the mid-fourteenth century. All the same it was in the last years of the fourteenth century that Tarascon had a *grande maison* built at public expense. The brothel in St Flour was bought by the municipality during the 1440s; in 1439 the councillors of Bourg-en-Bresse presented their town with a *maison*; in 1440 those of Villefranche-sur-Saône bought the *prostibulum* which they enlarged 14 years later, while in 1447 the aldermen of Dijon converted their *maison de fillettes* into a large and comfortable dwelling. The 1440s, when peace was restored at the end of the Hundred Years War, seem to have been a key period for such takeovers by town councils. We may observe that the enlargement and improved comfort of these houses were not carried out purely for material reasons or profitability; these undertakings also served to set an example. Finally, it is significant that the 1440s were demographically 'hollow'; they were years of relative equilibrium between urban and rural wages, of minimum competition for vacant jobs. After 1440 real wages reached a higher point than ever before; economic recovery had not wiped out the nominal increases of the previous 30 years, while grain prices were at a record low. In Tours, towards mid-century, a master mason earned half as much again as his ancestors during the years 1380–1420, and the city's manual labourers did even better. In 1460 the journeymen of Lille were able to earn, in three weeks, enough to pay for a year's supply of wheat, and only the fathers of very large families suffered from poverty. For all those workers who had the first offer of jobs at local building sites (i.e. men of that town), for the journeymen and apprentices who ate at the master's table, this new affluence was all the more agreeable in that it gave genuine hope of social advancement; for apprenticeship was not very expensive and there were plenty of masterships available. But prosperity was not evenly shared: new arrivals without qualifications, the widows of journeymen, girls without a solid family background, swelled the ranks of the poor, a poverty that was however alleviated by the charitable institutions. This period was brief: it lasted for a single generation in Paris, though much longer in Montepellier, Lyons and Tours, but it lasted long enough for the new ways of life, which had been slowly leavening the social mass, to become firmly implanted.

This enhanced prosperity had two complementary effects on behaviour. It accounted for the intense *joie de vivre* apparent everywhere after the 1450s, a newly awakened response to nature and attention to the trappings of life, to the pleasures of the table, the flesh and the countryside, a love of worldly joys condemned by the preachers with ever-increasing vigour: pleasures which only the wealthy had been lucky enough to enjoy between two outbreaks of plague. Secondly, as things were going well, as the townsfolk were fully employed and the charitable institutions were functioning, widows and working-class girls were in no danger of sinking into prostitution, nor was the community liable to be corrupted by the public prostitutes. Some of these earned more than domestic servants, but only the courtesans of the wealthy could flaunt their success with impunity; as for the others, fines and protection money severely limited their chances of betterment, unless matrimony and retirement from 'the profession' restored them to respectability.

There were various signs of this lively and easy-going sensuality even outside the precincts of the brothels: not merely the calm assurance with which men of all conditions openly admitted to an occasional frolic with the girls; but also the decision taken by the leaders of the council to turn the *prostibulum publicum* into a haven of peaceful fornication, which could accommodate clients overnight and be open on Sundays. Their regulations, which merely confirmed officially what was already common practice, were exemplary in two respects: they helped to establish a daily routine for the bath-houses which closely followed that of the *prostibulum*, and they made a strict ruling, to be universally observed, that the one and only forbidden period was during the celebration of the mass.

This social ethic, this culture which was beginning to assert itself and which had individual characteristics that varied sometimes even from district to district, was a product of the actual structures of urban society and the pressures that activated it. While the country was recovering from the wars and the population was growing, it was the local worthies and the *confréries* who set the tone. They sang the joys of work and an active life, but above all, where newly arrived couples were concerned, they assumed the right to decide if their marriage was genuine or not, and denounced them if it was not; they decided what sort of behaviour was permissible and what not, and in short acted as moral trendsetters to the community. The clergy and the mendicant friars had the final say, but during the 1450s there was no clash between a popular culture and a church one. The town dweller's culture was far removed from that of the peasant, while the priests and friars who were in touch with people's daily life were quite unaffected by the fulminations of the great preachers. The mendicant friars, especially the Franciscans, had been inculcating a sexual ethic which over the years had steadily undermined the ancient taboos, amending the list of the sins of the flesh and reducing their heinousness, first in married life and later on its fringes. What was more, they allowed the *fillettes* to join their processions, and, if they so wished, to be buried in their churches.

This moral emancipation for men was based on a body of opinions widely shared by different classes. Of course there was still a wide cultural gulf between oligarchs and artisans, but as a result of crises, wars and a high mortality rate, the municipal councils presented the spectacle of an unprecedented social mix. The old patricians had had to move over, and their heirs rubbed shoulders in the council with prosperous parvenus or representatives of the humbler classes. At all the city feast days 'nature' was celebrated and the 'kings of love' dressed up as 'king cocks'. A few bourgeois circles were beginning to acquire a certain refinement, but that did not stop their henchmen enjoying the fun of the fair in the indispensable company of the *fillettes joyeuses*.

Such were the components out of which had developed the behavioural patterns we have just described. After the period 1490–1500 some of the factors on which this state of equilibrium depended disappeared. Then a gradual change in public opinion led to its disintegration after 1560.

In the middle of the fifteenth century more and more people started flocking into the towns, and up to about 1480 they were assimilated without too much difficult, but after that the urban economy began to be seriously affected. There was an ever-widening gap between wages in towns, which were artificially maintained at a relatively high level, and those in the country which were depressed by the increase in population, thereby causing an influx of impoverished peasants into the towns. In the last 20 years of the century the immigrants were almost all very poor. The reaction of the authorities was to demand sureties, impose restrictions on entry and raise the qualifications for rights of 'bourgeoisie'. The towns went on letting in the poverty-stricken but felt no sense of obligation towards them, driving them out if necessary: the blessings of charity were reserved for genuine citizens.

Wage rates in towns were quickly affected by these developments. Face values may have remained stable, but purchasing power was eroded by a rise in the price of basic foods, which varied by regions. In Rouen the real value of wages was diminished by

25 per cent during the first third of the century, while in Paris the manual worker's wage only bought half the amount of corn it had previously. The lower paid town workers were the worst hit by the reconstruction that was now under way. During the 1500s a brewery worker in Tours or Lyons had to spend 70 per cent to 80 per cent of his earnings on feeding his family — not particularly well. It had become very difficult for him to start his son off on the road to a professional qualification, while wage-earning craftsmen found it harder and harder to gain masterships. Socially the gap between the prosperous and the victims of prosperity, the elite and the common herd, was growing wider. Internal tensions were beginning to build up between the leaders of the proliferating craft bodies and the 'oligarchs', who were against monopolies, and between the solid groups of traders, who were excluded from the more profitable lines of business, and the big dealers who managed the taxes and had their figures in the municipal till. The feelings common to all those who felt their economic, territorial or professional situation to be rather shaky were a mistrust of outsiders, whom they saw as potentially dangerous competitors, and hostility mingled with fear towards paupers and vagrants.

Almost everywhere there were increasing swarms of prostitutes. This was not the first time townsfolk had experienced periods of depression when their gates and hiring fairs were besieged by crowds of paupers or women reduced by want to selling their bodies; but this time the proliferation of vagrant and homeless women seemed never ending. It soon appeared, moreover, that the gangrene was not confined to casual workers from the countryside but was affecting the families of recently established citizens, sometimes even of residents of long standing who were sinking into poverty. In Avignon, Lyons and all the towns of the Rhône valley there was great suffering during the years between 1520 and 1530 and hundreds of well-known families were reduced to beggary.

In Paris, that trendsetting city, the cobbler Jean Tisserand founded around 1490 the *Refuge des filles de Paris*, later known as the *Refuge des filles pénitentes*. Poor girls would prostitute themselves so as to qualify for entry there, while others, at their parents' suggestion, tried to get in on the grounds of having been kept women. In 1500 candidates, after being inspected by matrons, were made to swear they had not sold themselves in order to get in; and paradoxically these poor wretches were asked for proofs, not of repentance, but of previous lechery — certificates of depravity, in fact.

At the same time city councils far and wide were bombarded with complaints against male and female vagrants and denunciations of this blight that was poisoning society. Thus at Dijon in 1540 'that the greater part of the said male children of poor families are beggars and, being ignorant of any trade, betake themselves to stealing and evil living, so that many have been convicted of crime, birched, imprisoned, banished or hanged, and many girls of the same kind take to whoring, frequent brothels and lead idle and wanton lives.' The authorities began to take measures against the red light districts. Not only were 'vagrant girls', formerly left alone, being picked on as criminals simply because of their vagrancy, but after 1500 even public prostitutes started appearing more frequently as offenders. They tended more and more to be accompanied by thugs, the *bonshommes* who lived with or on them. In Dijon brawls round the *grande maison* between barbers', butchers' and weavers' assistants were on the increase. The bloody encounters were between organized groups of men who worked in the trades that were worst hit by the depression or by controls imposed by the city authorities. This ended pimping as an ancillary to the prostitute's profession: the violence of the competition forced it into the world of delinquency, so that from before 1530 it was the managers of the *grande maison* who attributed the troubles overwhelming the profession to the proliferation of thugs.

The *maisons publiques*, the bath-houses, continued to exist, but it was becoming risky to frequent them, whilst elsewhere fornication with private or casual prostitutes could involve practices hitherto unknown. In 1518, for the first time on record, two weavers of Dijon were banished and their property confiscated 'for a certain great and horrible crime called sodomy', which they had for several weeks inflicted by force on the body of a 13-year-old apprentice 'telling him this was a good way to have girls'. Nine years later the father of a shop girl was banished for the same reson. He had committed the crime of sodomy with a young servant girl.

Needy young bachelors certainly had more reasons for violent behaviour than in the fifteenth century, and their brutal nocturnal adventures went on; but they were getting very dangerous for those who took part. Legislation against violence was being tightened up, the disciplinary rules affecting servants and apprentices were becoming stricter, and the arm of the law reached out not only to vagrants but to locals as well. It was getting harder to evade the law: its officers were more numerous and the old local professional bodies, which once had both punished and protected, had lost their keenness and strength. The authorities were suspicious of all such kinds of 'private' or 'people's' justice, which might be a cover for all sorts of illegal undertakings, and the clergy were beginning to accuse the fraternities and 'abbeys' of encouraging debauchery; meanwhile the various community bodies were also being crippled by internal dissension. Finally, the relaxed moral standards that the 'merry brotherhoods' and their festivities encouraged were beginning to seem pernicious to those who were hoping for society to be 'called to order'.

The basis of such order was to be the family. Let us consider this from the point of view of marriage. If the difference in age of partners can be used to throw light on the conjugal order, the slight narrowing of this gap in first marriages (falling from an average of four years between 1440 and 1490 in Dijon to less than three between 1490 and 1550) may be taken as an indication that there has been a shift in the ranking order of the partnership in favour of the woman. This is reflected by more frequent references to 'disorderly', i.e. unauthorized, marriages — marriages that took place without parental consent or discussion with brothers or mother. In Lyons, during the years 1520 and 1530, it certainly seems that the possibility of a daughter being free to make her own choice of a husband was seen as normal in middle-class circles. Inconceivable fifty years earlier, this sort of alliance could still suffer the consequences of paternal disapproval — a dowry reduced by half — though not disinheritance of the daughter. Leaving a girl freedom of choice was good for her brothers, who thus got a larger slice of the heritage. In Avignon, on 16 June 1546, twenty years after Henri II's famous edict on the marriage of children of noble families, a complaint was laid before the city council that 'since a short while the young women of Avignon have made so bold as to give themselves in marriage without the endorsement or consent of their fathers and mothers, and other kinsfolk, which is a thing most wonderfully scandalous and injurious to the public well-being.'

Paradoxically, one may see in this the consequence of the work of the 'merry companies', who had gradually clarified and imposed acceptance of the ancient rules of social control, and had greatly increased the number of occasions for boys and girls to meet. Sometimes they had allowed girls to join their groups; in the larger middle-class 'abbeys' the girls were sometimes allowed to choose the 'abbot', a person who in earlier days had tried to supervise their morals. They had acted as judges between rival suitors and encouraged marriages that previously would have been considered out of the question. These 'abbatial' manifestations always expressed a creed of enjoyment, but a creed which, at least in some circles, attached more importance to shared pleasures than to bought frolics with the *fillettes*.

Such goings on seemed all the more scandalous in the light of the new reformist zeal of both Catholics and Protestants who disapproved of festivities and gatherings of young folk, and considered the family to be the proper place for the education of the young. The Church, the authorities, the magnates, the Protestants, certain groups of women, all had their own personal motives for condemning immorality. There was no immediate combined attack on prostitution, whether public or merely tolerated. The Catholic reformers wanted to stop priests having concubines, the city councils wanted to suppress disturbers of the peace, respectable women wanted to preserve their children's virtue and force the whoreshops out into the outskirts of the towns; finally the zealots for reform wanted to extirpate the sinfulness which one day would bring down a terrible doom on the community. Little by little, helped on by some periods of crisis, these forces all came together, and between 1490 and 1550 the mood of the public slowly changed. In Dijon, some time after 1500 a journeyman remarked that 'one feels rather ashamed' in going to a *prostibulum*. During the 1530s private brothels were more firmly suppressed; later the more scandalous bath-houses were closed, and the municipal brothels were removed to the outskirts of the town before they were totally suppressed. The Edict of Amboise merely rubber-stamped a process that had long been under way. In Dijon, in 1573, the local hangman lived in the house once known as the *maison des filles communes*. Total moral freedom — for men — had had its day, but a specific form of public enslavement for women had disappeared too.[1]

---

[1] The principal themes of this study were expounded in Philippe Ariès's seminar in February 1980. It is an enlarged version of the subject matter of two articles, 'Prostitution, jeunesse et société dans les villes du Sud-est', *Annales ESC*, 1976, pp. 289–325, and 'Fraternités de jeunesse et niveau de culture dans les villes du Sud-est à la fin du Moyen Age', *Cahiers d'histoire*, 1976, 1–2, pp. 67–102.

8

Eroticism and social groups in sixteenth-century Venice: the courtesan

Achillo Olivieri

Eroticism, with its much-repeated stories and its lack of visual records, is rooted in oral culture and is present in the drawn-out couplets of popular balladry and the chronicles of priestly and monastic life. Its sexual vocabulary talks about the body, especially the female body; but it does not touch on family life, which is only concerned with reproduction and the defence of the home, nor is it interested in sexist hierarchies. The beauty of the female body matters less than its erotic and reproductive faculties. Even the very earliest erotic stories with a popular background stress the same subordination of woman that the modern world is maintaining.[1]

The *Sei Giornate*[2] of Aretino illuminates, in the history of Italian sensibility, the maturing of a process already started in the courts and diffused by Venetian culture. The dimensions of erotic language, established by Aretino, fit into a traditional narrative form. As with Boccaccio and the story tellers of the sixteenth century, it is essentially in the monastic world that one glimpses the outlines of an eroticism that revolves round the power of 'courtesans'. These figures fit into a picture that shows the *curés*, the lawyers and the courtiers as caricatural embodiments of social fashions. This attempt to place the courtesan at the heart of society makes use of traditional language. For Aretino, the courtesan is

---

[1] Emphasized (p. 557) by C. Klapisch-Zuber in 'Genitori Naturali e Genitori di Latte nella Firenze del Quattrocentò', *Quaderni Storici*, 44, 1980.

[2] P. Aretino, *Sei Giornate*, ed. G. Aquilecchia, Bari, 1969.

not a phenomenon on the margin of society, but one of its essential components; she constitutes an important stage in the diversification of social roles and of labour. So his attempt at interpretation, of which the intellectual and publishing centres were Venice and the Parisian court, expresses the leanings of a capitalist, mercantile society. Around the body of the courtesan and her magic there takes shape the erotic background against which Aretino sketches the features of a sexuality which has played a considerable part in the formation of the mental and domestic mechanisms of European societies. Aretino's eroticism does not place sexuality and its diffused power at the heart of city life; but at the same time he seems to see it as one of the numerous instruments for the creation of capital. and in fact Antonia asserts: 'See, see where the secrets of witchcraft go to nestle!' And Nanna replies 'They nestle at the fundament, which has as much force for lugging money from breeches as the money itself has for founding monasteries.' Aretino insists and repeats emphatically that the strength of sex resides in its power to influence social groups and their hierarchies without having any recourse to magic or philtres:

> Not to appear a hypocrite I can tell you that a good pair of buttocks is possessed of greater power than all that has ever proceeded from philosophers, astrologers, alchemists and necromancers. I experimented with as many herbs as would fill two meadows, with as many words as traders exchange in ten market days, and I never managed to stir the tiny heart of one whose name I must not mention. Well, with a little waggle of my buttocks I made him so crazy about me that it caused a sensation in all the brothels; yet they see something strange there every day, and they are not easily surprised.

These dialogues bear witness to an undeniable transformation of traditional urban behaviour. Outside the structures created by the family and the system of upbringing, like the *baliatico*,[3] which dominated Florentine society in the fourteenth and fifteenth centuries, but which also influenced the Venetian world, sex appears, with all its allure and power, devoid of the circumlocution and the polished mask that hide and distort. Sex and money are both caught up in the same game. 'If the fundament' adds Antonia 'is endowed with as much power as money, it is stronger than Roland who slaughtered all the Paladins.' And Nanna:

---

[3] Possibly emphasizing an especially masculine system of handing down family tradition, Klapisch-Zuber, 'Genitori Naturali'.

That was a whorish civility, and no less agreeable than the one I did for a sugar merchant. This fellow left even his casks with me for something sweeter than sugar, and so long as his passion lasted we sugared everything down to the salad. When he smacked his lips with the honey that came out of my little cask — if you know what I mean — he swore that his sugar was bitter beside it.

So the pages of the *Sei Giornate* can be seen to be at the very heart of the changes that were taking place in European societies between 1530 and 1580: a hierarchy of types of urban and social specialization which were rooted in sexual life, delegating to the prostitute and the courtesan the knowledge and creation of the erotic arts.

It may be that this definition has no connection with the spread and multiplication of courtesans in Venice and the principal Italian cities. However, behind the modern machinery of production and the internal development of towns there was an authentic *civiltà puttanesca* which progressed and developed, with its code of what it would and would not do, its corporeal rites and symbols. Through the medium of the courtesan the whole body and temperament of woman are symbolically brought into play. And Nanna says it herself:

Some like it boiled, some roast. They have devised a way of getting in from behind — legs on one's neck, à la Jeannette, stork-wise, tortoise-wise, the church on top of the steeple, the browsing sheep, and other positions that are weirder than any acrobat's. So that I can well say 'To hell with you!' In short, today any Signora has her anatomy well dissected. That's why, Pippa, you must learn how to please, how to perform; otherwise I'll see you in Lucca.

This new way of looking at the body, to which sixteenth-century civilization invites us, goes together with its sexual embodiment as a producer of capital. This function manifests itself symbolically in the very clothes worn by the courtesan. In the second half of the sixteenth century the Venetian and Florentine courtesans wore underclothes of a generally erotic character:[4] 'Voglio il core', as if to emphasize a reversal of outlook, whereby the magic of

[4] R. Bonito Fanelli, 'Produzione Italiana' (Veneziana?) from *Palazzo Vecchio: Committenza e Collezionismo Medicei*, Florence, 1980, p. 361.

sexual attractiveness has lost its relevance and the language of the
body has taken over. So, in her rediscovery of a function in the
world of the town the courtesan is led to pretend to be an investor,
so as to avoid the side effects her profession holds in store for her:
sickness, the woes of old age, poverty. Stingy people, says Nanna,

> don't give presents, or leave their valuables lying around: so
> take a chance and heed my advice, and if the peace of Marcona[5]
> doesn't come to pass, tell me I am an idiot of the same kind
> as those who stand there with their legs apart, and provided
> they are the first to be chosen, imagine they have organized
> their lives by selling their skin, without any more help from
> magical practices. Poor, wretched creatures. They have no
> idea that they are going to end in hospital or on the bridges
> where, full of the French Evil, broken in half with disease
> and repulsed by all the world they will make everybody
> sick to look at them. I can tell you, my girl, that all the
> treasure those brave Spaniards found in the New World is not
> enough to give a whore her due, however horrible and ugly
> she may be; and anyone who considers how they live sins
> damnably if he doesn't admit that's true.

The developing city is inevitably accompanied by these new
faces, the courtesan and the prostitute. The power inherent in
bodily gesture and the anatomy of woman affects every aspect of
a form of gestural 'civilization'. It undoubtedly forms part of the
domestic and sexual politics of Italian cities: hence a *civiltà
puttanesca* — such as Aretino illustrates, repeatedly using religious
phraseology — with its rules and its rites, with its 'ventures' and
its special language. One may well imagine that this *civiltà
puttanesca* is connected with the Church's encouragement of
prostitution after the thirteenth century so as to combat sodomy.
In the complex web of sectional interests that the modern city
gives rise to, the courtesan and the prostitute also become instruments of power and the source of further exclusivities. A particular
anatomical jargon of life and love; the resemblance to Jews
attributed to them in literature; their insatiable greed for money;
all these things underline their material role in the urban world.
As Nanna maintains,

---

[5] The peace treaty that is signed between the sheets (NdT).

The pride of a whore is worse than a peasant in his Sunday clothes. A whore's covetousness eats up whoever has it in her bones . . . I promise you, by the good fortune I wish for Pippa, that lust is the least of the urges a whore can feel, because she is for ever thinking up ways of tearing the guts out of others.

A whore seems to have unlimited power, like a magician. 'I won't deny that we use every sort of trick to throw dust in people's eyes: we even give them our turds to eat . . . I know of one who, to make a lover run after her, gave him a handful of scabs from the French Evil she was riddled with.' During the great religious festivals like Lent or Good Friday the courtesan stopped her 'bewitching' work; then the city, deprived,[6] became silent and empty.

All the same, this power had the effect of keeping woman in the background, secluding her either in the confinement of the courtesan's houses, or in her domestic functions. It also endowed sexuality in all its shapes with an anatomical or technical dimension, a sexual 'technology' which has survived[7] and refined itself right up to the present day. Sodomy also gained a significant role alongside this progressive institutionalization of the social and cultural forms of sexuality. The nobility and the merchants were responsible for the social upgrading of this traditionally deviant form of sex. It had an extensive cultural backing. From 1620 to 1650[8] we find an increasing number of treatises on 'friendship'; they depict a new gallery of heroes; 'great' or 'heroic' friendships assume more and more importance in Venetian culture and social life. Types of antique hero tend to disappear: even sodomy can be transformed into an 'heroic friendship' and be raised to a sexual activity in its own right. Wills have survived, such as that of Marco Trevisano in favour of Niccolo Barbirigo, which illustrate such tendencies: family wealth, the profits from trade, personal belongings, are all left to the friend, the hero of an increasing sexual habit. Thus, in daring to write of sodomy, friendship has emancipated a form of

---

[6] P. Britti, *El Venerdi Santo*, in M. Dazzi (ed.), *Il Fiore della Lirica Veneziana*, Venice, 1956, 2, p. 226.

[7] Which is linked to this same urban set-up where all these varieties of sex are liberally displayed and indulged in. Apropos the use of these 'technologies' and their spread, in contemporary sexuality, see N. Abbagnano's interview, 'Il Papa e i Discorsi sul Sesso', in *Gente*, 43, 24 February 1980, p. 14.

[8] An article by G. Cozzi, 'Una Vicenda della Venezia Barocca: Marco Trevisano e la sua "eroica amicizia" ', *Bolletino dell Instituto di Storia della Società e dello Stato Veneziano*, II, 1960, pp. 61–154, offers full documentary evidence for this.

behaviour in the shape it will assume in the eighteenth century.[9] This is another case of the development of influences outside the family, whose rigidity from the sixteenth to the eighteenth centuries was also demonstrated by the speed of the clandestine marriages.[10] Meanwhile woman's social and domestic role was undergoing a progressive regulation in the social hierarchy — one stage in the management of their lives by city dwellers as they adapted to merchant society.

Appendix to chapter 8:

The will and testament of Marco Trevisano

Intus vero
In the name of Our Lord Jesus Christ, March 16, 1626,
in Venice, in the house where I now live, at the Crosechieri

I, Marco Trevisano, being desirous of making my testamentary dispositions according to my free and firm wishes as to what shall be done with my possessions after my death, finding myself by the grace of God sound in mind and up till now in body, after mature deliberation and prayer to the Holy Spirit, have decided to write the present will in my own hand, in order to prescribe what follows. First, with the utmost humility, I commend my Soul to God, beseeching Him in His infinite mercy to pardon my sins and to receive me in the heavenly company of Our Lord Jesus Christ.

I should have not possessions, nor anything in the world had God not granted me the great boon of allowing me to find my very remarkable friend, the most illustrious Niccolo Barbarigo, son of the late Lorenzo, in whose house I have dwelt for so many years; for this reason, that all the wealth left to me after the apportionment made with my brothers according to the deeds drawn up by the late Dominico Adami, public notary of Venice, amounted to 5,848 ducats only and that I was indebted to the aforementioned Niccolo for 4,000 ducats that he had lent me, as legally certified, on which ducats any interest that he might have asked me to pay, as is commonly done, even between friends, would have swallowed up all my small capital and much more beside. But my incomparable friend, the aforementioned Niccolo Barbarigo, made me a present of the 4,000 ducats and paid the aforementioned out of his own pocket. And I can say that that was one of the least signs of

---

[9] Round this theme of 'friendship' one glimpses the beginnings of the idea of homosexuality being used as a distinguishing feature of individuals, something we shall find in the London clubs of the eighteenth century, as has been well described by N. Zemon Davis in 'Les Conteurs de Montaillou', *Annales*, I, 1979, p. 68.

[10] See G. Cozzi, 'Padri, Figli, e Matrimoni clandestini', *La Cultura*, 2–3, 1976, pp. 169–213.

incomparable love. And if there still remain to me any possessions I can dispose of I owe it entirely and solely to the pure kindness and magnanimity of my old friend and benefactor, whose goodness towards me has been more divine than human . . . For this reason I appoint and desire that my heir and legatee should purchase two basins and two jugs of silver at the cost of a hundred crowns each, that is one basin and one jug each engraved with my forename and surname and that they should be given, one pair to the most illustrious Zuanne Venier, son of the late Francesco, and the other to the most illustrious Giovanni Antonio Zen, son of the late Bartolomeo, in that order, with whom I have contracted a most cordial and devoted friendship, and asking them kindly to use them to wash their hands in memory of our true, sincere and virtuous friendship . . . All else that remains of my possessions, movable and immovable, present and future, stocks and shares, and all that will or could accrue to me I leave to the most illustrious Niccolo Barbarigo, my greatest friend, a friend unequalled by any that I have read of in history; a friend who has been more to me than human intelligence can imagine. And I desire that he should own and freely dispose, as sole legatee, of all my possessions. To him I commend my soul and charge him to consign my body to the same grave in which his is to be interred, feeling great joy at the idea that just as we have always been in perfect accord with one another and more united in our lives than any human mind can comprehend and that in the heavenly kingdom one of my supreme joys and part of my felicity will be to find myself united with his generous, pure and sincere spirit, who has shown by his constant love towards me, God's creature, what should equally be his love towards God the creator, so that our bodies should remain united after death so long as this earthly world exists . . . And if they (my brothers) have abandoned me in such a fashion I take it as an act of divine Providence that has allowed me to show the world and especially our country such an illustrious and remarkable example of a true and perfect friendship the like of which has never been seen . . . But I know he will carry out my wishes more than willingly on account of the special love he always bore towards me and the great trust he had in me, having, during life, entrusted to me all he possessed, his life and his honour, sure and necessary signs of his unceasing kindness and his good opinion of my faithfulness and honesty . . . Niccolo Barbarigo having been everything to me, after God and the oracle of the Holy Scriptures, and being fully confirmed in the case of our friendship . . .

Amicus fidelis protectio fortis, qui autem invenit illum invenit Thesaurum, Amico fideli nulla est comparatio, et non est digna ponderatio auri, et argenti, contra bonitatem fidei illius. Amicus fidelis medicamentum vitae et immortalitatis, et qui metuunt Dominum invenient illum. Qui timet Deum aeque habebit amicitiam bonam; quoniam secundum illum erit amicus illius (Eccles. 6, 17).

Si duo, hac in tabula videre corpora existumas, Nicolaum Barbaricum Marcum Trevisanum, duo vides membra unius corporis, unus est enim spiritus utrumque regens.

L'Heroica et incomporabile amicitia de l'Illustrissimi Signori Niccolo Barbarigo e Marco Trevisano, gentilhuomini venetiani . . . Venice, 1629 (Bibl. Naz. Marciana, Venezia, Misc. 190).

9

Two English women in the seventeenth century: notes for an anatomy of feminine desire

Angeline Goreau

Reconstructing a history of feminine sexuality in England more than three centuries ago very nearly excludes any document written by a woman. Women rarely referred to such matters in their private diaries or correspondence (though admittedly those references would most likely be the first deleted in afterthought) and mentioned them even less in print. On the basis of the evidence from women themselves that has survived, one might almost conclude that feminine desire was an entirely uncharted realm, if indeed it existed at all; that is, if the exigencies and absolute necessity for chastity, modesty, feminine 'honour' and reputation were not so repeatedly and universally insisted upon. Entire innocence of motivation, it seems, would eliminate the importance of such rigid constraint. It is a measure of the effectiveness this censorship exercised over women of that time, that any discussion of their sexual lives, whether imagined or practised, must pass through indiscretion.

The following poem, written by Lady Elizabeth Carey about 1613, describes the chaste posture that was generally represented as model feminine behaviour:

> Tis not enough for one that is a wife
>   To keep her spotless from an act of ill:
> But from suspicion she should free her life,
>   And bare herself of power as well as will.
> 'Tis not so glorious for her to be free,
> As by her proper self restrain'd to be.

When she hath spacious ground to walk upon,
    Why on the ridge should she desire to go?
It is no glory to forbear alone :
    Those things that may her honour overthrow:
But 'tis thankworthy, if she will not take
All lawful liberties for honour's sake.

That wife her hand against her fame doth rear,
    That more than to her lord alone will give
A private word to any second ear;
    And though she may with reputation live,
Yet tho' most chaste, she doth her glory blot,
And wounds her honour, tho' she kills it not.

When to their husbands they themselves do bind,
    Do they not wholly give themselves away?
Or give they but their body, not their mind,
    Reserving that, tho' best, for other's prey?
No, sure, their thought no more can be their own,
And therefore to none but one be known.

Then she usurps upon another's right,
    That seeks to be by public language graced;
And tho' her thoughts reflect with purest light
    Her mind, if not peculiar, is not chaste.
For in a wife it is no worse to find
A common body, than a common mind.

Many of Lady Carey's female contemporaries similarly testified
to the social hegemony of 'modesty': her poem is characteristic
both in language and content. Though her cautions are specifically
addressed to wives, the principles they were based on also held true
for women as a whole, for as *The Lawe's Resolution of Women's
Rights* (1632) expressed it, 'all of them are understood either
married or to be married . . .' Even widows long past the age of
childbearing and unlikely to remarry were still subject to the
confines of modesty. Lady Carey's poem is of particular interest
for its clear delineation of the process through which a specifically
sexual interdiction expanded to cover every aspect of a woman's
life.

The practical source of the requirement of chastity in women,
acknowledged by most seventeenth-century commentators, was the
importance of unquestioned paternity in a society whose whole
economic and social structure was based on the patrilinear,

primogenital inheritance system. The first Marquis of Halifax wrote to his daughter, who had complained of her husband's infidelities, to explain that sexual adventures might be countenanced in a man, which must be 'criminal' in a woman — because her unquestioned 'honour' insured the 'preservation of families from any mixture which may bring a blemish to them'. According to Lady Carey, however, feminine chastity encompassed a much larger territory than mere abstinence from any illegitimate sexual activity — ' 'Tis not enough for one that is a wife/To keep her spotless from an act of ill.' A woman who is truly chaste, she says, will divest 'herself of power as well as will', and forgo 'all lawful liberties for honour's sake'. Chastity is thus reinterpreted as passivity; the central characteristic of femininity becomes power- lessness — or impotence. By the same token, the expression of sexuality itself is equated with the exercise of power and will, or aggression. Violation of the prescribed inaction, the language of the poem unwittingly suggests, came dangerously close to acting as a man: a woman who desired to 'go on the ridge' (to rise to heights) betrayed a desire to usurp male erection.

Through the abstraction of the concept of chastity, Lady Carey sets up an infinitely expanding architecture of self-restraint. If sexual significance was to be applied to every sphere of a woman's life, then modesty placed inhibitions on her way of speaking, looking, walking, imagining, thinking. *The Whole Duty of a Woman*, a seventeenth-century book of advice for young women, specified that

Modesty . . . spreads itself in life, motions and words . . . Your looks, your speech, and the course of your whole behaviour should own a humble distrust of yourselves; rather being willing to learn and observe, than to dictate and prescribe . . . As you value your reputation, keep us to the strictures of this virtue . . . give no occasion for scandal or reproach; but let your conversation set an example to others . . . Let neither your thoughts nor eyes wander.

Manifestly, wandering eyes or even thoughts came to stand for unchastity. 'Discreet women have neither eyes, nor ears,' a seven- teenth-century proverb went.

The spatial imagery of enclosure that is so closely associated with feminine identity in Lady Carey's poem, depends on a very clearly defined sense of sexual territory: male and female domains of experience were two contiguous but irreconcilable universes.

The phrase 'the feminine sphere' comes up repeatedly in letters, diaries, etiquette manuals, and other contemporary texts; it is used synonomously with the 'private domain', or 'the home', while the male province delineates 'the world'. Any foray into what was seen as male preserve, whether real or imagined, verbal or actual, was seen as a negation of femininity. The sexual implications of this terminology are evident: woman's 'sphere' confines her to her 'inner space', while man's projecting sex naturally propels him into a larger, aggressive theatre of activity.

The equation of a 'common mind' with a 'common body' helps to explain in part why so few Englishwomen published any literary work before the eighteenth century: it was a symbolic violation of feminine modesty. To publish one's writing (one's thoughts) was to make onself 'public': to expose oneself to 'the world'. It was, of course, a penetration of a woman's 'private circle'. To protect themselves from scandal, many chose anonymity. The unidentified female author of a feminist tract published in 1696 states quite explicitly her reasons for keeping her name a secret: 'nothing could induce me to bring my name upon the public stage of the world . . . the tenderness of reputation in our sex . . . made me very cautious, how I exposed mine to such poisonous vapours.' Dorothy Osborne thought the Duchess of Newcastle mad for signing her name to her writing. In a private letter to her fiancé, she commented 'her friends are much to blame to let her go abroad . . . there are certain things that custom has made almost of absolute necessity, and reputation I take to be one of those; if one could be invisible I should choose that.'

The attitudes expressed in women's letters, diaries, literary works and other texts for the most part support Lady Carey's estimation of modesty as central to the feminine ideal. It is difficult to estimate exactly to what extent this ideal was internalized by women and to what degree it actually determined sexual behaviour. Part of the problem, of course, is that the moral stance one was willing to commit to writing might very well be at variance with morality practised in private. The paucity of evidence from women, however, argues that if the strictures of modesty did not prevent women from acting on their sexual desires, it at least kept most of them from writing about them.

There were occasionally rebels: if many women were forced to agree with Lady Carey on the social importance of modesty, not all of them saw it as a virtue. Certainly not all agreed with her that the experience of sexual passion was unnatural to women, or that its absence was an inherent feature of femininity. The author of a poem called *Sylvia's Complaint of her Sex's Unhappiness* (1688) evidently regarded modest restraint as oppressive:

> Our thoughts like tinder, apt to fire,
> Are often caught with loving kind desire,
> But custom does such rigid laws impose,
> We must not for our lives the thing disclose.
> If one of us a lowly youth has seen,
> And straight some tender thoughts to feel begin . . .
> Custom and modesty, much more severe
> Strictly forbid our passion to declare.

Despite her brave acknowledgement in print of her own sexual impulses, the author of the poem chose to protect her reputation from further damage by identifying herself by no more than the pen-name 'Sylvia'.

An extraordinary exception to this rule of invisibility was Aphra Behn. A contemporary of 'Sylvia', she was the first Englishwoman to become a professional writer, that is to say, to earn her living through the production of literary work. In seventeen years, seventeen of her plays were staged in London; in addition, she published several volumes of poetry and translations, and thirteen short novels. Her writing appeared without apology or denial of responsibility and she actively sought to take her place as a writer among male colleagues rather than as a lady who scribbled for her own amusement, as the few other women writers who published before her had claimed.

Aphra Behn's open confession of desire made her still more remarkable: she frankly addressed the question of sex and was not afraid to bring it on the stage. Her second play, *The Amorous Prince* (1671), opened on a seduction scene which had just been brought to fruition — the couple rising from their love-making. According to the stage directions, she is dressed in her 'night attire' and he is dressing himself; the setting is her bedroom. Not only has the act taken place outside the sanctity of marriage, but the gallant in question is not even the young lady's fiancé. Behn was not merely writing racy scenes to scandalise and entertain the theatre audiences of her day; she actively rejected feminine modesty as fundamentally oppressive and believed that physical passion was an inseparable part of love. Women as well as men, she held, experience desire and are equally capable of its intense expression.

Perhaps Aphra Behn might not have the courage or stamina to defend such a position had the Restoration not created a favourable climate. Born about 1640, she came of age in the 1660s, when Charles II's return to the throne had effected an abrupt and deliberate reversal of the Puritan ethic that Cromwell had attempted to impose during the Interregnum. The King's need to distinguish himself in every way from his predecessors — added to his natural inclination — created an atmosphere in which promiscuity was adhered to as a social norm as dogmatically as the more severe of the Puritan party had adhered to godliness. Part of the point was to demonstrate one's loyalty to the Royalist cause: Francis North was counselled to 'keep a whore', because he was 'ill-looked upon (at court) for want of doing so'. The movement primarily affected the fashionable society of London — the court and aristocratic circles, the playhouse, the taverns, coffee houses. The new breed of libertines were Aphra Behn's literary colleagues, audience, and patrons. There are many references to the scorn for traditional feminine modesty they professed. The hero of one of her plays chastises a lady he is trying to persuade to bed by telling her that her concern for her reputation is out-of-date: 'Fy, fy, Laura,' he says, 'a lady bred at court, and yet want complaisance enough to entertain a gallant in private! This coy humour is not a-la-mode . . .' The heroine is warned by her own brother, however, not to accede to such persuasions: 'beware of men,' he tells her, 'for though I myself be one, yet I have the frailties of my sex, and can dissemble too. Trust none of us, for if thou dost, thou art undone.'

Despite their espousal of sexual liberty, the promiscuous Restoration gallants still more or less unconsciously held on to the very ideas about woman's modesty they claimed to repudiate. This double impulse put women in an impossible position. Aphra Behn, in a poem entitled 'To Alexis, in answer to his Poem against Fruition', complained that men of her generation fled from women 'if honour take our part/. . . And Oh! they fly us if we yield.' Her poem, 'The Disappointment', describes in undisguised detail the difficulties a woman who attempted to escape the restrictions of modesty might encounter. I give the text in full here:

I

ONE day the Amorous *Lysander*,
By an impatient Passion sway'd,
Surpriz'd fair *Cloris*, that lov'd Maid,
Who could defend her self no longer.
All things did with his Love conspire;

The gilded Planet of the Day,
In his gay Chariot drawn by Fire,
Was now descending to the Sea,
And left no Light to guide the World,
But what from *Cloris* Brighter Eyes was hurld.

II

In a lone Thicket made for Love,
Silent as yielding Maids Consent,
She was a Charming Languishment,
Permits his Force, yet gently strove;
Her Hands his Bosom softly meet,
But not to put him back design'd,
Rather to draw 'em on inclin'd:
Whilst he lay trembling at her Feet,
Resistance 'tis in vain to show;
She wants the pow'r to say — *Ah! What d'ye do?*

III

Her Bright Eyes sweet, and yet severe,
Where Love and Shame confus'dly strive,
Fresh Vigor to *Lysander* give;
And breathing faintly in his Ear,
She cry'd — *Cease, Cease — your vain Desire,*
Or I'll call out — What would you do?
My Dearer Honour ev'n to You
I cannot, must not give — Retire,
Or take this Life, whose chiefest part
I gave you with the Conquest of my Heart.

IV

But he as much unus'd to Fear,
As he was capable of Love,
The blessed minutes to improve,
Kisses her Mouth, her Neck, her Hair;
Each Touch her new Desire Alarms,
His burning trembling Hand he prest
Upon her swelling Snowy Brest,
While she lay panting in his Arms.
All her Unguarded Beauties lie
The Spoils and Trophies of the Enemy.

V

And now without Respect or Fear,
He seeks the Object of his Vows,
(His Love no Modesty allows)
By swift degrees advancing — where
His daring Hand that Altar seiz'd,
Where Gods of Love do sacrifice:
That Awful Throne, that Paradice
Where Rage is calm'd, and Anger pleas'd;
That Fountain where Delight still flows,
And gives the Universal World Repose.

VI

Her Balmy Lips incountring his,
Their Bodies, as their Souls, are joyn'd;
Where both in Transports Unconfin'd
Extend themselves upon the Moss.
Cloris half dead and breathless lay;
Her soft Eyes cast a Humid Light,
Such as divides the Day and Night;
Or falling Stars, whose Fires decay:
And now no signs of Life she shows,
But what in short-breath'd Sighs returns and goes.

VII

He saw how at her Length she lay
He saw her rising Bosom bare;
Her loose thin Robes, through which appear
A Shape designed for Love and Play;
Abandon'd by her Pride and Shame
She does her softest Joys dispence,
Offering her Virgin Innocence
A Victim to Loves Sacred Flame;
While the o'er-Ravish'd Shepherd lies
Unable to perform the Sacrifice.

VIII

Ready to taste a thousand Joys,
The too transported hapless Swain
Found the vast Pleasure turn'd to Pain;
Pleasure which too much Love destroys:
The willing Garments by he laid,

And Heaven all open'd to his view,
Mad to possess, himself he threw
On the Defenceless Lovely Maid.
But Oh what envying God conspires
To snatch his Power, yet leave him the Desire!

IX

Nature's Support, (without whose Aid
She can no Humane Being give)
It self now wants the Art to live;
Faintness its slack'ned Nerves invade:
In vain th' inraged Youth essay'd
To call its fleeting Vigor back,
No motion 'twill from Motion take;
Excess of Love his Love betray'd:
In vain he Toils, in vain Commands;
The Insensible fell weeping in his Hand.

X

In this so Amorous Cruel Strife,
Where Love and Fate were too severe,
The poor *Lysander* in despair
Renounc'd his Reason with his Life:
Now all the brisk and active Fire
That should the Nobler Part inflame,
Serv'd to increase his Rage and Shame,
And left no Spark for New Desire:
Not all her Naked Charms cou'd move
Or calm that Rage that had debauch'd his Love.

XI

Cloris returning from the Trance
Which Love and soft Desire had bred,
Her timerous Hand she gently laid
(Or guided by Design or Chance)
Upon that Fabulous *Priapus*,
That Potent God, as Poets feign;
But never did young *Shepherdess*,
Gath'ring of Fern upon the Plain,
More nimbly draw her Fingers back,
Finding beneath the verdant Leaves a Snake:

XII

Then *Cloris* her fair Hand withdrew,
Finding that God of her Desires
Disarm'd of all his Awful Fires,
And Cold as Flow'rs bath'd in the Morning Dew.
Who can the *Nymph's* Confusion guess?
The Blood forsook the hinder Place,
And strew'd with Blushes all her Face,
Which both Disdain and Shame exprest:
And from *Lysander's* Arms she fled,
Leaving him fainting on the Gloomy Bed.

XIII

Like Lightning through the Grove she hies,
Or *Daphne* from the *Delphick God*,
No Print upon the grassey Road
She leaves, t' instruct Pursuing Eyes.
The Wind that wanton'd in her Hair,
And with her Ruffled Garments plaid,
Discover'd in the Flying Maid
All that the Gods e'er made, if Fair.
So *Venus*, when her *Love* was slain,
With Fear and Haste flew o'er the Fatal Plain.

XIV

The *Nymph's* Resentments none but I
Can well Imagine or Condole:
But none can guess *Lysander's* Soul,
But those who sway'd his Destiny.
His silent Griefs swell up to Storms,
And not one God his Fury spares!
He curs'd his Birth, his Fate, his Stars;
But more the *Shepherdess's* Charms,
Whose soft bewitching Influence
Had Damn'd him to the *Hell* of Impotence.

The poem begins traditionally enough: it is Lysander, the man, who initiates the sexual encounter, who is 'swayed' by passion, who seizes the maid. Cloris cedes to his *will*, as she can no longer 'defend' herself against his *power*. Even the woods that hide the lovers take on her 'charming' passivity: through metonymy, they become 'silent as yielding maid's consent'. Here Behn reverses herself. The young woman 'permits his force', and yet usurps it at the same time. She too 'gently strove'. She actively draws him near her rather than feigning modesty by pushing him away. In the third stanza, Cloris rather feebly protests the compromise of her 'feminine honour', but whatever passing reservations she might have entertained are quickly removed by the awakening of her own desire. Although Behn later (stanza VII) describes her as a 'victim' offering up her 'virgin-innocence', Cloris is hardly unaware of the seat of her own pleasure: 'That Fountain where Delight still flows/And gives the Universal World repose.' Nor does Behn seem unfamiliar with the mechanism of clitoral erection, for in stanza XII, when she describes the extinguishing of Cloris's desire, 'The Blood forsook the hinder place' — the hinder place designating her sexual parts.

Intensity of desire, however, renders the would-be lover impotent. He tries to recall his 'power' by masturbating himself, but 'No motion 'twill from motion take . . . the insensible fell weeping in his hand.' His desire for the young woman rapidly turns to fury. Doubling his humiliation, Cloris puts her hand on his flagging member (stanza XI) and exposes its deflation. Behn's imagery underlines the transmogrification of the penis from instrument of pleasure to emblem of danger: she discovers a snake.

In rejecting the sexual passivity that ought to have been her part, Cloris has prevented her lover from exercising his 'power' over her. He clearly considers her responsible for his impotence. Behn does not attempt to draw any moral from the failed encounter; she is not counselling a more modest stance for Cloris by any means, but merely analysing the complex interaction of roles in an equal meeting of desire. The imperative of feminine chastity could not be eradicated from social consciousness, she implied, by women alone.

10

Sex in married life in the early Middle Ages: the Church's teaching and behavioural reality

Jean-Louis Flandrin

Few of our sources provide so much detail on sex in marriage as treatises of moral theology, records of cases of conscience, confessional manuals, etc. So I propose to start from these ecclesiastical documents, devoting special attention to those instructions that seem most strange to us today. Then I shall try to find out how much this literature has to tell us about the actual sex life of husbands and wives of long ago.

A basic tenet of Christian morality is an overwhelming disapproval of the pleasures of the flesh, because it trammels up the soul in the body, preventing it from aspiring towards God. We must eat to live, but we must be careful not to enjoy the pleasures of the table too much. We are obliged to embrace the opposite sex in order to produce children, but we should not get too fond of the pleasures of sex. Sexuality was given for the purpose of reproduction. We abuse it if we use it for other ends, such as pleasure.

In our society, as in all others, say the Christian moralists, the institution of the family is the best one suited for the bringing up of children; and one can only beget legitimate children — that is children legally entitled to succeed us — in lawful marriage. All sexual activity outside marriage has necessarily some purpose other than procreation and constitutes a sin. Hence, no such activity may be permitted. We are more familiar with the notion of this ban than with the theologians' reasons for it, to say nothing of the historical reasons, which deserve careful study

What seems even stranger to us, on the other hand, is that even within marriage sexual union was only lawful if it was performed for its rightful object, i.e. to beget children and render to one's partner what had been promised to her in the marriage contract. To these two good reasons for marital coition the theologians after the thirteenth century added a third, rather less laudable, intended to fight against shameful desires. As St Paul had written to the people of Corinth: 'It is a good thing for a man to have nothing to do with women; but because there is so much immorality, let each man have his own wife and each woman her own husband. The husband must give the wife what is due to her, and the wife equally must give her husband his due' (1 Cor. 7, 1–3). So marriage was a kind of preventive medicine given by God to save man from immorality. In other words — the words of these theologians — if either spouse is tempted to commit adultery or to masturbate, failing any better alternative, he can have recourse to the antidote to temptation that marriage provides.

After the fifteenth century some theologians considered that it was not sinful for husband and wife to have intercourse with this intention. Earlier they had all rated it as venial. The imagination had to be carefully controlled for fear of falling into mortal sin: even to imagine intercourse with anyone other than one's spouse was to commit adultery. The majority of early theologians deemed that husbands and wives who copulated for pleasure were committing mortal sin. Of course there is a moment when the simple animal enjoyment, which is the pleasure of sex, drowns all other feelings; or so said the theologians. And many, including Pope Gregory the Great in the sixth century, believed that it was almost impossible to be pure after marital copulation. But what was certainly a mortal sin was to embrace one's spouse solely for pleasure. Almost all medieval theologians emphasized this, following St Jerome rather than St Augustine.

We have to wait until the end of the sixteenth century for another opinion, and the appearance of a fresh problem, both expounded by Thomas Sanchez. Husbands and wives who embrace with no particular object in mind, but simply as a married couple, commit no sin; so long, of course, that they do nothing to impede procreation, which still remains the ultimate and only objective of the sexual act. Getting pleasure from it is not condemned, but only 'pleasure alone': in other words, copulation deliberately separated from its procreative function. So long as there was no other justification for sexual intercourse than the begetting of children it went without saying that any contraceptive or abortive device was utterly reprehensible. The more marital behaviour of this kind was extenuated, the more explicit became the condemnation of such devices. The formula put forward by Sanchez, 'for pleasure alone', is an important landmark in the history of these two arguments and shows how closely connected they are.

It would appear that after the sixteenth century — but this needs confirmation by more intensive research — theologians were urging couples not to be afraid of having too many children. So Benedicti in the sixteenth century,[1] Fromageau in the eighteenth,[2] and Pope Pius XI in the twentieth.[3] On the other hand, at the end of the Ancient World and the beginning of the Middle Ages they were being encouraged to give up sexual intercourse once their succession was assured. Large families have not always been a Christian ideal.[4]

[1] 'The good man need never fear to have too many children, but should think it God's blessing and trust in the saying of David: "I have been young and now am old: and yet saw I never the righteous forsaken, nor his seed begging their bread" (Ps. xxxvii, 25. AV). 'For since God has bestowed them He will provide the means whereby to nourish them, for it is He who feeds the birds of the air, and He will never fail him' (*Somme des péchés*, liv. II, chapter ix, N. 63, p. 227, 4to ed. of 1596). For a commentary on this text, see 'L'Attitude à l'égard du petit enfant' in J.—L. Flandrin, *Le Sexe et l'Occident*, especially pp. 153 and 180.

[2] '*Case XXXVI*: 'Ausone was a poor man, and seeing himself burdened with six children, although his wife was still young, had resolved more than a year earlier to abstain from intercourse and had even refused his wife her due many times for fear of increasing his family and that he might totally lack the means of feeding them. Can he pursue his resolve without committing mortal sin?'

Answer: Some authorities consider that in these circumstances a husband can, without sin, abstain from intercourse, and consequently refuse his wife her due, provided there is no danger of incontinence, or risk of recriminations, but it would seem wrong to follow this opinion in practice. If God, as Jesus Christ has told us, and David long before him, "giveth food to the young ravens", a Christian is insulting divine providence if he doubts His goodness and believes that if God gives him children He will not provide for their needs . . .' Fromageux, *Dictionnaire de cas de conscience*, 2 vol., 1733 and 1746, 'Devoir conjugal' col. 1202.

[3] 'Christian parents should, besides, realize that they are not only called upon to propagate and sustain the human race on earth, they are not just intended to produce worshippers of the true God, but to give their sons to the Church to join the fellowship of the saints and be the servants of God so that the number of those who worship God and our Saviour should increase daily. We are touched to the heart by the groans of poverty-stricken couples who find it so hard to feed their children. But . . . no obstacle can absolve man from the obligation created by God's commandments which forbid actions that are wrong by their very nature; in all circumstances married couples, strengthened by God's grace, can always faithfully fulfil their duty and preserve their conjugal virtue from any such shameful slur: such is the unshakeable truth of the pure Christian faith, as expressed by the authority of the Council of Trent: "it is forbidden by the Fathers, under pain of anathema, for anybody to pronounce these reckless words — that it is impossible for the righteous man to obey God's laws. For God does not demand the impossible, but He admonishes you to do what you are able, and to ask for what you are unable, and He helps you to be able" ' (Encyclical *Casti Connubii*, 31 December 1930).

[4] 'The young often profess a desire to have children and think to excuse the heat of their youth by their wish to procreate: so much the more shame to the old to behave in a way the young are ashamed to admit to! And even the young, when their hearts

Another difficulty concerned 'the crime of Onan' or coitus interruptus, which was to become the great family contraceptive of the eighteenth and nineteenth centuries. It is seldom mentioned in the period between the Ancient World and the beginning of the fourteenth century, it is then mentioned more frequently, particularly from the sixteenth century onwards. In the seventeenth and eighteenth centuries all the theologians and confessors discuss it, finding that it raises new problems, such as the complicity of the wife. She, as we know from St Paul, must give the husband his due whenever it is required of her. But does she have to — and has she even the right to do so — when he is in the habit of practising coitus interruptus? By the seventeenth century theological literature was full of arguments about this, long before the fecundity of married couples had begun to fall off at all significantly.

In addition there had been, ever since the fourteenth century, a number of theologians who had given some thought to the problem of couples with over-large families. Pierre de la Palu was the first to suggest controlled coition, that is penetration without ejaculation, a practice which still has its supporters in the Church today. Pierre de Ledesma in the sixteenth century put forward as his contribution a simple refusal to grant conjugal rights.

What has come to seem even odder to us today than the ancient injunctions about what should guide copulating couples are the notions of creditor and debtor in married life. This idea of conjugal indebtedness goes back to St Paul. In his first Epistle to the Corinthians he writes, as we know: 'because there is so much immorality, let each man have his own wife and each woman her own husband. The husband must give the wife what is due to her, and the wife equally must give the husband his due. The wife cannot claim her body as her own; it is her husband's. Equally, the husband cannot claim his body as his own; it is his wife's' (1 Cor. 7, 2–4).

Interpreting this text very literally the medieval theologians and their successors up to the beginning of the twentieth century have put the notion of debt in the centre of the sex life of married couples. In treatises of moral theology, in the canonical *summae*, in works more particularly devoted to the sacrament of marriage, everything concerning sex is to be found under the heading *debitum*, that which is 'due', the 'debt'.

---

have been calmed and moderated by the fear of God, often abandon, once they have prosperity, the ways of their youth' (St Ambrose, *Treatise on the Gospel of St Luke*, 1, 43–5).

In the course of everyday life one would imagine that to achieve coition one partner had to ask the other to discharge his or her debt, and the other had to pay up. Thus, in every case of conscience relating to sex in marriage, one always had to investigate separately the case of the partner demanding payment and that of the one who paid. One could never imagine that they might have been drawn to each other simultaneously and by mutual impulse.

One also has to bear in mind that the woman, no less than the man, might be in the position of wanting to claim her due. Outside the marriage bed man was always woman's master. And in the sex act itself he was assumed to be the active partner, hence superior to the woman, who was expected passively to undergo his on-slaughts. But where the debt was concerned — and in that only — they were equals, each of them, in the words of St Paul, having a claim on the body of the other. The theologians were so attached to the idea of this equality that — contrary to all normal patterns of behaviour, not to mention their own powers of imagination — they did not hesitate to favour the woman as compensation for her weakness and the inherent timidity of her sex. She was bound to pay her due if her husband explicity demanded it according to his rights. In return he was bound to 'pay' as soon as he saw from his wife's demeanour and attitude that she desired to make love, though she lacked courage to ask for it or express her desire aloud. This principle of favouring the woman could be counter-productive, by encouraging her timidity and confirming her passivity. If she depended wholly on her husband to divine her wishes, she risked losing their fulfilment altogether. Finally there was the risk that strict observance of the conjugal indebtedness, although in principle it made the wife the equal of her husband, could in reality bear more heavily on her than on him.

One would like to know to what extent the wife had the right to any pleasure in this trade which rated her own desires so cheaply. Actually the theologians did not put the question in those terms. Pleasure for the woman, as also for the man, seemed to them to be felt automatically at the moment of ejaculation. The problem was — was the woman supposed to emit her 'semen' at the time of copulation?[5]

---

[5] For further details on this question, see Anne-Catherine Ducasse-Kliszowski 'Les théories de la génération et leur influence sur la moral sexuelle du xvi au xviii siècle' (University of Paris master's dissertation, June 1972). This work has been summarized in 'Homme et femme dans le lit conjugal' in J−L. Flandrin, Le Sexe et l'Orient, chapter 8, pp. 127−36.

First question: was female 'semen' essential for procreation, as Galen had maintained, or was it unnecessary as Aristotle had said? After lengthy arguments in the course of which some favoured Galen and others Aristotle, all our theologians agreed that there did exist a form of female semen which was emitted at the moment of orgasm; that it was not necessary for the conception of a child; that it was a considerable help and made the child more beautiful. In fact, why should God have made it enjoyable for women unless it helped to propagate the species? Too Aristotelian a viewpoint in this matter might have undermined the whole Christian teaching on sex.

Various moral problems arose from this point. Was the woman bound to emit her 'semen' during copulation? Discussion of this question normally followed after that of coitus interruptus and controlled coition, and suggested that by refusing to emit her 'semen' the woman avoided or diminished the risk of conception. Of the 15 authors (out of twenty-five examined) who took up this question eight thought that the wife who deliberately abstained from orgasm committed venial sin, and three that she committed none.

Second question: was the husband bound to prolong copulation until the wife emitted her 'semen'? Four theologians thought it a moral obligation, and the rest decided that he was not so bound. All 'allowed' him to prolong his embrace until his wife attained orgasm, although a child could be conceived with less effort, and with less enjoyment of course.

Thirdly: should husband and wife make their emission simultaneously? Only six out of our twenty-five took up this question. But all six agreed that every effort should be made to achieve this, for simultaneity increased the chances of conception and helped to make a more beautiful child. None, however, laid it down as an obligation, though several doctors, including Ambroise Paré, asserted that conception could not take place unless there was simultaneous emission. The male partner does not control the female orgasm, and through confessions or by other means our authors might have realized this. None, however, in this debate referred to this experimentally verifiable fact.

Fourth and final question: is it lawful for the wife to achieve an orgasm by fondling herself when her husband has withdrawn before she has made her emission? Of seventeen theologians who discussed this problem only three forebade this post-coital manipulation, and fourteen allowed it. A noteworthy point raised by the minority three: an independent emission by the wife prevented her from being one flesh with her husband. Not one of them, including the three, made explicit mention of the word 'love' in this discussion.

In contrast with the wayward and passionate ways of lovers, marital behaviour was supposed to be stable and rational: intercourse was lawful only on certain occasions and in certain places.[6] It was objectionable on all fast or feast days, periods of uncleanness in the wife, such as menstrual periods, forty days after childbirth, during pregnancy or while breast-feeding. But there have been many changes between the ancient world and the present day in ideas about periods of continence. The rules were originally based on female uncleanness during periods or after giving birth, but after the twelfth and thirteenth centuries there was an emphatic shift to the view that intercourse could harm the wife (after childbirth), or her child (during periods or pregnancy). This new solicitude for the safety of the child led the theologians of the sixteenth, seventeenth and eighteenth centuries more and more to ban intercourse during breastfeeding, though none of their predecessors except Gregory the Great had worried very much about it. On the other hand the number of feast days and fast days had dwindled from about 273 in the seventh century to about 140 in the sixteenth. And while during the High Middle Ages continence was most solemnly enjoined, at the end of the Middle Ages and in modern times it was merely recommended.

Intercourse in public or consecrated places was more strictly forbidden than in earlier times. This was doubtless due to a general increase in modesty and a livelier sense of the holiness of ecclesiastical precincts, just at the time when observance of feast and fast days was falling off.

Intercourse between husband and wife was supposed to take place in the 'natural' position, the wife stretched out on her back with the man on top. All other positions were considered scandalous and 'unnatural'. The one known as *retro* or *more canino* was unnatural because it was the way animals performed. The position *mulier super virum* was at variance with male and female characters, the woman being passive 'by nature' and the man active. In this position, said Sanchez, 'it is obvious that the woman acts and the man submits.' It was because 'women had gone mad and abused their husbands in this way' that God had sent the Flood to destroy

---

[6] On this question see J.–L. Flandrin, *La doctrine de la continence périodique dans la tradition occidental*, thesis presented to University of Paris, IV, 1978, TS. See also 'L'attitude à l'égard du petit enfant et les conduites sexuelles' in Flandrin, *Le Sexe et l'Occident*, pp. 193–201.

mankind, alleged another theologian. It was, besides, particularly suspect as inhibiting conception, in spite of the attractive force attributed to the uterus. More generally, all these 'unnatural positions' seemed to be characteristic of a pursuit of pleasure which was as excessive as it was likely to be uncreative. All the same, after the fifteenth century, some theologians allowed them when the couple had good reason for indulging in them; for example when the husband was too fat to be capable of the natural position, or when the wife was nearing her confinement and the unborn child might be damaged. This indulgent attitude of the theologians often shocked laymen who knew about it. According to Brantôme some said 'Husbands had better keep away from their wives when they are carrying, as animals do, rather than pollute their marriage with that sort of vileness.'

It is hardly necessary to add that sodomy was forbidden under the direst penalties, as much between husbands and wives as between members of the same sex. It was the unnatural sin *par excellence*. So were kissing and caressing the 'shameful' parts of the body if there was a likelihood of being 'polluted'. Sanchez alone, so far as I know, allowed them as manifestations of love, even where such a risk was present . . . so long, of course, as 'pollution' was not the objective.

With the exception of Sanchez and Francisco Vitoria, the former in his chapter on kisses and caresses, and the second on forbidden times, not one of the ancient theologians ever introduces the subject of love in these discussions of sex in married life. Nor did any of them try to find out if one of the partners were not simply reducing the other to the condition of a mere object! Twentieth-century theologians, in the same context, are always thinking in terms of love and the realization of the partner as an actual being. In fact, it is clear that each was seen by the other as an object, as witness the whole question of conjugal indebtedness. Occasionally it was softened by the notion of kindness; but it was on the level of justice – not kindness – that the theologians normally conducted their debates. The wife's body belonged to the husband and he could do what he wished with it, provided he committed no serious transgression. The same applied to the woman in respect of the husband's body.

What was more, when the idea of love occurred in these discussions, it was firmly disapproved of:

A man who is too passionately in love with his wife is an adulterer, says St Jerome. Any form of love of another's wife is disgraceful, and so is excessive love of one's own. The wise man loves his wife prudently, not passionately. He should withstand the temptation of sensual pleasure or of importunately seeking intercourse. Nothing is so vile as to love one's wife as if she were a mistress . . . Men should come before their wives not as lovers, but as husbands. (*Contra Jovinium*, I. 49).

This attitude, derived from the Stoics and more generally from philosophers of the Ancient World, constantly recurs in the writings of the medieval and later theologians, who are always quoting from this text. Thus Benedicti in 1584:

A husband who is so immoderately in love with his wife and takes his pleaure of her so heatedly that, were she not his wife, he would like her as his mistress, is a sinner. And it seems that St Jerome confirms this when he cites the words of Sextus the Pythagorean, who says that a man who shows himself to be more violently in love with his wife than a husband is an adulterer . . . Whereby a man should not treat his wife as if she were a harlot, nor a woman her husband as if he were a lover, for the holy sacrament of marriage should be treated with all honour and reverence.

Why this hostility? Was it only the pursuit of excessive pleasure that they criticized? Lovers were evidently expected to pursue sexual pleasure more ardently than they have since the days of the Romantic Age. But there was something besides — a fear that too passionate a love between husband and wife could damage social relations and the duty we owe to God. Two laymen of the sixteenth century expressed this. First Montaigne:

The love we beare to our wives is very lawful; yet doth Divinitie bridle and restraine the same. I remember to have read in St Thomas, in a place where he condemneth marriages of kinsfolk in forbidden degrees, this one reason among others: that the affection a man beareth to such a woman may be immoderate; for if the wedlock or husband-like affection be sound and perfect as it ought to be, and also surcharged with that a man oweth to alliance and kindred, there is no doubt but that surcrease may easily transport a husband beyond the bounds of reason. (*Essais*, I, xxix, trans. Florio)

The reference is only to *amitié*, friendship or affection, which rules out any idea of wantonness. Brantôme talks about carnal love and not *amitié*, but he too is not exclusively concerned with worries about forbidden practices:

> We learn from Holy Writ that it is not necessary for husband and wife to love each other so violently. This is what is meant by wanton and lascivious loves. Lovers of such a kind apply themselves with all their might to those sensual pleasures, so that their minds are full of them and they indulge in them so much that they forget the love they owe God; with my own eyes I have seen many women who were so much in love with their husbands and their husbands with them, and burned with such ardour that both of them forgot what they owed to God, so that all the time they should have devoted to Him was just what was left after their lustful behaviour. (Brantôme, *Dames galantes*, First discourse)

From this one has the feeling of a possible rivalry between the love of one's partner and the love of God, something that Philippe Ariès has already noticed in Chaucer's *Parson's Tale*. Noonan thinks that one should not pay much attention to this, for all mortal sin sunders man from God. His view is that the object of all these denunciations is simply the search after guilty pleasure.

My own view, on the other hand, is that, following the Stoic tradition, what the theologians were opposing was love for a particular person, and that the reference to wantonness was nothing but a polemical tactic which helped them to convince their audience that wantonness was a sin and that married folk should not behave wantonly with each other.[7]

What do all these moral precepts tell us about the way married people behaved in those days? I will try to explore this question, looking at the precepts from two different angles: first as standards of behaviour in a Christian community, secondly as reflections of the mental attitudes and behaviour of olden times.

Most historians have adopted the first method. They see the sexual behaviour both of married people and bachelors as conforming to Christian morality, at least up to the middle of the eighteenth century or even to the French Revolution. Their evidence is the minute figure for illegitimate births, and the very small number of pre-nuptial pregnancies; the size and consistency of

---

[7] See 'Contraception, mariage et relations amoureuses dans l'occident chrétien' in Flandrin, *Le Sexe et l'Occident*, especially pp. 118–24.

fertile marriages; the significant dips in Lent in the curve for marriages, and even for conceptions — something which tells us a little more about the secrets of the marriage bed.

One would like to know, all the same, if all this signified a genuinely deep adherence to Christian doctrine, or was just an outward show of respect — a face-saving performance. None of the demographic data I have referred to gives one any feeling of certainty about this. The fact that there were very few pre-nuptial pregnancies and illegitimate births is no proof that bachelors were chaste in the Christian sense of the word; especially as confessors of those days all remark on the forms of contraception practised outside marriage and the solitary pleasures of adolescents. The Lent fall in the conception curve seems in general to have been fairly slight and at best only bears witness to the continence of a minority of those lawfully married. But in any case this no longer had much bearing on the question of the observance or non-observance of the Church's precepts, for after the end of the Middle Ages the theologians ceased to demand continence in Lent.

This question is very often explored in terms of Christianization and de-Christianization. The fall in fertility of married couples and the increase in the number of illegitimate births and pre-nuptial conceptions have been put forward as symptoms of a de-Christianization which has gone on steadily from the mid-eighteenth century to the present day. On the other hand, many historians, taking their cue from militant Catholic reformers, have asserted that the bulk of the peasants had not really been Christianized until the seventeenth century, and up till then had remained basically pagan. Once one begins to study the history of how people behaved and thought one finds these ideas quite unconvincing. The French people, including the country folk, had been Christian ever since the High Middle Ages, and since that time had given all sorts of proofs of their faith; worshipping, paying tithes, making pious bequests, going on pilgrimages and crusades, getting involved in heresies and wars of religion. What the champions of Catholic reformism call paganism seems to me more a special kind of Christianity, rather archaic and marked by a peasant-like outlook.

The peasants had been Christians for a thousand years after their own fashion, as other social groups had been after their's. The aristocracy either made war with each other or made love with the ladies of the court. Were they more Christian? Or better Christians? And what about the bourgeois, whose cardinal virtue was their avarice? Or the Conquistadores, whose greed and cruelty were notorious, but who refused to have sexual relations with the Mexican women who were provided for them until they were baptised, and who obstinately insisted that their allies should be instantly converted and made to destroy their idols, despite the political inconveniences of such a demand, and against the advice of the ecclesiastics who had accompanied them? See, in this connection, the diary of Bernal Diaz del Castillo, who recorded the conquest of Mexico by Cortes. All of these were Christians after their own fashion — which was neither our's nor that of their theologians.

Perhaps there were married folk to be found who accepted the theologians' marriage doctrines and tried to live up to them, those who were known as *dévots*, the devout. In the country as a whole they formed a tiny group, even in the most exalted circles. But it is a group whose existence is confirmed by contemporary evidence, and its social heterogeneity is of little importance to our analysis. In fact I imagine that 'devout' behaviour could be found in both town and country, in all social classes, and among women more often than men. St Francis of Sales's *Introduction to a Devout Life* is addressed to women. What gave the casuists the hardest problems was how a wife should behave towards a husband who was addicted to sinful habits. Husbands were less often troubled by such difficulties and in confession it was mostly women who raised them. See, for example, what Father Féline had to say about this in the eighteenth century. Few as were the *dévots* who conformed strictly to the Church's doctrine on marriage, its impact was probably reinforced by the total lack of co-operation from their husbands.

Society in these early times was very different from our's in that, generally speaking, marriage was not the consecration of a loving relationship but a family matter, a contract drawn up between two individuals, not for their personal happiness, but after taking the advice of their families and consulting the good of these families. For two people thrown together in such circumstances to manage to spend their lives together there had to be a set of rules which they could apply to one another. Even in bed; perhaps especially in bed.

There is a good deal of evidence to suggest that husbands and wives were sometimes inclined to be rather bashful with each other in the marriage bed. There might be a certain amount of embarrassment — at least in some circles — which was a good thing for 'Christian morality'. In many households the husband might have had to cope with a wife's refusal, and, if she persisted, be forced to face the intervention of her confessor. He would have to submit to this intervention under pain of being refused absolution and the sacrament. In fact, despite what present day habits might suggest, the couple were not alone in the marriage bed: the shadow of the confessor loomed over their frolics.

The fact that theologians and canonists discussed the sex life of married couples down to the last detail and devoted so much attention to cases of conscience was not simply because it was an intellectual game, or because they wanted to inject some Christian spirit into every corner of married life; it was also to provide what couples expected of them, or, more precisely, to answer questions put to them in the confessional. Behind all these discussions lay the anxious desire of couples, married at the will of their families, to learn the rules of the marriage game. So, faced with the spectacle of this marriage trade which seems so astonishing to us today, we cannot write it all off as the wild imaginings of churchmen who were quite out of touch with the realities of married life.

Let us now try and see how far the ancient doctrine of marriage actually reflected the mental attitudes and behaviour of married couples in those days. I have deliberately emphasized those aspects of this doctrine which seem the most peculiar to us today. For the extent to which it differs from the doctrines of modern theologians is, in all probability, a measure of the wider difference between the mental attitudes of those days and today.

Of course the celibacy of priests and their book-oriented culture distorted their outlook and set them apart from married folk. This became very obvious in the eighteenth and nineteenth centuries over the question of birth control;[8] and even more so in the eighteenth century with the development of the 'theory of good faith'.[9] Another piece of evidence, found from the fourteenth to the eighteenth century, is the endless series of discussions on how to question married people during confession. In fact these were almost entirely taken up with the problem of relations between priests and female patients, but they do suggest a certain inability of churchmen to provide married couples with guidance.

So we have to find out on what points theologians and laymen shared the same views and on which they differed — always

[8] See J.Y. Noonan, *Contraception et mariage*, Paris, 1969, especially chapter XIII. A résumé of this lengthy work is to be found in Flandrin, *L'Eglise et le contrôle des naissances*, Paris, in the series 'Questions d'Histoire', 23, 1970.

[9] J.Y. Noonan, *Contraception et mariage*, pp. 479ff and 507–11, and J.–L. Flandrin 'Contraception, mariage et relations amoureuses' in *Le Sexe et l'Occident*.

remembering that there were many different sorts of laymen, and one has to allow for geographical, social and cultural differences among those who expressed their views. Take for example Montaigne and Brantôme. Both seem to have considered it completely normal for an ordinary man to have extra-marital affairs, a view which seems to have been widespread among the nobility up to the seventeenth century and even later. So on that point they were at variance with Church doctrine.

Both of them considered it scandalous to behave with one's wife as one would with a mistress. In this their reasoning followed that of St Augustine and the medieval theologians. They went even further than the theologians and confessors of their time in objecting strongly to the idea that husbands should be permitted to have intercourse in 'unnatural positions' on the pretext that their wives were pregnant or they were themselves too fat. We have already seen what Brantôme had to say about this, and Montaigne wrote as follows:

> Those shameless endearings, which the first heat suggests unto us in that sportful delight, are not only undecently, but hurtfully employed towards our wives. *Let them at least learn impudencie from another hand*. They are broad-waking when we need them. I have used no means but natural and simple instruction. Marriage is a religious and devout bond: and that is the reason the pleasure a man hath of it should be a moderate, staid and serious pleasure, and mixed with severitie; it ought to be a voluptuousness somewhat circumspect and conscientious. And because it is the chiefest of generation, there are that make a question whether it be lawful to require them of copulation, as well when we have no hope of children, as when they are over-aged or big with children. (*Essais*, I, xxix, trans. Florio)

Montaigne was all the more ready to accept the Church's teaching in that it coincided with that of the Ancients, and he had found a similar attitude in many different societies: the Moslems, the ancient Persians, the Greeks, the Romans, etc.[10]

He may have thought that a prudent husband should not let his wife acquire a taste for the more exotic pleasures of love-making.

[10] The ethnologist Luc Thoré maintains that our contemporary society is the only one in the world to have made love the basis of marriage. All others are suspicious of love matches because they disrupt society. Cf. 'Langage et sexualité' in *Sexualité humaine*, Collection RES, Paris, 1970, pp. 65–95.

Brantôme is very explicit on this point. His own views follow aptly on the previous quotation:

> What is worse is that these husbands teach their wives, in their own marriage beds, a thousand lubricities, tricks, counter-tricks and new ways, and try out those monstrous devices of Aretino; with the consequence that for one little flame that was in their bodies they generate a hundred and turn them into such famous lechers that 'tis scarce to be wondered at that with such initiation they are apt to look beyond their husbands and go and seek other cavaliers. Whereupon their husbands are aggrieved and punish the poor women; but in this way they do great wrong . . .

One could quote endless examples relating to this social class; on the other hand it is much harder to find out what the peasants' idea of marriage was. Descriptions of some marriage ceremonies suggest a rather similar attitude; for instance the following, found in l'Ille-et-Vilaine round about 1830.

> At this point the tears of the bride are redoubled: she runs away with her companions and the husband runs after her with his groomsmen. There follows a struggle which has every appearance of being in earnest. The attempt to drag the bride back to her husband's house often results in her clothes being torn, and this redounds enormously to her credit, for the more a girl resists on this special occasion, the greater is her reputation for chastity in her canton, and her husband's confidence in her fidelity. (Abel Hugo, *La France pittoresque*, II, p. 82)

It is as if what was admired was not the bride's love for her husband, but her resistance to the consummation of the marriage.

One cannot draw any very definite conclusions from these few scraps of evidence, but it would appear that in all classes of medieval society the idea of behaving too incontinently with one's wife was considered shocking, and that a chaste wife was to be preferred to an amorous one. This seems to be an admission of the distinction drawn by the theologians between marriage and love affairs. The first was only meant for procreation, while the second were concerned with a search for immoderate pleasure.

But, at the same time, at all social levels, a sharp distinction was drawn between ideals of masculine and feminine behaviour.

This was quite contrary to the doctrine of the Church as expounded by the most expert theologians.

I have a feeling that the convergence of views on the first point derives from the fact that here the Church's traditional doctrine was inspired by the wisdom of the Ancient World and the attitudes that prevailed in pagan societies. The divergence on the second point comes perhaps from the fact that equality between men and women in sexual behaviour was a Christian invention that was at variance with ideas traditionally accepted in the western world, and has only managed to get itself accepted quite recently. This is pure hypothesis, given the present state of research.

11

Love in married life

Philippe Ariès

Nowadays we tend to forget about an absolutely basic phenomenon in the history of sexual behaviour, which remained quite unchanged from earliest times up to the eighteenth century and which Jean-Louis Flandrin has done well to recall — the distinction that men of nearly all societies and all ages, except our own, have drawn between love within and love outside marriage. There are endless examples. We will take a few from texts illustrating Judaic and Greek culture. There is nothing like a straight reading without the intrusion of commentators' views.

Elkanah (1 Sam. 1, 4–19) had two wives, Hannah, whom he loved but who was barren, and Peninnah, of whom he was less fond, who had children and would cruelly mock and humiliate her barren rival. In spite of his preference Elkanah, when he sacrificed, was in the habit of giving several portions of meat to the mother of his children, and only one to his beloved. She was upset and wept, whereupon he tenderly remarked: 'Hannah, why are you crying and eating nothing? Why are you so miserable? Am I not more to you than ten sons?'

Here one can see clearly the two reasons for marriage: procreation (the fecund wife is honoured) and love. But this love involves a degree of constraint and bashfulness, well illustrated by Rebecca's behaviour (Gen. 24, 63–7). She leaves her parents' home and sets off with her camels and her servants to the land where she will henceforward live. She arrives in the evening and Isaac comes to meet her. She asks 'Who is that man walking across the open towards us?' The servant replies 'It is my master', that is to say her future husband. Then, with a gesture of modesty not displayed among other men 'she took her veil and covered herself.' Thus apparelled 'Isaac conducted her into the tent and took her as his wife.' The wife-to-be had had to remain veiled up to her wedding night, and till then she had to be more concealed from her future husband than from other men.

This custom lent itself easily to substitutions. Thus Jacob, in the house of Laban, had chosen Rachel to be his wife; but Laban wanted to marry off his elder daughter Leah first, and slipped her into the bridal bed instead of Rachel. Jacob never noticed until the next morning, which shows how lovers' personalities and appearances may vanish during the physical act of love. Such cases of substitution are a literary commonplace, and it would be interesting to make a study of them. It would also be interesting to compare them with what we know about the *ancien régime*'s views on the automatic character of the sexual act, with or without previous love. Love is blind indeed; but a feeling of indifference towards the other party at the moment of copulation must undoubtedly have been furthered by the woman's determined modesty.

Our own western societies have certainly not hidden their young women behind the impenetrable veil of the east. They did, however, invest them with a modest reserve, a code which prevented a wife from giving herself with the wild abandon of a mistress, to a point where a husband might be deceived over an identity, a mistake which a lover would never make.

The perfect woman of the Old Testament (and also of the *ancien régime*) is not merely fertile and a mother; she is mistress of the house and the head of a domestic enterprise:

> Who can find a virtuous woman?
>   for her price is far above rubies;.
> She will do him good and not evil
>   all the days of her life.
> She seeketh wool, and flax,
>   and worketh willingly with her hands.
> She is like the merchants' ships;
>   bringeth her food from afar.
> She riseth also while it is yet night,
>   and giveth meat to her household,
>   and a portion to her maidens.
> She considereth a field and buyeth it;
>   with the fruit of her hands she planteth a vineyard. . .
> She layeth her hands to the spindle,
>   and her hands hold the distaff.

She stretcheth out her hand to the poor;
  yea, she reacheth forth her hands to the needy . . .

She maketh fine linen and selleth it . . .

Strength and honour are her clothing;
  and she shall rejoice in time to come.

Here is another example from Greek culture: the *Alcestis* of
Euripides, perhaps the most beautiful celebration of conjugal love
in all literature. The story is well known. Apollo has persuaded the
Fates to let King Admetus escape the death to which he is destined
if he can find a substitute to go down to the Underworld in his
place. His aged father refuses: he is much too fond of life. His wife
Alcestis is the only one willing to make the sacrifice. She becomes
an object of universal admiration. The Chorus says 'Her death will
make her famous as the most noble of all women in the wide earth.'
'Truly,' replies the Servant 'who can question that . . . How could
any wife give clearer testimony that she honours her husband,
than by freely dying for him? This the whole city knows, but it
will touch your heart

To hear how she has spent these last hours in her home.
She knew that her appointed day had come. So first
She washed her white body in water from the stream;
Next, from her store-room lined with cedar-wood she took
A gown and jewels, and dressed herself becomingly;
Then stood before the altar of Hestia, and prayed:
'Goddess, since I am going below the earth, I now
Pay my last worship to you. Watch over my children,
I beseech you'; Then she went to every altar
In the whole palace, and before praying decked each one
With garlands of green myrtle she had picked herself.
No tear fell, not a sigh was heard. Her lovely face
Did not change colour, gave no sign of what must come.
Then to her room; and now indeed, flinging herself
Down on the bed, she wept. 'O marriage-bed,' she cried,
'Farewell! Here once I gave my maidenhood to him' . . .

Kneeling beside her bed, she kissed it; and the tears
Streamed from her eyes till the whole coverlet was wet.

And it is here, in this symbolic place, that she says farewell
to all her household, her children and all her servants: 'She took

each one by the hand, and spoke to each, and each to her, even the humblest.'[1] Then to her husband who, without her sacrifice, would have died:

> . . . But to live
> Parted from you, and these children unfathered — that
> I would not bear. My youth filled with delight and joy,
> I gave up.

If only his father, too old to beget another son, had not failed him, they could have 'lived their length of years . . . but all this some god has ordained for us.' Then she makes a solemn request, that Admetus should not marry again, as would normally happen, as not to give her children a stepmother. And Admetus replies: 'Have no fear. While you lived you were my wife; and dying alone will bear that name', and with a strange and anachronistic vow which, two thousand years before its time, proclaims the romantic rejection of the idea of the other's death, the desperate attempt to construct a substitute likeness:

> I shall bid a cunning sculptor carve your image in stone,
> . . . and I shall kneel
> Beside it, and throw my arms around it
> . . . Then in my dreams you'd come and go,
> Making me glad.

> I shall command these children to entomb us both
> in one coffin of cedar-wood, and to lay out
> My body close to yours. I will not even in death,
> Be parted from you, who alone are true to me.

Thus it is to the bed which has seen their love and perhaps the birth of their children that Alcestis comes to collect her thoughts before dying, without uttering one word that oversteps the bounds imposed by the reserve of the perfect woman, a reserve, however, that does not exclude love but bears witness to it, even openly affirms it.

Fecundity, the modesty of the wife and mother, the dignity of the mistress of a household, such are the enduring qualities which, right up to the eighteenth century, have marked the contrast between married love and love outside marriage. These qualities

---

[1] In his description of the death of Madame de Montespan, Saint-Simon states that feeling the approach of death, she summoned all her servants 'even the lowest' to bid them farewell.

and the value attached to them have varied in the course of time, but whether in fact, in ideas, or in imagination, only within narrow limits.

Certainly in the first centuries of our era, before the spread of Christianity, the moral philosophy taught by the Stoics saw procreation, the propagation of the species, as the object and justification of marriage, in contrast no doubt to the free union, commonly practised and not always very clearly distinguished from marriage. The Christians took over Stoic ethics, to the extent that some Stoic texts are known to us through quotations in the texts of the Early Fathers; for instance a lost text by Seneca (*Contra Jovinium* I, 49) on marriage is quoted by St Jerome:

Any love for another's wife is scandalous (so much for adultery); so is too much love for one's own wife (too much love simply means love without restraint, the passion lovers feel outside marriage). A prudent man should love his wife with discretion, and so control his desire and not be led into copulation. *Nothing is more impure than to love one's wife as if she were a mistress* . . . Men should appear before their wives not as lovers but as husbands.

The tone is urgent, that of a commandment. The ancient and commonplace distinction between modest love in marriage and passionate love outside it is here expounded by Seneca no longer as the description of a custom, but as part of a moral code.

Christianity inherited some of this moral code. In St Paul love outside marriage, fornication and uncleanness are condemned. Christianity was tempted to go further and proscribe even marriage — there was a tendency in that direction — but, resisting at once the pull of sensuality on one side and of asceticism on the other, it maintained the right to marry, though rating it below virginity in the scale of values. The principal reason for marriage was to solve the problem of human concupiscence by means of a mutual obligation that bound the two partners, the *debitum.* Clearly, in this sort of moral climate the *debitum* had nothing to do with the feverish pleasures of passion and eroticism. The juridical nature of the expression bears witness to the limits of the transaction. The aim was to suppress desire, not to increase it or make it more lasting. But although the Fathers adopted the Stoics' rule that marriage is justified by procreation, St Paul seems noncommittal on the subject. The problem does not seem to interest him. He mentions it *en passant* while discussing woman. It was she, not man, who brought sin into the world. The woman was tempted, not Adam; all the same she will achieve salvation by bearing children. Here, once more, we find the ancient tradition of fecundity, but obliquely, as compensating for the original inferiority of the sex.

Although he thought virginity was best, St Paul, who according to St Clement was married, unreservedly accepts the institution of marriage and extols the perfect union of man and wife: 'Men are bound to love their wives, as they love their own bodies. In loving his wife a man loves himself.' Nevertheless it is noteworthy that, if husbands are asked to love their wives, wives are bidden to be subject to their husbands. The distinction is considerable. Subjection seems to be the female expression of conjugal love. But in spite of their difference and because they complement each other, husband and wife 'shall become one flesh', a formula which does not merely mean sexual penetration, but also mutual trust, fondness for each other and identification of one with another.

Such love which means each possessing the other ('My true love hath my heart, and I have his') does not come suddenly like love at first sight, or the result of a love potion, or the love of Tristan and Isolde, an essentially non-conjugal love. It does not have to exist before marriage, though it may do so, especially where there are no material interests at stake to frustrate personal inclinations. This is why there was nothing shocking, even by the strictest moral standards, in arranged marriages based on family connections and property. The Church merely preferred that such an arrangement should be accepted by the couple and not forced on them. All the same it was generally hoped, and often happened, that love was born after the marriage and grew in the course of life together. Such perhaps was the case of Admetus and Alcestis, Ulysses and Penelope . . . The Christian Pantheon can hardly offer anything to equal these. The Duc de Saint-Simon, at the end of the seventeenth century, provides one of the best historical examples of married love. That great memorialist makes no secret of the fact that he chose his wife for purely material reasons without any pretence of sentiment. But in the course of time husband and wife became so devoted to one another that, contemplating the prospect of his own death, Saint-Simon did not hesitate to open his heart in his will and express his deep love for his wife who had died before him. He asked that their two coffins should be chained together, that they could be united in death as their bodies had been in life.

Such revelations are rare; it seems that men preferred not to speak of the love they found in marriage, except in wills where such testimony becomes more frequent. It is hard for the historian to penetrate the silence that reigns over vast areas of human life. Such silence may indicate indifference or ignorance, a sense of propriety or a desire for secrecy. 'There are some things one does not talk about.' Married love was one such.

This silence is occasionally broken, nearly always at the time of death. Archaeologists have found in Merovingian cemeteries tombs where the skeletons of husbands and wives are lying embraced in the same sarcophagus. In portrayals of the Last Judgement we see the Resurrection re-uniting husbands and wives whom death has parted, but these are exceptional testimonies, tiny signposts in the immensity of time. They are evidence that there were individual cases which differed from a common, more discreet pattern. Even so, one may assume that there was scope within these patterns for original and divergent forms of behaviour. What is original in the case of Saint-Simon and a few other wills of the period is the moving, public manifestation of feelings normally kept hidden.

Sex life is also hidden from us by the same veil of discretion. Hints are to be found in the sort of *risqué* story that is not much given to sentimentalizing over married love. A good marriage forms the background of the *fabliau* 'Desire frustrated': the couple are very fond of one another. The goodman leaves his country on business and is away for three months. On his return his wife welcomes him warmly 'as her duty bound her, and never felt such joy'. She gave him a sumptuous meal with plenty of wine: 'she had great desire to do all to please him, for she expected the like in return and hoped for her reward.' Unfortunately the goodman had eaten and drunk so much that 'when he came to bed he forgot the other pleasure.' His wife who 'was all ready to set to work' was distraught. She might have shaken him and woken him up. But she was incapable of such action. 'He would have thought her shameless. She ended by giving up her desire for him and went to sleep full of vexation.' One sees why the early Church texts impose a duty on the husband to anticipate the wife's desires, because she is too inhibited to show them and ask for what is owed her.

Thus marriage existed where a vast area of public life touched on a tiny secret place, secret rather than private. Privacy implies an enclosed space, withdrawn from the external world but known and sought out, accessible in certain conditions. But that which is secret is hidden away, except from a few initiates, as if it did not exist, protected by its cloak of religious silence, which binds the initiates also to silence. Revelation would destroy it: more than unspoken, it is the unutterable. So conjugal love could be one of the secret places of the old society. Today it has lost, generally speaking, this secret character.

But in a sense marriage did become public — a subject to which we shall return later — and it needed this publicity for its continued existence, that is for its continued recognition by the community in which the married couple lived. The fact that secret marriages continued shows the restricted power of such publicity and its functioning. They became more frequent just at the period when the community began to have its right to recognize marriage usurped in favour of a juridical body — the Church. The Church assumed the business of publicizing marriage with the declaration of banns. All the same, in both these acts performed in public, sanctioned by the community or the Church, there was originally a choice — one or several transactions; and this choice and the transactions involved were permanently binding. Was this the juridical influence of the Church? It is hard to say. But here I must underline the status attached to 'precedent' in the conjugal choice. Marriage was one of many precedents. Medieval and modern societies are always in the habit of attaching a religious significance to precedent, the original signpost marking a series of actions which may thereafter be lawfully repeated. It was precedent that lent sanction and constituted legitimacy. By virtue of it particular events were singled out from the anonymous flux of time and dedicated to a special status. Dedicated by whom? By the totality of those whose recognition and endorsement were essential for making something endure. Such recognition saved the event from fading from people's minds or being changed; it fixed it for ever. The moment it had reached this stage it could not be abolished; it was fated to last, i.e. it was to be repeated, to become the start of a series of events. The indissolubility of the marriage bond is closely linked with the respect paid by a custom-loving community to the concept of precedent.

Things changed after the eighteenth century. From then on society began to reconcile the two traditionally opposed kinds of love. The west gradually adopted an ideal of marriage requiring husband and wife to love each other (or appear to), like real lovers. Extra-conjugal erotics found their way into the marriage bed, expelling traditional prudishness in favour of real feeling. Today, thanks to Jean-Louis Flandrin, all this is well known. Nevertheless, we still find it hard to believe that the change is so recent, and so limited to western civilization. There is now only one kind of love, powerfully eroticized; and the original former characteristics of conjugal love that we have recalled have been abolished, or thought of as awkward relics, standing in the way of the triumph of passion, the only form of love and sexuality.

It is true that at the beginning of this change the special quality of conjugal love disappeared. But at a later stage the successful fusion of the two forms may well have provoked a spontaneous reaction in favour of the earlier dualism. I am not thinking of such survivals as the Prince of Lampedusa who begat goodness knows how many children without ever seeing his wife's abdomen. I am thinking of more recent phenomena.

Passionate love was love at first sight: one fell in love. A feverish beginning, a flowering and an end. Cupid's dart was as sudden and unforeseen as death's sting. Passionate love does not last, marriages based on it do not last either. So divorce cannot be regarded as a means of retrieving a mistake, but simply as the normal write off of a feeling which cannot and should not be expected to last and must yield to its successor. Our young contemporaries cannot tolerate lengthy commitments, whether in marriage or the priesthood. 'Long term' is an unfashionable expression. But one wonders if it may not make a comeback, and if love in marriage, as distinct from the other, may not take shape again round the idea of 'long term', long term in fact rather than in intention. A couple is long in the making, and each layer of time accumulated attaches its partners that much more closely and makes them feel their union is stronger — 'and they shall be one flesh.' They love each other because they have loved each other for a long time, and their love goes on growing with time up to the dread moment when it comes up against the wall of death, unbearable because it means separation, the end of what they have built up together. Jean Baechler goes so far as to suggest that 'there can be an almost neurotic reinforcement of the marriage bond.' After death the survivor tries to force a way past the barrier and to continue beyond it the interrupted evolution of their union. This is not a legacy from the distant past. Ancient society had a high regard for precedent, but not for long-lastingness. As it was in the beginning so will it always be, without the question of duration coming into it. It was because it *had been*, and not because it had lasted, that a precedent was seen to be of value.

Today it matters little what is the origin or nature of the bond; what matters is how long it lasts. On the whole, unofficially speaking, a real marriage — not all that different from a free union that stands up to wear and tear — is not created by a ceremony at the *mairie* or in church, nor by a previous, precarious choice, but by the fact of its duration. The true marriage is a union that endures, with a living, fertile lastingness that defies death — a hidden renewal of the dynamic of continuity in a civilization that inclines to the sudden and the destructive.

12

The indissoluble marriage

Philippe Ariès

The outstanding fact in the history of western sexual behaviour is the persistence, over many centuries and right up to the present day, of the pattern of marriage as a binding tie, monogamous and indissoluble. This contrasts with other patterns which preceded it in the Roman era and which still exist beside it today. These involve, at least for the man, the right to dissolve the union and start again. The form of marriage in which a man can repudiate his wife and remarry is undoubtedly the most widespread and normal, except in the western world. The indissoluble union seems to be the exception, but a very vigorous exception, which continues to resist the powerfully eroding effect of contemporary moral laxity.

How did the change from marriage with the right of repudiation (of the wife) to the binding union take place, as it certainly did in the Middle Ages? This is a very large question, going to the heart of our civilization: a question to which there can be no sure answer, though one may put forward various hypotheses.

The reader may find this uncertainty surprising. Why see a difficulty when the answer is so obvious? Everyone thinks they know that the indissolubility of marriage is a Christian invention, and in its most radical form an invention of western, Latin Christianity. The Church only had to impose it by compulsion on the peoples who lived under its governance and were bound by its rules. Belief in this version is shared by friends and enemies of the Church alike. Indissolubility came in with the rise of the power of the Church and began to fade with the decline of Christianity today. This accepted view should be treated with total scepticism.

Firstly, because a tendency towards the *stabilization* of marriage (*stabilitas* is the Latin word which corresponds very closely with what we mean by indissolubility) was beginning to appear in Rome before Christian influence began to be felt. P. Veyne suggests that during the early centuries of our era a profound change in morals and values had injected more sentiment, more moral strictness, more appreciation of the importance of durability into Roman married life; in short there was acceptance of a moral code which was to become Christian, but which was pagan in origin and powerfully influenced by Stoic doctrine. The mental and spiritual revolution which preceded, then accompanied, and without doubt furthered the cause of Christianity, makes this period (called by H.–I. Marrou 'Late Antiquity' rather than the more traditional 'Late Empire') one of the great turning-points in the history of our civilization. Recent research has shown that it was not simply a feature of the spread of Christianity, but that Christianity itself was rather its culminating point.

The moral principles of this period were inclining people to perceive a value in the stability of a union that was no longer dependent on caprice or the wishes of the spouses, and more particularly of the husband. But this was only a *tendency* that did not aspire to upset at once the norms of contemporary behaviour. In fact it did not upset anything.

If one wants to understand this mutation, we must see how it developed, first in the aristocratic classes and in the Church between the ninth and the twelfth centuries. It was in this period and in these circles that Christian marriage began to take the shape in which we practise it today – in a secular structure, modified by the possibility of divorce, but formally legalized. We have useful guides to help us in this enquiry, especially G. Duby's *Medieval Marriage*[1] and P. Toubert's *La Théorie du mariage chez les moralistes carolingiens*.[2] which we shall follow.

At the end of the Carolingian period we have clear evidence of two opposing forms of marriage, that of the nobility and that of the Church. Contrary to what one might suppose the secular model is the easiest to grasp, although our evidence for it comes largely from clerical sources. It was also the simplest of the two. As in ancient Rome, marriage was essentially a private function; it took place in the house, where, in a limited and wordly sense, it was public, for the couple and their parents were surrounded

---

[1] Baltimore, 1978. Duby has since published *Le Chevalier, la femme et le prêtre*, Paris, 1981.

[2] *Il Matrimonio nella Società altomedievale*, Spoleto, 22–28 April 1976, Centro italiano di studi sull' alto medievo, Spoleto, 1977, pp. 233–85.

by spectators, who acclaimed them and by their presence bore witness to the reality of the act and the approval of the community. All the same this half-private, half-public function was not endowed with all the symbolism of marriage. It had none of that formal and immediate character that it assumed later on and which it always has today, when one ceremony, one word, one signature, create a legal right, so that one minute one is not yet married and the next one is entirely immersed.

The formalities of marriage were stretched over a variable period, sometimes quite lengthy; they began with the *desponsatio*, the promise, the *foedus* or *pactum conjugale*, the origin of our betrothal, and the contract ceremony which was very important in France up to about 1914. Marriage was a treaty requiring a pledge from the two contracting families. One family bestowed a wife, the other received her on her parents' payment of a *dos*, a dowry (*donatio puellae*). The final stage of the marriage formalities was the bedding of the young couple, which took place in public in fairly ceremonial conditions, and was endorsed by the applause of the company, who thus bore witness to the genuineness of the function. What was in fact being celebrated was the key moment when boy and girl were in bed together with the aim of begetting children as soon and as often as possible. The importance and urgency of their task depended on the wealth or power of the family and the seriousness of the matrimonial strategies that depended on it. One might ask to what extent the reality of a marriage thus openly celebrated before numerous witnesses was not to be reckoned simply in terms of the values at stake. In cases where they were negligible there would not be such publicity or so striking a ceremony; consequently there would be no real marriage, but only — and it amounted to the same in the end — a marriage in outline, the juridical reality of which depended on the impression it left on the collective memory. If the impression was faint it was interpreted as a passing liaison; if strong it was considered a legitimate marriage.

Originally not all alleged marriages had the same value. The marriages in noble families, where the stakes were high or the union set the seal on an alliance or furthered some policy, were always real. They were reserved for the powerful and for only some of their children.

The big moment was when the family gathered in the room of the heir, round the bed. The father of the groom, the *caput generis*, officiated. It was he who called down the blessing of God on the young couple, who were undressed and put to bed together.

Later the priest wormed his way into the ceremony to bless the bed with incense and holy water. This was certainly the first and only ecclesiastical intrusion into a private ceremony, private because a family affair, though rendered public by the essential presence of a social group, but quite without legal sanction or regulation. One is struck by the correspondence of the marriage bed and the death bed, which had the same collective character and also ended with incense and holy water. The nuptial ceremony took place in the evening and the hours of darkness, the most fitting for love and procreation. The celebrations began the day after, lasting generally for three days, during which custom sometimes demanded that the couple should refrain from sexual relations.[3]

Now it became the business of the scribblers, the family chroniclers, to draw up the indispensable genealogies which would fix for posterity the state of the family alliances and relationships, forefathers of *The Artisans of Glory* described by O. Ranum.[4]

In such conditions, among the aristocracy and its dependents, *marriage was not universal. It was neither necessary nor desirable* that all should marry. Other means were available for satisfying *voluptas*, such as rape or abduction, a passing affair with a prostitute, or a peasant girl, or the daughter of a vassal, or a bastard, all easy and socially acceptable prey. There must also have existed intermediate states between a brief rape and an unstable, that is unwitnessed, union. It was important that not all children should get married. Otherwise there could be too many claimants to a share of the patrimony and a risk of the family losing wealth and power. At the same time it was necessary to have a reserve of unmarried boys and girls to draw on if needed to fill the gaps caused by the high mortality rate, sickness, disease, and the accidents of war or the tournament. Celibacy had to be enforced on younger sons so as to avoid disadvantageous marriages, but a watchful eye had to be kept for matches that could lead to profitable connections, and for this a reserve of girls was needed, as much or more than one of sons. Female bastards formed what Duby calls 'the pleasure stock' of noble houses. Other girls were confined to *moutiers*, castle annexes, set up by heads of families to keep guard on their daughters and widows. The young men

---

[3] Is there a connection with the three days, after death, during which the soul wandered round the body and the house?

[4] O. Ranum, *Artisans of Glory: Writers and Historical Thought in Seventeenth Century France*, N. Carolina 1980.

condemned to celibacy formed bands of bachelors (*juvenes*) to
seek adventure, military, sporting or amatory, hoping one day to
achieve some honourable goal, i.e. become *senior*, by marrying
an heiress, sometimes having made her pregnant, or in becoming
the 'seneschal', the officer or confidential vassal of some powerful
head of a family.

The sort of marriage we have described above would have been
arranged by the families concerned for clearly defined aims. If,
through sterility or some other reason the aims were not achieved,
the whole *raison d'être* of the marriage was lost, and it had to be
dissolved, and the wife returned to her family or to the *moutier*.
Another marriage had to follow at once.

During the period when this kind of marriage was customary in
aristocratic societies, the Church was elaborating a very different
sort of marriage which, by the thirteenth century, it had managed
to elevate to the lofty status of a sacrament, equal to baptism and
ordination. This was an extraordinary enhancement of a private
function, a sexual union, organized with a view to family alliances,
to be made or broken in accordance with family interests. However,
the very fact that the union once performed and consecrated could
not be dissolved made such family arrangements all the more
definitive and irrevocable. Material interests still counted and of
course the Church admitted as much, but they were no longer all-
important and had to come to terms with serious risks, in particular
misconduct or sterility, which had to be accepted with resignation.
Even so it is remarkable that the Church should have taken so long
not only to get a refractory aristocracy to accept its lead, but to
decide what its doctrine actually was, to express it clearly and arrive
at a simple description of what it conceived marriage to be.

Within the Church there were, in fact, two increasingly opposed
trends of thought. One, the ascetic, harked back to St Jerome:
hostility to marriage, which was seen as an inferior, barely tolerable
condition. Support for this current of thought fluctuated violently.
It seemed to gain ground during the twelfth century among clerics
who wanted to prevent the Church from trying to control marriage,
or from having anything to do with it. The Church should stand
apart from these mundane and common matters in which it had
no concern. There are signs of the same tendency in Languedocian
Catharism, exceeding the bounds of orthodoxy.

The other tendency, deriving from St Augustine and St Paul,
was the one which triumphed, seeing in marriage the *remedium
animae*. In the twelfth century, no doubt in answer to the violence
of the opponents of marriage, St Bernard gives his reason: 'to

attack marriage is to open the door to concubines, incest, *seminifluels, masculorum concubitores.*' St Bernard fears that depreciation of marriage will lead to the spread of masturbation and male homosexuality.

Consequently the Church elaborates a marriage doctrine in texts aimed at the laity, but the aristocratic literate laity, the only ones it can hope to influence. It lays stress on the need for the prior assent of husband and wife, which played a very minor role in lay thinking, so much so that much later in France the family viewpoint that parental consent was just as important as that of the couple was upheld by royal and parliamentary authority. The Church no longer held this view after the Council of Trent. A ninth-century text by Hincmar, Archbishop of Rheims, is a good example of this new approach to Christian marriage: The lawful bond of matrimony exists (*est vera*) when it is solemnized between free and equal persons (consequently, free to make their own decisions) whom it unites in public nuptials (*publicis nuptiis*), by an honourable sexual union (*honestata sexuum commixione*), with paternal consent, a man to a free woman, lawfully endowed. One should note the epithet *honestata*, showing the essential difference between *sexuum commixtio* in marriage and the alternative, *luxuriosa*, outside marriage.

At no time did the Church or its priests attempt to interfere or organize any legal control. However, according to P. Toubert, 'the conjugal state is . . . defined as something essentially religious, whose very name, as Hincmar says, has a sacred meaning', so that the union of the sexes becomes a *mysterium*, a sacrament of Christ and the Church, whereby the woman should know (*noscitur*) that marriage assures her this honourable status.

All the same this ninth-century model lacked one feature, which in our eyes lies at the heart of Christian marriage, namely its indissolubility, its *stabilitas*. Or, if it existed, it was vague and ill-defined, though the comparison between the sacramental union of the married couple with the eternal union of Christ and his Church was suggestive. But this same Hincmar, in the text *De Coercendo Raptu* (the title is explicit), quoted by P. Toubert, gives an example of a good marriage – Ahasuerus repudiating his first wife to enable him to marry Esther! This second union is quoted as a model for Christian marriage.

No doubt repudiation was common. The Church strongly disapproved but took no action against it, because it was unsure of its legal right to interfere in natural communities, governed *per leges publicas*, and answerable to lay courts. So there was still some uncertainty both about the Church's right of intervention and about its idea of marriage.

During the eleventh and twelfth centuries the Church was inclined to interfere more and more in marriages, to control them and make them conform with the sacramental pattern that was being worked out and established. It was no longer content, as it had been in Hincmar's time, to give advice that risked being simply ignored; from now on it had no hesitation in backing up its beliefs with sanctions such as excommunication, even when it was dealing with the King of France. The next stage was very curious and shows how difficult it was for the Church, even at this time, to enforce on the secular aristocracy restrictions that were totally at variance with their traditional habits, in particular the right to repudiate a wife in certain circumstances. When the Church started to interfere in matrimonial affairs it was not, initially, to win acceptance for indissolubility. Hesitating to launch a head-on attack on a hitherto unchallenged right, it had recourse to a pretext. One has the impression that nobody dared appeal openly to the principle of total indissolubility. It was pursued, but by indirect methods, and one of these was incest. A seventh degree of consanguinity was enough to label a marriage incestuous, and even if contracted and consummated it had to be dissolved, however long-lasting and fertile it had been. It was only dissolved after consummation, sometimes long after, since at that time the Church had no control over the betrothal or the ceremony itself. It could only step in afterwards – when asked to do so.

One may suppose that bans on such remote blood relations were extremely irksome for the matrimonial plans of great families. But the Church was inflexible on this point. So it is evident that contemporary opinion tolerated, or at least did not reject, objections on the grounds of kinship more readily than it did a ban on repudiation. Thus in the eleventh century one finds in episcopal circles great reluctance to condemn divorce and remarriage as adulterous and bigamous, yet some hesitation in letting them pass unquestioned. Hence the temptation to condemn a failed marriage as incestuous. In the case of King Philippe I of France, the Pope hesitated to denounce him as a bigamist, but cheerfully excommunicated him for having married too close a blood relation.

In the course of the twelfth century things changed, as Duby has shown. Incest became of secondary importance, while *stabilitas* became the prime consideration. St Bernard, in his usual blunt fashion, states that consanguinity is man's affair, but indissolubility pertains to God. The moment a marriage had been given lawful consent (*consensus* was mandatory) it became unique and indissoluble. At the Fourth Lateran Council in 1215 the Church brought the incest ban down to the fourth degree of relationship; but it came down heavily in favour of *stabilitas.*

The final, exemplary clash between the Pope and a King of France over a repudiated wife was the case of Philippe Auguste at the beginning of the thirteenth century. In the year 1190 this King found himself the widowed father of a three-year-old son. The whole line of succession hung on the slender thread of a child's life. In 1193 he took Ingeborg of Denmark as his second wife, then alleged that he was prevented by witchcraft from having intercourse with this young woman. She denied this. To resolve the difficulty it was suggested in ecclesiastical circles that a distinction could be drawn between *commixio sexuum*, the penetration that undoubtedly took place and the *commixio seminum in vase muliebri*, that is the ejaculation, which did not – an involuntary arrested coitus.

Philippe tried to have his marriage annulled by pleading a degree of consanguinity, which was not upheld by the ecclesiastical courts. That did not prevent him from marrying Agnès de Méran, who presented him with two children. The Pope refused to recognize this marriage, but temporized, and things remained in abeyance until a more energetic character, Innocent III, succeeded to the papal throne and excommunicated Philippe. In the meantime Agnès de Méran had died in 1201. Finally Philippe submitted in 1213 and took back Ingeborg, twenty years after repudiating her! He was 48, the five children born of his union with Agnès had been conveniently legitimized by the Pope, and he had no need to worry about the future of the dynasty. But the Church had won the argument. Within certain limits *stabilitas* was gaining ground: the Church's model was slowly ousting the lay one. Soon no wordly prince would dare contest it – until the time of Henry VIII in the sixteenth century.

Nevertheless it is remarkable that it took several centuries to move from the lay pattern of marriage, still practised by the Carolingian aristocracy, with its customs of privacy and repudiation, to the ecclesiastical pattern, whose most significant features were indissolubility and openness.

All that we have said so far relates to the world of the gentry, the aristrocratic classes and the Church. What was going on among the huge, silent mass of lesser folk in town and country? We will pass over the case of the towns, whose sexual behaviour, or certain aspects of it, have been described by J. Rossiaud. While listening to him I thought — and here I am sure I am going beyond what he is evidently prepared to offer as his opinion — that at the end of the Middle Ages the mentality of town dwellers was still imbued with some of the feelings we have observed in the early Middle Ages, namely a general tendency to see the marriages of the rich and powerful as more real than those of the poor. In other words, to speak anachronistically, there were more marriages on one side and more *concubinages* on the other.

If we look at the rural communities, one prime fact immediately stands out . . . so vast that it escapes the eyes of the historians, so inclined to see the near and miss the distant object. That is the apparent ease with which the indissoluble 'ecclesiastical' marriage became established in the country. One has the impression (misleading perhaps) that there was less resistance to *stabilitas* in rural communities than there was in aristocratic circles. It seems to me that if the Church had been forced to fight an obstinate opposition, the battle would have left its mark. We have a general idea of how hard the Church had to fight to gain recognition of the veto on consanguinity, and to impose on its parish priests a celibacy in which their parishioners were not interested. But 'bigamy', that is to say *instabilitas*, does not seem to me to have caused a grave social problem. Here again, this impression needs to be confirmed by more detailed research. All the same, let us assume that the indissoluble marriage *was* readily accepted.

There are three possible reasons for this. First, that it had already existed in the Romano-Gallic world and that no change was involved. This hypothesis, which is not susceptible of proof, would imply a difference between peasant marriage on the one hand and urban marriage such as we know existed in Rome and which was characterized by the right to repudiate, often enjoyed by both parties, and to take concubines. But we must not allow ourselves to be duped by points of law introduced two or three centuries before in considering contemporary mentalities. It is likely that in the country socio-economic conditions worked in favour of *stabilitas*, while in the towns, as in Rome, they worked in the opposite direction, towards repudiation, without contemporaries having any idea of the existence of such a deep cultural divide.

The second reason is the one most commonly accepted today: the Church imposed its model of marriage as well as its views on sexual behaviour on a society that could be stubborn, but lacked resolution and submitted. In the end, it is true, the pattern stuck. Personally I disagree with this interpretation. As I said earlier one does not feel that the Church exerted itself very strongly in this direction. The texts quoted by P. Toubert for the Carolingian period chiefly concerned the military aristocracy, and the Church was addressing them because they formed the only audience it could influence. It could hardly have much influence in country districts. Some still had no parish organization, others were served by clergy who, I imagine, were probably very quick to adopt the ways of life of their parishioners, beginning of course with marriage. How could they expect to battle successfully against an entrenched habit of 'bigamy'?

That does not seem a very likely hypothesis to me, and it imputes to historians an excessive belief in the powers of the Church over society before the end of the Middle Ages, and up to the Council of Trent. It conforms to an idea held by some of our contemporaries that the indissolubility of marriage was a serious obstacle to sexual freedom (an innate and natural right) and therefore could only be imposed by force.

Finally there is a third hypothesis, contradicting the second, the power of the Church, but not the first, the anteriority of *stabilitas*. The restraining force came, not from some outside power such as the Church, but was accepted and upheld by the communities themselves. If there was a transition from repudiation to indissolubility it was deliberate, not consciously so perhaps, but imposed by the general will, with no sense of doing something new but more with the idea of paying respect to the customs of its ancestors. This is why I am tempted to assume that something of the kind was already in existence in the Romano-Gallic period or during late antiquity.

The difference between this trend towards *stabilitas* and rejection of remarriage on the one side, and the function of repudiation among aristocracies (whether Roman or Gallic) on the other, is perhaps explicable in terms of their different matrimonial strategies. In rural communities strategies were simpler and *stabilitas* would be rated higher than fecundity or other considerations. They may have had other ways of getting round such problems. The basic principle was that one did not go back on one's word. One was not allowed to change one's plans, one's alliances, one's transactions too often or too quickly. One's venture took place within the fixed time — all too short in that period — of one generation. That was the only way of managing the stock of girls. Even in conditions of complete stability it was difficult to maintain equilibrium.

The *stabilitas* of the community seemed to depend on the

stabilitas of marriage, and society had to make sure that this was strictly observed. One may assume that this task was entrusted to the young, that is the bachelors, who had an interest in the business. They formed the local sexual vigilantes. They saw to it that the girls were chaste (or at least kept their virginity), that wives were faithful (up to a point), that husbands were masters in their own house, and finally — what interests us — that there was no remarriage, even of widowers, so radical were they. The Church, when finally it had the power, was forced to intervene to gain acceptance for the remarriage of widowers.

The community weapon was 'rough music', in which not only the young but the whole neighbourhood took part. If a man or a woman wanted to marry again, there was only one way to gain their freedom and shed their obligations — flight, which in practice meant leaving all their belongings behind — or murder. Certainly flight caused fewer complications for the boy or the girl without possessions. Yet the girl lost her reputation and landed herself in a world of easy morals, verging on prostitution. Boys had more freedom of choice. Here again we can see the connection between the *stabilitas* of the family home and the marriage, and that of possessions, one's portion of the inheritance, the right to a share in the togetherness of village life — the last a very important factor. Until proof to the contrary turns up I shall provisionally adopt the hypothesis that indissoluble marriage was a spontaneous creation of rural communities, a choice uninfluenced by external pressures but conforming to the ecclesiastical model and reinforced by this probably chance convergence.

Although we know very little about these rural communities, in which far the larger part of the population lived, some much later evidence, dating from the fifteenth and sixteenth centuries, gives us an idea of what went on on earlier times. My material comes from J.–L. Flandrin's latest book, *Le Sexe et l'Occident.*[5] During his research in the archives of the *officialité de Troyes*, i.e. the episcopal court, the author has worked on the cases concerning promises of marriage, called in Champagne *créantailles* (in Champenois dialect *créanter* meant to promise marriage).

Here are some examples. We know that in actual fact the commonest sort of marriage was one negotiated by the families. It does not feature very often among the lawsuits because it was the least often contested, so did not have to appeal to the court. However the records give us an idea of a typical scene. It took

5 Paris, 1981.

place at the house, to which come friends and relations, especially an uncle of the girl, no doubt a maternal uncle, who has a special role to play in the ceremony. The father invites the young man to sit down beside his betrothed and offer her a drink. The handing over of the drinking cup has the symbolic value of a gift. The young man invites the girl to drink solemnly and deliberately; he says it is 'in the name of marriage'. They drink in silence. Then the maternal uncle says to his niece 'Give Jean a drink in the name of marriage, as he has given you to drink.' After she has done so the young man replies in turn 'I desire you to receive a kiss from me in the name of marriage.' He kisses her, and the company, confirming the deed by acclamation, shout 'You are *créantés* (pledged) to one another. Bring wine.' There, we have witnessed a true marriage. It takes place at the house in the presence of the bride's family and in the company of guests who play the part of the choir of earlier days and the witnesses of today.

The Troyes lawsuits disclose other scenes of this kind, not in a house, but in a public place such as a tavern. The part of father or uncle is played by some public figure, often picked out at random from bystanders. One young woman, Barbe Montaigne, has just accepted, in formal terms, the proposal of her betrothed, Jean Graber. They are probably in the street, or more likely in the tavern, but certainly in the midst of a group of friends. One of them takes the initiative and, in the name of those present, exclaims 'Good, then I declare you *fiancés*.' But the husband is not inclined to listen. His marriage deserves something better than that, and he says bluntly 'You can't even read; you aren't going to declare us *fiancés*.' Luckily at that moment the schoolmaster appears on the scene, just the sort of person he needs: 'Here's the headmaster: he'll do us proud'. The words *créanter*, *fiancer*, *marier*, were synonymous. Then there is conflicting evidence. The schoolmaster states that he refused the invitation and advised the young couple to pledge each other alone together, without any intermediary. Witnesses claimed, however, that the schoolmaster had well and truly carried out the *créantailles*, and, what was more, had done it on the steps of the church, a place henceforth reserved for the priest.

Among the Troyes cases a few others crop up, which are more frequently mentioned in the records of proceedings than actually occurred, because they gave rise to argument. In these cases the ceremony, which seems derisory though it was in fact taken seriously, was reduced to the exchange of a few ritual words between the two lovers in secret, without any public performance.

It seems possible that these secret commitments became more frequent at the end of the Middle Ages and at the beginning of modern times: contemporary moralists denounced them as a serious danger. If these documents are to be believed, in order to be recognized as committed or married, it was enough for the lovers to have exchanged the following words: 'I swear to thee (*te*), Marguerite, that I will love no other woman but thee (*toi*) to the day of my death — Paul, I pledge my word that I will have no other husband than you (*vous*) to the day of my death.' (Note the change from *tu* to *vous* when the woman speaks.)

This exchange would be accompanied by a symbolic gift: something of value, a drinking cup, some music on the flute. The exchange of words and the gift were ratified by a handshake and possibly a kiss too. This handshake seems like a glimpse of the *dextrarum junctio* of the Roman marriage ceremony, surviving across the ages. This ritual could be performed absolutely anywhere, outside or inside, in the house or in the street, in public or in private. All that mattered was the intention and the correct form of words. Sometimes, at the final perilous moment with the girl clasped in her lover's arms, he might say 'Now, Marguerite, so that you won't think I'm just taking advantage of you (things had almost gone that far), I put my tongue in your mouth in the name of marriage.'

The judge of the *officialité*, questioning Guillaumette, who complains that her lover has abandoned her, asks very emphatically 'Did you give him anything in the name of marriage?' He meant that any gesture (like the tongue in the mouth?) was equivalent to a commitment. She said No, but that when he had intercourse with her, he told her he was doing it in the name of marriage, and that was enough. And the court decided that was indeed enough.

According to these documents, marriage in rural communities does not seem to have been very different from marriage among the aristocracy, in that both were private and domestic affairs. However, where indissolubility was concerned, it must be admitted that there were very different attitudes. One huge phenomenon, which has escaped the myopic vision of historians and anthropologists, is the ease with which the ecclesiastical model of indissoluble marriage became established in country districts. One gets the impression that *stabilitas* did not come up against the obstacles that faced it in the halls of the mighty. Moreover at first the Church had no way of asserting its influence. If it had had to cope with obstinate resistance, the fight would surely have left some traces.

Judging from the *crèantailles* in Troyes it seems that any inter-
ference by the Church before the Council of Trent was extremely
mild. It was not seeking to displace the *crèantailles*; it recognized
the value of commitment, though in doubtful cases it might demand
a religious ratification. Thus two lovers may be required to have
the marriage they have contracted and physically consummated
solemnized by the priest at the doors of the church. The Church
merely solemnized; it was not taking over.

The Church had no need to impose *stabilitas*; the communities
themselves insisted on it. A young French historian, Gérard Delille,
has just finished a brilliant study of matrimonial strategies in the
rural communities of southern Italy. This doctoral thesis should
be published shortly by the *Ecole française de Rome*. It emphasizes
the binding character of the alliances between families, the inter-
change of sons and daughters. So delicate and so carefully organized
a balance of exchange would have been upset if marriages could
have been broken easily and wives repudiated. Sterility did not
pose a problem, for it could be compensated by an increased rate
of marriages and fecundity. One gets the impression that the
stabilitas of early marriage was the basis for the *stabilitas* of the
whole community; and the community had to see to it that it was
respected. In many places the policing of sexual roles fell upon
the young, in other words organizations of bachelors. 'Rough
music' was one of their weapons.

After the twelfth century indissolubility ceased to be a problem.
It was grudgingly accepted by the aristocracy and certainly more
spontaneously adopted by rural communities. In any case, from
then on, the notion of indissolubility gained general acceptance,
apart from a few places, England in particular, where social and
religious contracts were more relaxed and a few cheats and even
some honest bigamists were still to be found. Basically nothing
changed: the battle for indissolubility had been won.

There was still a problem, but with a change of emphasis.
Henceforward, after the thirteenth century and the Council of
Trent, it was the public and institutional character of marriage
that was in question. The sort of marriage I have been talking
about up till now was essentially a domestic function, taking place
in the house or even the bedroom. But now a new phenomenon
appears. There is to be a great change of scene, and marriage will
move from the private to the public area. A very considerable
change, which has so far largely escaped notice.

The ritual of the marriage ceremony appears in the twelfth
century.[6] In its oldest form it continues to recognize the validity

of the domestic contract, and faced with the way it was still
being carried out in Troyes in the sixteenth century, the Church
contented itself with adding a touch of religious formality; but not
yet inside the Church, only in front of it, *ad januas ecclesiae.* What
was the significance of the doors of the church? This meant the
most public part of the village, the churchyard, the open air
meeting place for the whole community, where justice was meted
out, news proclaimed and gossip exchanged. The great change,
marked by the marriage ritual, consisted of the removal of the
marriage ceremony from its traditional location, the house, to
the door of the church. Henceforward that is the place where
all that mattered for the marriage was to take place. It was a
real revolution.

In the ninth and tenth centuries all that the priest was expected
to do was to bless the nuptial bed and the couple in it. The aim was
to ensure the fecundity of the 'seed', a word constantly repeated.
After the twelfth century the role of the priest, from being rather
sporadic, became important and even essential. After the thirteenth
and fourteenth centuries the ceremony in front of the doors of
the church consisted of two quite separate parts. One, which was
the second in point of time, corresponded to the traditional and
central act of marriage, formerly the only one, the *donatio puellae.*
First the parents gave their daughter to the priest, who handed her
over to her future husband. In the next stage the priest took the
place of the father of the family and himself put the hand of one
into the hand of the other, the *dextrarum junctio*. A little later,
between the fourteenth and the sixteenth centuries, this vital
act, the *dextrarum junctio*, underwent a change which involved
an alteration in the role of the priest. It no longer signified the
traditio puellae, but the reciprocal commitment of the couple,
their mutual *donatio*, evidence of a profound change in human
feeling, a landmark in the history of civilization. 'I, Jean, give thee,
Marguerite, my body, to be thy husband.'

The second part of the marriage ritual, which actually took
place at the beginning of the ceremony, was more administrative
and modern-seeming. This was the completion of the enquiry
the Church had carried out to make sure there was no impediment
to the marriage, and that the parties to it had freely consented.
What is curious is that this part, which had been added later to the
ceremony, became in the long run its most important component,

---

6 J.–B. Molin and P. Mutemble, *Les Rituels de mariage en France du XXIIe au XVIe
siècle*, Paris, 1974.

at the very heart of the marriage, and carried all its symbolic meanings. Modern forms of marriage ceremony, both religious and secular, derive from this, while *traditio puellae* has disappeared. Then came the last stage, towards the seventeenth century, when the whole ceremony was moved from outside the church doors to within, where it has remained ever since.

If one confined one's attention to this brief analysis of rituals, one could be left with the idea that, ever since the thirteenth century at least, the ceremony of marriage underwent a firm and authoritarian clericalization. The reality is quite different. Domestic commitments like the *créantailles* of Troyes went on despite the spread of the religious ceremony, and the Church took a long time to deprive them of their official character and merge them with *fiançailles* in their present day sense. In fact the first result of the clericalization of marriage was simply to tack on an extra piece of ceremony to the existing domestic one, and consequently extend the wedding over a longer period of time.

From now onwards what counted was not so much the religious ceremony as the written record of it. The writing confirmed the proceedings at the same time as it controlled them. The church service had two vital effects: it publicized the marriage and it recorded the event in writing. It therefore now appeared in a new light: on the one hand an exercise of power and control, on the other a time factor with a sharp limiting point. At five to eleven one is not married, at five past one is. Children born before eleven are illegitimate, those born after are legitimate. Signing the register had changed everything, replacing with a moment of time a vague period of indefinite duration that began with the first commitment and ended with a final blessing in church.

It is not surprising that such a sharp change should have provoked resistance and refusal among old-fashioned and conservative groups who clung to the customs of former days and to the greater freedom that these customs allowed. In contrast, zealous and reformist parish priests in charge of the register were tempted to treat the old customs as forms of *concubinage*, and in their baptismal register they would record as bastards children born of what they considered a free union, when it was simply the older form of marriage. Peter Laslett discovered resisters of this kind, and thought he had found a subculture among them. Why not, in fact, a subculture of non-indoctrinated resisters? In the course of a colloquium in historical demography an English research worker told me that there were still parts of Scotland where people objected to written registration. The apparent increase in illegitimate births at the end of the eighteenth century may be partly explicable in terms of a difference of cultures between parish priests who wanted to record and villagers who objected.

Victory went to the register. The cause of its opponents faded away, although continuing in France at the beginning of the nineteenth century among immigrant workers, whose determination to live in a state of cohabitation was denounced by French social workers. If the opposition had continued, western Europe would have seen a South American type of family life.

Later on the state took over from the Church and made its own rules. But none of the changes that have affected couples and families, e.g. the closing of the gap between passionate love and conjugal love, the replacement of the arranged marriage by the love match, the legal easements of indissolubility, the limited right of remarriage for divorcees, none of these have released marriage from its legal restraints or put it back into the private domain. It has remained a public function.

However, in the last twenty years, we may have seen the beginnings of change. In France and in the post-industrial nations one notices a slump in matrimony. When asked, the young say they do not want to make a concession to the system, amounting to a mere formality. Marriage is their affair and not society's. Though free, a union of this kind can last. One hears malicious stories about mistresses who become intolerable when eventually married. But in fact there is a big psychological difference between the free union of today and the private marriage of former times. The latter meant domestic ceremonies, the participation of the community, of relations, of neighbours. The free union of today wants to be quite unattached, entirely spontaneous. All the same the institution of public marriage comes into its own when a child is born. A free union is changed into a legal marriage, sometimes even sanctioned by religion. It is as if the presence of a child has brought the parents back into a less private and more universal region. The link between marriage and the outside world may have become looser and weaker; but it survives.

In this chapter I have tried to throw some light on three important aspects of marriage in the western world. One is indissolubility, which confers on it a unique quality. It has seemed to me that this came not only from above through the Church, but from below, from the rural communities which had taken it up and absorbed it totally. However, and this is the second point, the inhibition of indissolubility succeeded for a long time in preventing the movement of marriage out of the private area, or at least out of what was most private in a vast domain of communal life and private sociability.

Lastly, first the Church in the twelfth and thirteenth centuries, then from the eighteenth century the state, dragged marriage into the region where the fundamental institutions of our written culture and public life, of which it is now one of the pillars, have their being. It is still there today, despite the centrifugal forces which are acting on it and pushing it towards the region, not exactly of the private, rather of the intimate and the spontaneous. How far will it go in this direction? That is my last question. I shall leave it to the future to reply.

13

The extra-marital union today

André Béjin

In contemporary western society more and more young men and women live together without getting married. Louis Roussel, who has written some illuminating books on this subject,[1] suggests that, since this phenomenon cannot be called 'engagement', 'trial marriage', 'concubinage', 'free union', a new label must be found, perhaps the relatively (for the moment) non-committal one of 'juvenile cohabitation'.

This phenomenon is already quantitatively significant in France. A survey carried out by INED in May 1977 among the age-group 18 to 29 showed that 10 per cent were cohabiting. In the same group 30 per cent of those married had lived together before their marriage, very often with their future spouse. (In Sweden 99 per cent of married couples cohabit before marriage.) In 1977 this type of union was found most frequently among women of 20 to 21 and men of 22 to 23, all fairly well-to-do. Very often the desire or the attempt to have a child leads to the union being 'regularized'.

Roussel's difficulty in finding a label for this phenomenon is enough to show how hard it is to place it in the traditional scheme of reference of conjugality. Are we talking about a 'quasi-marriage'? Should it be seen as a sort of pre-conjugal 'affair'? I think the difficulty arises from the fact that the young who attempt this mode of life are trying, without being aware of it, to reconcile modes of behaviour that our ancient western society and most other cultures have traditionally found incompatible. Philippe

[1] See, especially, Louis Roussel, 'La cohabitation juvénile en France', *Population*, I, 1978, pp. 15–42, and Louis Roussel and Odile Bourguignon *Générations nouvelles et mariage traditionnel. Enquête auprès de jeunes de 18–30*, Cahier 'Travaux et Documents' de l'INED no. 86, Paris, 1978.

Ariès and Jean-Louis Flandrin have emphasized the importance of the great divide between love in marriage and love outside marriage, seeing it as a crucial aspect in the regulation of sexual behaviour up to the eighteenth century, even in certain circles right up to our own time. My aim here is to show that contemporary juvenile cohabitation can look like an attempt to make a synthesis of the almost irreconcilable features of the two sorts of love. I propose to consider nine points of comparison which will help us to distinguish quite clearly between these two modes of social life. I can hardly avoid being rather schematic, ignoring the finer nuances, the short-lived cultural variations that are the very stuff of history. I shall, in fact, be looking at three ideal types of love: a sedate married love, durable and fecund; an extra-marital love, trying to combine passionate love with an avoidance of childbirth; thirdly, young folk cohabiting, determined to win on all counts without making any sacrifices.

First criterion:
The possibility of a lasting union

Married life, in principle, ended only with the death of one of the partners, but the extra-conjugal couple in the past had no prolonged life together, only furtive embraces and fugitive pleasures. Only those who lived in select circles, or on the outside edges of society, could openly cohabit, extra-maritally. Juvenile cohabitation today lies somewhere in between. It is not so ephemeral as the illicit affairs of earlier days; on the other hand it is hardly regarded as a very solid relationship. It is almost as if its duration has to be renegotiated daily by the partners.

Second criterion:
The social ratification of the union

Whether formally contracted in the presence of a civil or religious authority, or more simply ratified by the community, marriage was a rite of passage sanctioned by society, while the extra-marital union, generally regarded as wrong, though occasionally tolerated as a lesser evil, pretty well escaped any ritual treatment. Today juvenile cohabitation receives partial blessing from society. It is not ranked with prostitution or sexual promiscuity, but it does not carry the official, ceremonial character of marriage. It constitutes a sort of preliminary rite foreshadowing the genuine social transformation that marriage entails, and it acquires its meaning only in relation to this further ratification.

Third criterion:
The basic aims of the union

It is well known that in the western world, at the time of the Industrial Revolution, there were restrictions on entry to the matrimonial market-place. The confirmed bachelor was more common than he is today, and the age of marriage was later — a situation hard to understand for those who imagine that, even at that time, people got married for love and the pleasures of love. In fact, although love might spring up between the pair, and even pre-exist marriage, this was not normally the sole reason for a matrimonial alliance. One got married mainly for economic reasons (increasing one's property, begetting children to look after one in old age), or to acquire useful family connections. One needed to insure oneself against hardship, poverty, sickness, but also, if one was a believer, against sin — the lusts of the flesh ('marry or burn', in the words of St Paul). Absence of love or sexual incompatibility constituted no great obstacles to marriage. On the other hand the extra-marital affair was primarily sought after for the pleasures and sexual satisfactions it was capable of providing. It did not have to worry about class distinctions and could disregard considerations of rank and fortune.

Juvenile cohabitation today offers a curious mixture of these rather diverse features. Choice of partner is not much influenced by material considerations. Frequently they are both earning money or receiving allowances from their parents. They are comparatively monogamous, a restriction more cultural than economic. There is not much of the sexual free-for-all that some regard as ideal. Behind this type of cohabitation one senses a concern to guard against those modern ills, loneliness and boredom; but there is also a feverish search for pleasure. Sexual compatibility is seen by cohabitants as the indispensable, nearly all-sufficient basis for their liaison.

Fourth criterion:
The division of labour in a shared existence

Married life, which initiated a partnership in both production and reproduction, implied a fairly well-defined division of labour between the partners, essential for establishing the mutual dependence of their respective contributions. The extra-marital union, on the other hand, more ephemeral and devoted exclusively to sexual satisfaction, called for no such differentiation.

Juvenile cohabitation fluctuates between these two poles: the establishment of a complementarity conducive to a fairly long life together, but one which leads each partner to specialize in certain tasks, and thus lets some of his or her potentialities fall into disuse; and, on the other hand, the search for 'equality', the perfect balance, the occasional illusion of what is kept going by the perfect union of two bodies in a voluptuous embrace. Symptomatic of these fluctuations is an unceasing argument over the form the sharing is to take – the unavoidable disagreements of 'equals'.

Fifth criterion:
How faithful are we expected to be?

Lovers should decide to be faithful to one another, but this was not expected of them as a principle. They did so freely, not in obedience to some moral or religious rule. Husband and wife, on the other hand, were required to be faithful to one another. Of course there were ways of getting round this social imperative, especially for husbands. This is what has been called 'the double standard', strict fidelity demanded of the wife, relative fidelity accepted for the husband. This double standard, so reviled today, was well adapted to the culture and mechanisms of pre-industrial societies. In the last resort it meant that one knew who one's mother was, while one's paternity was a matter of belief. To convert this act of faith into a strong presumption, if not total conviction, all sorts of protective measures were devised, for example the elimination of rivals, surveillance of wives (with eunuchs, duennas, chastity belts etc.), not to mention the inculcation of ideals of self-control (virginity, faithfulness and so on). Things are very different today for reasons we need not examine (e.g. the advance of medical knowledge), but also because husbands have abandoned certain marital and paternal functions to their most dangerous rival, the welfare state. Today a wife finds it much easier to adopt a double standard of morality in her turn, or give free rein to her desires. She knows that the third party in the threesome she forms with her husband, i.e. the state, is there to look after the material and psychological consequences of her behaviour.

Juvenile cohabitation today occupies an intermediate position. It is no universally accepted, let alone observed, standard of absolute faithfulness. On the other hand it is no total moral void. Cohabitants mostly want to be faithful to one another, not merely to honour their commitments, but also because they think fidelity pays. The delicate balance of the 'egalitarian' situation, on which their union stands or falls, tends to increase the danger of reprisals by the 'deceived' partner, hence risking the destruction of their relationship. Cohabitation exists by virtue of a contract whose terms are endlessly renegotiated, and which both parties realize can be broken at a moment's notice. All this tends to make it paticularly fragile, and it has been found necessary to modify the demands of fidelity and go back surreptitiously to expedients which one cannot help comparing to the old 'double standard'. In fact both parties fall back on what one might call a 'dual morality', a morality which to all appearances rests on the dualism of body and mind. On the one hand there may be a purely 'physical' form of sexual behaviour, the simple satisfaction of a bodily desire with the occasional partner without any wish for a lasting relationship, and on the other a total amalgam of carnal and spiritual love.

Women are still believed to find it harder to separate body and mind, though this may change. It is this all-inclusive love which is deemed the most genuine. Consequently the woman's infidelity is a greater threat to the relationship than the man's. This line of argument takes one to the establishment of a new dichotomy, if not between the rights and duties of the two sexes, at least of two types of behaviour. In the realm of so-called physical sexuality lapses need not matter very much, but in that of love — that mixture of sex and sentiment — they are much more serious. So what we are left with is not the ancient hierarchic opposition of carnal versus spiritual, but another, equally sharp dichotomy, which inevitably reminds us of the ancient confrontation.

Sixth criterion:
Ways of expressing feeling

The extra-marital relationship — because it could more easily escape the restraints of the community, because it was often ephemeral and was entirely given over to the lovers' craving for pleasure — was a world where it was easy to behave recklessly, to surrender oneself totally to passion; the world of love at first sight, of utter abandon; a sheltered haven where restraint could be thrown to the winds. In marriage, on the other hand — built to last, to procreate, concerned with inheritances, business matters, family connections — it was much harder to seem to abandon oneself solely to the heart's affections. Love might be there but it had to manifest itself in different ways. A certain reserve had to be maintained, one had to be modest, undemonstrative, at least in public. To show one's infatuation with one's wife in front of others was to reduce her to the level of a mistress, even a prostitute, and thus detract from her honour and dignity. Desire, love and tenderness (that indefinable mixture of the two) could only be shown secretly, in those rare moments of intimacy shared by the couple alone.

Faced with these two totally opposed standards, young cohabitants today try to have it both ways, as if they want to be 'madly in love', but within reason. They express their feelings at once restrainedly and excessively. Restrainedly, in that they do not want, or appear, to be too deeply involved. Excessively, in the way they flaunt their love openly, making no secret of their passion and physical desire for each other. This 'excess' also appears in a requirement of loyalty to each other, of total openness: demands which would probably have seemed improper, even shameless to our grandfathers. Ideally there should now be no secrets between partners, everything should be told, all infidelities confessed, all fantasies divulged, even masturbation admitted. It is a heavy burden to be at once the lover, husband, friend, father or mother, brother or sister, confidante, confessor, to the person with whom one shares one's life. One can well understand why some of our contemporaries look on a relationship that lives up to this ideal, and lasts, as a considerable achievement.

Seventh criterion:
Standards of sexual behaviour

In western societies of the past the physical union of husband and wife was traditionally legitimized in terms of a kind of 'marital indebtedness'. Each was looked upon as the owner of the other, and by right of this could exact his or her due in the observance of various social proprieties, rituals and religious obligations — which could be very restrictive. This was a firmly established right and applied to these two beings, and to them alone.

The extra-marital relationship rested on no such supposition.

There was no socially recognized mutual appropriation of bodies and hearts, only a unilateral or reciprocal loan, usually kept secret. Each retained a total ownership of what it put temporarily at the disposal of the partner, for love, money or any other reason.

Today cohabitants try to reconcile these two ideas. On the one hand they consider that simply deciding to live together does not mean that they have abandoned the full possession and enjoyment of their persons ('our bodies are our own'). Furthermore they consider themselves endowed by nature with the right, albeit abstract and vague, to sexual fulfilment; the right, not to a specific act (e.g. copulation), but the right to a climax, that is to say to the physical and psychological result of all kinds of actions rated as more or less equivalent. One no longer claims one's 'due' rights from one's partner, but the right to 'consummate unrestrictedly' with or without one's partner's help. However, since starting from such assumptions, one can hardly expect any lasting harmony of sexual interests, the cohabitants try to introduce qualifications by pretending to be bound by duties no longer so definite or so clearly defined, such as 'marital indebtedness', but as abstract as the right to 'sexual fulfilment' ('we owe love, fidelity, frankness etc. to x, y, or z, whose life experience we share'). This uneasy attempt at a compromise leads either to a fluctuation between selfish laxity and stern moral restraint, or to a mixture of both.

Eighth criterion:
To procreate or not to procreate

In the extra-marital union the partners could express their desires more openly and unashamedly than in marriage. But one essential act was excluded from this relative freedom — the sexual act itself, particularly in its capacity to lead to pregnancy. Precautions against venereal disease had to be taken, and it seems likely that, originally at least, the use of condoms originated from this necessity. But the avoidance of pregnancy was paramount, which led to coitus interruptus and forced lovers into considerable control of their reflexes during coition.

In marriage, on the other hand, it was less necessary (and for many 'unthinkable', according to Philippe Ariès) to have recourse to such 'cheating', at least prior to the eighteenth century. Social life in the west (at first in France at the end of the *ancien régime*) was heavily affected by the spread of coitus interruptus, which led married life to be infected with extra-marital habits such as the greatest freedom of expressed feeling combined with the greatest physical restraint at the moment of intercourse.

Where the question of pregnancy is concerned, young present day cohabitants do not indulge in any of these types of relationship exclusively, but try to harmonize them. Unlike extra-marital couples of the past, they do not totally exclude the possibility of having children, because it no longer involves, for the couple, and the woman in particular, the consequences that an illegitimate birth could have in the past. Nor is their attitude derived from ideas which once prevailed in traditional marriage. For unless they totally rule out the possibility of a child, the cohabitants like to give themselves a moratorium by postponing its birth. Hence much vacillation between the desire for and the fear of paternity, not to mention maternity. So the birth of a child may be indefinitely postponed without either of the partners plumping for a total refusal of progeny. What frequently happens is the resolution of the dilemma by a period of procrastination followed by an anxious pursuit of conception. They worry about periods, not through fear of pregnancy, but because they want a child; and they are nervous that a long period of voluntary childlessness may lead to real sterility.

Ninth criterion:
The affective environment

In earlier times the emotional atmosphere generated by 'lovers' could not be felt outside their own small world, because normally it was impossible for them to have children or to have their liaison recognized by society. In the case of marriage the emotional territory could be wider and more open. It was hard for a married couple to confine themselves within an 'egoism for two'. The relations, the children, the servants, the friends and neighbours, all formed a network, limiting but protective, of well-defined affective ties.

Today the cohabitants' situation is somewhere in between. their emotional territory is not limited to just themselves, as happens in an illicit liaison sworn to secrecy. It often includes their parents, who frequently accept the situation and lend their help; also their friends. Such temporary appendages as the child and the domestic pet are also admitted, often on an equal footing. In this emotional territory it is certainly the couple, and not the family or the child, who occupies the centre of the stage. The child, however, is not the justification and *raison d'être* of the family so much as its guarantor and cornerstone. An emotional pattern of this kind can lead to difficulties. One constantly hears of the tragedy of young children whose parents have endless rows and finally separate; but perhaps we should also worry about the more private problems of children whose parents love each other too much (or too ostentatiously) and who feel shut out from this love.

Of course it is not only among juvenile cohabitants that the couple occupies the centre of the stage in their emotional territory. Married couples are going increasingly this way. For many homosexuals the word 'couple' stands for an ideal. So it is that this 'tea for two' situation, which in some ways threatens to diminish the circle of normal sociability, exercises a considerable attraction. Anyway what other kinds of 'sexual sociability' do our contemporary communities or bureaucratized crowds have to offer? Mass orgies, rationalized prostitution, professionalized pick up spots. Such activities, born of social levelling and reeking of boredom, can be reduced to two paradigms: the crowd's watchword 'move on' and the queue's 'next please'. As our tutelary state becomes more and more dug in and burdensome, it is not surprising that some people reject the forced nomadism offered to them. The couple that resists the current of time presents a challenge to all these soul-destroying policies of forced displacement and mixing of peoples.

So juvenile cohabitation tries to synthesize the conflicting characteristics of married life and the extra-marital affair. The cohabitants' behaviour is extremely contagious. Young married couples conduct themselves more and more like cohabitants. They postpone having a child; they are fairly permissive about each other's behaviour; they tolerate occasional infidelity, or experiment with conventional forms of it (within a basic fidelity), such as wife-swapping. Others, after a life of random affairs, decide they have had enough and try to organize a retreat into something like cohabitation, for example shacking up with their most favoured connection, though not necessarily for good. The life style of young homosexual couples is rather like that of heterosexual cohabitants of their generation. What is the difference? A child? But we have already seen that the heterosexual relationship, at least at the start, is based on mutual attachment rather than on a child or the desire for one. Is it simply the difference of sex on one side and identity on the other? But when the heterosexual cohabitants stop wanting their union to be based on complementary roles, when the women want to play just as active a part (pro-fesionally and sexually) as their men, earning wages and behaving as their partners' mistresses rather than mistresses of the house and mothers, is there really such an enormous difference?

This similarity between the homosexual couple and the young cohabiting couple is perhaps symptomatic of a deeper yearning. It looks as if these overgrown adolescents who aspire to an 'egalitarian' relationship with their partners of the opposite sex want to find 'the other', and at the same time to find themselves in 'the other'; to be equals, each seeing their reflection in their *alter ego* and finding themselves magically endowed with that little different quality they need to create the perfect figure — autarchic, stable, liberated from the need to perpetuate themselves, androgynous.

14

Changing sexual behaviour in French youth gangs

Hubert Lafont

The unceasing efforts of our society to organize our existence have resulted in indigenous habits and customs, based on ways of life that have slowly developed into a natural culture, being replaced by artificial social patterns dreamed up by philanthropists and social engineers.[1] These efforts have drastically weakened the ability of the working classes to beget and perpetuate a native culture. However, certain groups, usually analysed in terms of their deviance from social norms or of social pathology, and proffered as favourite targets for social workers, have shown a remarkable capacity for side-tracking this sort of enterprise and largely evading the synthetic patterns that people have tried to impose on them.

In certain traditionally working-class districts of Paris there exists an indigenous form of social life, lively, imaginative and well insulated from the outside world. Its members resist conformity, thanks to a dense social and urban environment. The young play a determinant role in this culture, which offers them considerable freedom of movement and a highly communal mode of existence. From the eighteenth century onwards the social life and cultural patterns of such groups have obviously experienced many changes. But they have displayed an astonishing continuity right up to the present day, and what is so striking is that behind

---

[1] The text which follows is based on data collected over fifteen years of observation and work among groups of young adolescents living in the north and east of Paris. It has been written as part of a research project carried out in 1980 by the Groupe d'études des fonctions sociales on behalf of the Direction de la construction of the Ministère de l'Environment et du Cadre de vie.

all these changes a hereditary way of life has reproduced itself and been handed on from generation to generation, all the time preserving its own peculiar characteristics, its vitality and its richness.

To get an idea of what this sort of society is like one should read A. Farge's description of working-class Paris in the eighteenth century, or the realistic descriptions of nineteenth-century novelists and pamphleteers; or again the reports of worried philanthropists, of the teachers and doctors of the Third Republic, or the recollections of music-hall artistes, who drew much of their inspiration from it. All these seem more useful and relevant than the social statistics and other information about life on the fringe that we employ today. It is very difficult to get a grip on the content and form of a mass culture at the very moment it is living and reproducing itself. Basically commonplace and hence hard to grasp, changing and re-creating itself daily and hence completely fluid, it is only when it dies and becomes enshrined in folklore, or sufficiently far off for its details to become distinguishable, that one can think or say anything significant about it. Nevertheless we felt that the best way to direct attention to what goes on in these groups today was to try hard to impose some sort of pattern on a mass of detailed and rather trivial observations.

For it now seems that during the sixties there was a relatively sharp break in the cultural continuity to which we referred above. Adolescents, in particular, now no longer seem to acquire from their working-class birthplace and background the experience they need for their progress into adult life. At the same time they seem to play a diminishing role in the social build up and cohesion of the group from which they spring, a role which earlier on was especially theirs. One still found in the working-class districts of the sixties that those aged between 13 and 25 were provided with a traditional pattern of behaviour based on active social and sexual exclusiveness. With the boys' gangs this was particularly blatant, but it was fairly pronounced among the girls, just as for the group as a whole the culture of social differentiation was the principal means of identifying with a very well-defined milieu.

In a wider sense this identification was initially an assertion of urbanness, that is of being civilized, intelligent, 'clued up': in contrast with the *ploucs* from the country, the provincials, even the Parisian suburbanites. Unlike today, nature or the countryside seemed just a barbaric wilderness, inhabited by savages, who were in no way to be taken as the standard. On the other hand these city-dwellers could easily relate to other urban youth, who set the standard in their eyes. Young street urchins made it a point of honour to set themselves well apart from other groups of young, maybe just as wild as them, whether smart or drop outs, but 'bourgeois', not working-class, young toffs or students, whose appearance and habits they ridiculed. They despised them ostentatiously and regarded their colleagues who mixed with them as traitors, condemned to be expelled from the gang.

Where music, drink or more generally a common aspiration for greater moral freedom were concerned, the young hooligans of the sixties had more or less the same tastes as those other young whom they called *minets* (trendies) — a damning insult — but they were careful not to indulge them in the same way, frequenting none of the same haunts, bistros, *boîtes* or dance halls. They wore their own well-defined type of clothing, used a different vocabulary, smoked different brands of cigarettes and drank different drinks.

This assertion of distinctiveness, by which a group preserves and propagates its group identity, is in many ways traditional. One can find similar antagonisms early in the last century with the 'apaches' and the 'lions', or again round about 1830—40 between the young *voyous* (louts) and the dandies or the students.[2] Within the group, even between neighbourhoods, or more specifically between one block and the immediately adjoining one, this assertion of identity prevailed and grew until one could perceive very small differences, which were, however, sufficiently plain to enable their particular localities and attachments to be distinguished with a high degree of accuracy.[3] This search for an individual identity involved the degree of value attached to personal qualities such as the good, the true, the tough, the cunning, as distinct from the *minet* or trendy values — the beautiful, sophisticated, cultured, learned. Such were the qualities which lay behind and gave meaning not only to sartorial habits, to the sort of drink consumed, to favourite meeting places, but also to everyday behaviour and appearance. The meaning attributed to these qualities and their deployment derived from mechanisms that were far from unique to these working-class groups, but this way of deploying them and setting a high value on some and a rather low value on others was always characteristic of this world.

Cutting across this primary antagonism between working classes and bourgeois, the differentiation of roles and sexual attitudes

[2] For example Gavroche and his little group, Tortillard or the Martial family as described by Sue, or the 'Mohicans de Paris' of Dumas.

[3] For an English parallel see Richard Hoggart, *The Uses of Literacy*, chapters 2 and 3.

between boys and girls was played out around an internal and external conflict in behaviour and spheres of function.

The life of the *mecs* (guys) was lived totally out of doors. From the age of 12 or 13, apart from school, meals and sleep (and more and more frequently as they got older, at their own expense) the boys, willy-nilly, were drawn to live in the street. During the sixties there was no such thing in these neighbourhoods as a street gang after the American fashion with its rules, hierarchies, strict regulations and alliances. The supportive background of the boys' apprenticeship to this sort of life was a closely woven masculine network, a relatively informal horde of cronies, spending most of their time together, growing up in the same social and geographical universe and regulating themselves by customary uncodified rules.

This apprenticeship would be served mostly in the home district, in the street, where most of the time would be spent and where the majority of adults encountered would be men: barmen, café owners and their *habitués*, the local gipsies and tramps; the fair-grounds, flea-markets, scrap-merchants, music-halls, or any other favoured spot frequented by those who had not settled down or who, even after marriage, went on behaving like *mecs*. This small world of the street with its varied perambulations and meeting places had a character which was poles apart from the family — from its authority of course, but also from the sphere in which it had its being and its patterns of behaviour. As a tightly closed circle, sentimentalized and with a fair measure of physical comfort, the family was not the place for a boy: it was only good for kids and girls. When they joined a gang, most of the young boys lost their first names and saw themselves awarded a nickname,[4] followed no longer by a surname but by the name of the locality they came from, which also served as the tribal name of the gang. From now on, any mention of the family was to be banned, and if necessary wide detours would be made to avoid having to meet parents, younger brothers or sisters when on the street with one's pals. The gang network often made it possible to leave one's family for quite long periods, finding food and shelter with friends; or else one lived rough, finding a roof where one could, at the risk of spending several nights out of doors and missing a few meals.[5]

---

[4] Usually by a distortion of the forename — Dédé, Gégé, Nanard, Néné, Piépierre, less commonly by a physical reference — Nenoeil, Zorro, Buny, le Gros. Also Popaul des places, or Tarzan de la porte nord.

[5] A boy's independence of his family and home had long seemed quite natural. In the sixties people had scarcely begun to talk about 'running away' or 'truant children', and even then only in reference to the very young.

In contrast with family life, life in the street was lacking in warmth and comfort. It had no rules, no timetable; it had long periods of inactivity and boredom, sloth and indiscipline, occasionally interrupted by wild adventures. The gang all trailed about together, telling stories, killing time, waiting for something exciting to happen and often trying to make it happen. Often they would launch great expeditions, hell-bent for some adventure, ending up with a collection of raids and daring deeds, cheering each other on, learning how to deploy strength, courage and resourcefulness at much risk and sometimes expense. After such a sortie the piss-ups, beatings up, pick-ups, break-ins, the risks and dangers encountered, the way members of the gang acquitted themselves would be discussed and dwelt on for months afterwards, creating a sort of gang history and folklore.[6] Such a background gave a gang reason for thinking there was something special about itself; and its existence helped the whole neighbourhood to evolve and adapt itself to modern life without losing its identity. The values of the gang continued to be values of the street, exemplified by the unruly lives of the young. The orderliness of family life and its inevitable accompaniment, which meant regular application to a steady job, were accepted only as necessary evils, unhappy and unavoidable necessities that came of growing up. Although these adventures contravened all the family values they were supposed to stand for, even mothers and sisters gained something from them, inasmuch as they preserved and sustained a cultural world from which they themselves felt perforce excluded. So they were quite glad to turn a blind eye, even lend a hand, or simply get the boys to tell them about their exploits, which in turn gave them something to gossip about to the neighbours.

Finally, for the boys, street life was an apprenticeship for working life. Whether pushed out (unofficially of course), or leaving school well before the legal age,[7] boys learned very quickly how to survive on their own, first for pocket money, then for clothes, amusements (outings, drink, magazines, records, bikes or motor bikes), even food. To begin with they would just do such small jobs as cropped up without leaving the streets: picking up

---

[6] The majority of these exploits consisted of totally anti-social activities, held up as signs of delinquency and poor education for over a century. Performed outside their own district, normally entailing no serious consequences, they were taken completely for granted by the milieu, even when it thoroughly disapproved.

[7] In 'Les jeunes délinquants membres des bandes et l'école', a study carried out for Unesco in 1963, young delinquents of between 14 and 17 seem to have had a school attendance record consistently half that of the average for children of the same age.

bottles, clearing a cellar, helping to unload a truck, distributing leaflets, swilling down tiled floors. Even when, a good deal later, they gradually began to look for proper work, the vast majority of the jobs they found were in rather casual or free-and-easy occupations that made it easy to re-create or go back to the rather special 'all boys together' atmosphere of the *mec* world. Keeping well away from big business or office life, these young men would become messenger boys, chauffeurs, ambulance men, truck drivers, removal men, market-stall holders. With a bit of luck they might get apprenticed to a small craftsman, locksmith, plumber, printer or decorator.

Once they were grown up, they would leave the gang, but still try to live close to street life, taking the sort of jobs we have described above, and, even if leading a family life, developing alongside it (and often in a sort of protest against it) the life of the café frequenter, with its rounds of drinks, arguments and masculine ritual, or meeting their old chums in the evening for a game of *pétanque*. Among themselves they would continue to display total disdain for their life at home, nostalgically re-calling past exploits, and in a kind of way revenging themselves on their wives, who had 'got their claws' into them and who from now on would play a major part in their lives. For family life, the home, the housekeeping, were the undisputed world of wife and children. The man had no say in it, even if he was first to be served at meals. This woman who ruled the household had nothing in common with the girl one might have met in the street. She was neither the *minette* one kidnapped from the *minets* as she came out of the *lycée*, nor the girl one picked up at the movies, the dance hall or the café. Nor was she *la grosse* — a purely sexual object — found in village or suburban hops, nor one of those rare *filles de rue* one might find in the course of one's wanderings round the neighbourhood. The good woman, the really nice *nana*, kept well away from the street and all its works, which did not prevent her from gaining as high a reputation at home as the *mec* out of doors.

It was in this closed family world that the girls of the neighbour-hood learned how to become women and experts in all the de-partments of household management. When, quite early on, the boys were packed off to play out of doors, the girls were not allowed out into the street, even within sight and sound of their mothers at the foot of the building. They helped their mothers about the house, they did the shopping, they looked after their brothers and sisters. Their attendance at school was more strictly regulated, and they were only allowed out in company, generally for family visits or to see a girl friend in a neighbouring family. In order to stop being treated like 'kids' and get to know a world outside the narrow one of the family, where they seemed doomed to spend their lives, the girls had, apart from flight (risky, and only possible for very strong characters), only three escape routes: a job, a set-up with some other girls, or a 'fiancé'.

As soon as they were old enough, many managed to find a regular job: they became domestic helps, saleswomen, auxiliary nurses or junior officials. Often they had taken their schooldays rather more seriously than their brothers, and having staked a great deal to gain their freedom they would take internal examinations or educational courses that helped them to gain rapid promotion. The wages they brought home — for there would be no question of their leaving home — as well as the responsibility of character they showed in these worthy, even quite prestigious occupations, afforded solid grounds for demanding more independence. Even then it would be grudgingly accorded, and it was by using her friends, saying they were waiting for her, or by asking them to call for her, that a girl had the best chance of getting permission to go out. It was difficult to refuse if it meant offending a neighbouring family and letting people think that one did not trust one's daughter's chosen friends.

As they grew older, girls got more chances of going out. They would go out in two's and three's, each chaperoning the others. Unlike boys they did not just wander out of doors but left the house to go somewhere definite, meaning a point of departure, particular stopping places and a legitimate objective, all of which they could account for. They might stroll round the neighbourhood, go to the cinema, the ice rink or the fairground. Such trips gave them a chance to cast their eyes over the *mecs*, compare them and tell each other what they had learnt about them. But they were careful to keep out of trouble. For if they dreamed of being noticed by a real *mec*, sharing his glory and moving thus glamorously out of family protection, they knew that the possibility of leaving their family creditably was directly tied up with their reputations as good girls with a clean record. This was one reason why the solution of a 'fiancé', which might seem the most effective, did in fact involve the greatest risks.

The term 'fiancé', was only used because nothing else served. There was no formal engagement. It was a lengthy process, an increasingly assiduous and exclusive series of open visits, recognized and accepted by the whole neighbourhood, but without any clearly observable beginning or end. Marriage usually took place when a child was born, well after the time when the ménage had been set up and recognized as such by the local community. Before agreeing to live thus openly with a boy without being married to him, the 'respectable' girl had to make him give up his street life, his dubious company and his adventures and get him to look for a steady job, if he had not found one already. Only by accepting this kind of domestication could the boy be officially recognized by the neighbours with no loss of reputation for anyone. Boy and girl could then live together, very often within the girl's family, without anyone raising any objection.

Obviously, if a girl prematurely sought the company of *mecs* who were too young, she ran the risk of seeing herself in the course of time being dropped by her boy friend, who would go back to his pals and his street life; and she would be unable to keep him in her home, as convention and her reputation demanded. This would cost her her respectability and the boy his prestige as a *mec*, for having settled down too quickly and too young. Without actually being obstracized by their milieu they could not hope to reclaim the same place and the same role as they had occupied before. So girls had to be careful; this made them suspicious and reserved, even prudish − if not in speech, at any rate in their outings, in the way they dressed[8] and in their attitude towards boys. They kept an eye on one another and grimly defended their reputations.

On their side boys did not take readily to domestic life. In no hurry to return to family life they were not worried by the sexual segregation imposed by their way of life or the lack of opportunity for meeting girls. They preferred gang life and a collective introduction to sex. In the street and particularly in gang company there was a lot of masculine physical contact: they shook hands, prodded and punched each other, wrestled and barged about. This was all highly charged with sex, and their language and conversation was loaded with physically sexual references.

The boys who had been physically plunged into this communal existence, with its exaggerated ideal of virility, developed their own particular brand of machismo. It fell somewhere between homosexuality, which in action would have been a treasonable insult to *mec* standards, and a Don Juanism, which would have swiftly put an end to gang life and its time on the street; and it

[8] Mainly by using photographs, we have found that girls who try to follow fashion take more trouble over their hair and their clothes, and wear longer and less brightly coloured dresses than their contemporaries from *lycées* and colleges.

resulted in a form of sexuality which rested on the group's assertion of its own masculine and heterosexual vigour. This parade of virility in an all-male group gave rise to an ambiguity which the gang did its best to divert or expel. It purged its feelings by means of all sorts of jokes and clowning, both in talk and action. For instance it much applauded miming of lovers' behaviour or take offs of typical homosexual posturing.

Gang life, by its very essence, bred homosexual feelings, but its very intolerance of them caused it to move from jokes for private consumption to a public exhibition of insulting and aggressive behaviour. So a passer-by might have his virility challenged and be provoked into a fight to prove he was neither a *minet* nor a pansy — up to a point the same thing — and to see how his male prowess measured up to those of the gang. Or again the gang might go off on a hunting expedition to places marked down as haunts or pick-up spots for homosexuals. These ritual expeditions would be carried out with a cruelty that left their consciences clear; for they incurred no blame from the neighbours — rather the opposite in fact — and no awkward consequences.

In all this there was no real sexual activity, only an ensemble of behaviour patterns and references that were strongly charged with sexual significance. Being eternally in the company of the gang was narrowly inhibiting, making any progress towards the act of sex very difficult. Such progress was exceptional and could only happen collectively, for example mimed parodies of the sexual act that involved the whole gang and ended with a session of collective masturbation. To the extent that such goings on were simply a form of play activity nobody disapproved or worried about them. The boys (like the milieu as a whole), if taken unawares and not in a joking mood, were fundamentally rather modest in all that concerned their sexuality, their bodies and their nudity.

This very fact of the group's omnipresence and the difficulty of progressing to the sexual act would crop up in the heterosexual relations. Picking up a *minette* was a triumph much to be vaunted, but was likely to remain limited in scope thanks to the total lack of intimacy that gang togetherness imposed. One might tease the girls one met in the street, or lay on a party for them, or a trip to the movies. But the best one could hope to gain from that was a few kisses exchanged under the sarcastic or envious look of one's pals, which would cut short all prospect of any more sentimental exchanges; and, even in this, behaviour had to be regulated according to the conventions of the game with its rules, stages, points scored, winners, records and champions. Occasionally one came across a woman of the neighbourhood, usually rather older than the gang members, who would take it upon herself to initiate them, one after the other. Since it would immediately be known what she had done for one, she could hardly refuse the rest without a drama or a fight. Such women often ended by being regarded as 'public' by the whole neighbourhood; they were looked down on, even maltreated and subjected to all manner of blackmail.

Exceptionally it might happen that a girl acquired the reputation of being 'easy', because of things said about her, or because her general behaviour was seen as provocative, or because she let herself be petted by one of the boys and not the rest. She would be voted a *salope* (bitch) and ran the risk of being carried off, willingly or by force, and raped by the whole gang.

In all such behaviour the act itself was of less importance than the fact that it provided a sort of official recognition of one's membership of a sexual group which only the gang could bear witness to and validate. Women played no part in all this other than as objects of passing fancy or means of showing off; and the gang's jokes and antics ensured that they became nothing more. Once away from her home and her own specific role in it a girl became a *minette*, a piece of goods on a level with the clothes, *mobylettes*, records etc. which the gang treated as common property.

This brief description of a traditional way of life has all the disadvantages of a caricature that ignores the nuances and variety of real life; but it has some of the advantages of a caricature in that it shows up the salient features of this lower-class culture. It was rooted in a milieu that was clearly defined, both socially and geographically; sharply, almost hostilely distinct from other categories; with a pronounced division between the masculine world of the street and the feminine world of the home; a strongly traditional part played by older men, with customs handed down unchanged for generations; lack of interest in, and/or powerful repression of, genuine sexual activities, compensated by exaggerated sexualization of play, social attitudes and language.

Now these traditional characteristics are steadily fading out and yielding place to radically different behaviour patterns all revolving round a single wide and ill-defined model, that of 'youth'. The only criterion for 'belonging' has become age, the only opposition is between age groups; while feelings about sexual, social or geographical distinctions that indicated origin or class are in course of being wiped out.

Today, in the same neighbourhoods, girls go out into the streets as soon as they have reached the age of 12 or 13. They mix with boys of their own age; they come and go late in the evening. They all have the same clothes, the same jewellery, the same hairstyle. The old gangs of earlier days are splitting up into a variegated medley of *copains* (pals) and more and more frequently of *copines* (girl friends), who get together in cafés and discos, often far from home, students and working-class boys and girls all sharing the same tastes in music and clothes, the same crazes for *mobylettes* or motor bikes, doing the same jobs, carrying messages, cleaning windows, etc.

By yesterday's standards this kind of behaviour would not have been tolerated, and gang pressure would quickly have made everyone toe the line. But neighbourhood standards no longer decide what is and is not done. Sharing as they do in a whole series of widespread sources of communication with no particular territorial attachments,[9] the young live in an immediate and ever-changing modernity, with no past or future, and quite unattached to the society of the old and their tradition. The adoption of this 'youth' pattern means that one no longer displays, in a rather aggressive way, one's attachment to a particular social class or even an individual identity, but one follows and conforms to the ephemeral symbols of 'belonging', whose rapid renewal marks the departure of the present into the past, the ageing and the rebirth of age groups.

Boys and girls who follow this model label themselves as 'youth' and claim that they are liberated from all other constraints, moralities or loyalties. By denying any connection with family, social or geographical background, and taking no thought for their present or their future, they squat on the summit of a present that is always renewing itself, like a static traveller who has no point of departure, aim or destination.[10]

In this way of life it hardly matters to which sex one belongs. While behaviour, clothes and appearance become 'unisex', sexual activity is devalued, 'liberated' and shoots out in all directions: masturbation, homosexuality, partner swapping, heterosexual affairs, are to be judged by no other criteria — in principle, at least — than the immediate satisfaction of desire, or the intensity

---

[9] Radio, for example, the more or less specialized newspapers and magazines, the networks of juke-boxes and disc-jockeys, and — more rarely — television.

[10] Note, in connection with these stationary voyages outside time and space, the transformation in traditional types of delinquency among the remnants of the gangs. The mythology of the 'beating up', in its liturgy and language, has been displaced by the liturgy and language of the drug addict, the new archetype of mythology.

of pleasure. Traditional sexuality, genital and socialized, in as much as it depended on the pair bond and hence procreation, on the family and its social milieu, has given way to an eroticism that yields to a sensuality limited only by the extent of its desires and the demands of individual pleasure. Being young is no longer a passing phase of life, nor a social condition, nor an apprenticeship for life. It turns out to be a natural state, owing nothing to anybody but itself. It has to be allowed to run free and express itself in a kind of asocial, amoral and asexual *angélisme* (abnormal desire to escape from the conditions of bodily existence).

The widespread craze for T-shirts, blue jeans and 'kickers', with the fashionable accessories, hairstyles and bleaching, jewellery and badges, all fit in with this attitude. The development of rock music and its dance forms is also significant. In the districts we have described the stars who were most popular in the sixties were idolized as personalities, and their personae identified firmly with the lower-class world to which they claimed to belong.[11] They showed this in their tunes, their themes and their masculine song language, which was very different from the lyrics of their *minet* colleagues and even more so from that of female singers. This type of rock brought out partners of opposite sexes, who played very different roles in the dance. Today the presence of girls in the bands or the existence of entirely female rock groups no longer surprises anyone. The disco and its anti-stars present themselves as explicitly homosexual and the new wave scores hits with a brutal sound, tuneless and formless. Moreover, if one wants to join the dance, there is no need for a partner of the opposite sex. The enjoyment is individual and consists of pulsations, vibrations, intense and powerful — values no longer symbolic, but sensual, explosive and immediate.

The situation of homosexuality, which at the beginning of the seventies was condemned to total secrecy, has in the new conditions undergone a spectacular change. In what remains of the gangs it is absolutely accepted, even approved behaviour. It now decides the evenings out, the choice of clothes and activities generally. The younger brothers of the lads, who used to go to the parks or waited outside 'gay' cafés in order to 'do the queers', now go there 'for the cash', prostituting themselves with the same lack of scruple or sense of shame.

There was no lack of opposition or drama when this change first

---

[11] See, for example, the rapport between Johnny Holliday or Eddie Mitchell and R. Anthony, Adamo or Antoine.

took place. The earliest to adopt the new outlook were gangs without any clearly defined local or social affinity, and they came up against universal disapproval and contempt. There would probably be a great deal to be learnt in unravelling the history of this change. All one would have to do would be to follow up the gradual substitution of the traditional tattooing by the wearing of a gold earring by members of the various gangs. Paradoxically, some even burned their skins with acid when adopting the ring, and these symbolic changes reflect accurately the changes in behaviour patterns in this type of neighbourhood. They also demonstrate their significance and their consequences.

Tattooing is a very ancient practice, an indelible sign of attachment and loyalty. A life sentence no less than a consecration, it is significant that tattooing is associated with prison life or the sea or the armed forces, which restrict men to long periods of purely male company. It is a symbol of virility, initially because of the courage needed to endure for hours, days even, the pain of the tattooer's needle, but also because it is essentially an ornament of muscle, an advertisement for strength. Finally the presence of one or more tattooers, the choosing of a design, the drink taken to reduce pain, turn it all into a ceremonial affair.

The earring is also an ancient tradition in the armed forces, but it signifies something quite different. It symbolizes the freedom of one who has broken away from his background, the emancipated man, the initiate, or among wayfarers the gipsy, the corsair, the conscript returning from the wars. It is an adornment which can easily be taken off. The first hippies coming back from India or Nepal soon changed the simple ring hooked into the ear for more elaborate arrangements consisting of a tube which passed through the lobe and was only noticeable if an earring or some other decorative object was hooked into it.[12] The ring no longer stands for strength, but advertises the presence and importance of sensuality.

The antithesis, sensitive femininity/masculine vigour, has been replaced by 'the naturalness of youth', free and universal, lived not just socially but sensually too. The change has been abrupt and profound, and it is still too soon to calculate its scope, and especially its effect on the cultural traditions of the lower classes and the likelihood of their survival. It will be worth while pausing and watching the situation carefully.

---

[12] This adornment being detachable can be handier than a one-piece earring if one gets involved in a scuffle or one is taken along to the police station.

15

The decline of the psycho-analyst and the rise of the sexologist

André Béjin

Freud discovered 'sexuality' (especially the infantile variety) and invented the science of sex. This statement is of interest in only one respect: it is susceptible to proof or disproof, unlike most Freudian theories. As early as 1905 Freud was acknowledging what he owed to the research of the Hungarian paediatrician, Lindner, and 'the well-known writings of Krafft-Ebing, Moll, Moebius, Havelock-Ellis, Schrenk-Notzing, Löwenfeld, Eulenburg, Bloch and Hirschfeld'.[1] Sexology, the science of sex, seems to have had two births. The first was during the second half of the nineteenth century, the period between two significant dates, 1844 and 1886, the publication dates of two books with the same title, *Psychopathia Sexualis*. The first, by Heinrich Kaan,[2] is little known, and the second, by Krafft-Ebing,[3] is celebrated. The first sexology (or, perhaps, the 'protosexology') was developed during these forty years, being more concerned with scientific definitions than therapeutics, and concentrating on venereal disease, sexual psychopathology (the major 'aberrations' and their connection with 'degeneracy') and eugenics.[4]

---

[1] S. Freud, *Three Essays on the Theory of Sexuality*, London, 1953, p. 135.

[2] H. Kaan, *Psychopathia Sexualis*, Leipzig, 1844. See pp. 34, 41–3 in which Kaan attributes to both orthodox *copulatio* and to *aberrationes* a common origin, the sexual instinct, for which he uses various terms indifferently — *nisus sexualis, instinctus sexualis, Geschlechtsstrieb, Begattungstrieb.*

[3] R. von Krafft-Ebing, *Psychopathia Sexualis*, Stuttgart, 1886.

[4] According to the *Oxford Dictionary* the words 'sexology' and 'sexological' came into currency in the 1920s. As Auguste Comte with 'sociology', did some writer invent the words 'sexology' or 'sexologie', and realize that, in doing so, he was christening a new science? I cannot answer this question with any certainty, but I can provide two

I would be inclined to place the birth of the second sexology, the present day variety, during the 30 years following the First World War say between 1922 and 1948. It was in 1922 that Wilhelm Reich discovered what he called 'the true character of orgastic power';[5] in 1948 there appeared the first of Kinsey's two great works.[6] Between these two dates sexology marked out and defined its central problem, the orgasm.[7] In order to understand the meaning and the significance of this shift of emphasis one only needs to consider these three quotations:

> You must not forget that at the moment we are not in possession of any generally recognized criterion of the sexual nature of a process apart, once again, from a connection with the reproductive function, which we must reject as being too narrow-minded.[8]

---

pieces of evidence. The word appeared in the title of a work which I have been unable to consult, Elizabeth Willard's *Sexology as the Philosophy of Life*, Chicago, 1867. What is probably much more significant is that the expression 'sexualogy' appears, apparently for the first time, in a passage (written in 1885) in *The Ethic of Free Thought* London, 1888, p. 371, by the statistician and eugenist Karl Pearson: 'Not until the historical researches of Bachofen Girard-Teulon and McLennan, with the anthropological studies of Tylor and Ploss, have been supplemented by careful investigation of the sanitary and social effects of past stages of sex-development, not until we have ample statistics of the medico-social results of the various regular and morbid forms of sex-relationship, will it be possible to lay the foundations of a real science of sexualogy.'

[5] In his seminal work of 1942, very different from that of 1927, which has the same title (*The Function of the Orgasm*, London, 1942) Reich chronicles his own research as follows: 'The sexual economy originated within the framework of Freudian psycho-analysis between 1919 and 1923. It broke away from its source about 1928, though I myself did not quit the psycho-analytical organisation until 1934 . . . The discovery of the true nature of *orgasmic power*, the most important part of the sexual economy, made in 1922, led to the discovery of the *orgasm reflex* in 1935 and the discovery of *orgon radiation* in 1939 . . .'

[6] A.C. Kinsey et al., *Sexual Behaviour in the Human Male*, Philadelphia, 1953.

[7] Long before Reich and Kinsey, various writers, Dr Felix Riboud in particular, had certainly provided fairly precise descriptions of the orgasm, but they gave it none of the normative value it acquired later. Roubaud described the *orgasme vénérien* during coition (note the limitation later dropped by Kinsey and others): 'The pulse quickens, the eyes become dilated and unfocussed . . . With some the breath comes in gasps, others become breathless . . . The nervous system, congested, is unable to provide the limbs with coherent messages: the powers of movement and feeling are thrown into disorder: the limbs, in the throes of convulsions and sometimes cramps, are either out of control or stretched and stiffened like bars of iron: with jaws clenched and teeth grinding together, some are so carried away by erotic frenzy that they forget the partner of their sexual ecstacy and bite the shoulder that is rashly exposed to them till they draw blood. This epileptic frenzy and delirium are usually rather brief, but they suffice to drain the body's strength, particularly when the man's over-excited state culminates in a more or less abundant emission of sperm' etc. *Traité de l'impuissance chez l'homme et chez la femme*, Paris, 1855, p. 39.

[8] S. Freud, *Introductory Lectures on Psycho-Analysis*, London, 1963, p. 320.

The function of the orgasm becomes the measuring rod of psychophysical functioning, because in it the function of biological energy is expressed.[9]

The orgasm is a distinct and specific phenomenon which is usually as identifiable in the female as in the male. It has served therefore as a concrete unit . . . Orgasm is distinct from any other phenomenon that occurs in the life of an animal, and its appearance can ordinarily, if not invariably, be taken as evidence of the sexual nature of an individual's response.[10]

Orgasmology

A tremendous development. Instead of the uncertainties of Freud and the Reichian identification of orgasmic energy with organismic energy, and later with 'orgonic' energy, Kinsey provides behaviourist evidence about the orgasm, backed by a body of objectively clear physiological evidence. Henceforth the orgasm becomes a subject for calculation; orgasm therapies multiply; the 'rationalization of sex' is asserted; the influence of the sexologists grows stronger.[11] From now on sexology tends to become nothing more than 'orgasmology' and sex therapy simply 'orgasmotherapy'.[12] To the contemporary sexologist (the 'orgasmologist') what we may call 'perisexual' matters — contraception, pregnancy, abortion, venereal disease — are only of secondary interest. 'Deviance' and 'sexual perversions' have ceased to be focal problems and are not worth getting excited about. He really could not care less about deviance: his quarry is dysfunction. His overriding aim is to wipe out the troubles of 'everyday' sex, which are often contemptibly small but very common. In setting about this task

---

[9] Reich, *The Function of the Orgasm*, p. 299.

[10] A.C. Kinsey et al., *Sexual Behaviour in the Human Female*, Philadelphia, 1953, pp. 45–6 and 101.

[11] See two of my articles which throw light on the social processes that have contributed to the reinforcement of sexology's influence, and analyse the norm of 'ideal orgasm', the precept of orgasmic productivity and communication, and the rule of 'equal shares in orgasmic joy'. A. Béjin, 'Crises des valeurs, crises des mesures' in *Communications*, 25, June 1976, pp. 39–72, especially 53–6, 64. Also A. Béjin and M. Pollak, 'La rationalisation de la sexualité', *Cahiers internationaux de sociologie*, LXII, 1977, pp. 105–25.

[12] Reich appears to be the inventor of the expression 'orgasmography'. See *The Function of the Orgasm*.

of eradication he displays an impressive determination to heal, thus showing how different he is not only from the 'proto-sexologists' of the last century but also from his present day rivals, the doomed psycho-analysts, who have given up pretending to believe that they expect to cure their patients. It is precisely because they have managed to confront the psycho-analysts over the question of therapeutic success that the sexologists are on their way to winning a probably decisive advantage. This advantage is based, as we shall see, on two grounds, helped on by a general decline in the credibility of psycho-analysis: firstly therapeutic success and secondly reference to a whole body of experimental results.

Psycho-analysis and orgasmotherapy

Yet at first sight there seems to be much in common between psycho-analytic and sexological treatment. They both provide a more or less 'personal' form of service,[13] and their fields of action overlap a good deal. In the words of their own supporters it is not their business to deal with the troubles of psychotics;[14] on the other hand the sexual dysfunctions of 'normal' or 'neurotic' individuals are some of the ailments treated both by psycho-analysis[15] and sexology.[16] A fee is usually charged for the treat-

[13] For a social analysis of ideas about 'service' and 'personal service' see, especially, Talcott Parsons, *The Structure of Social Action* and E. Goffman, *Asylums* (1961).

[14] Freud says that, if one wishes to achieve definite results one has to limit oneself to people whose condition is normal (!) . . . Psychotics, the mentally disordered, profound, almost toxic, melancholics, are not amenable to psycho-analysis, at least not as practised so far (*On Psychotherapy*, 1904).

Masters and Johnson state that their Foundation is glad to treat neurotics, but not psychotics. *Human Sexual Inadequacy*, New York, 1980.

[15] See E. Glover, *The Technique of Psycho-analysis*, London, 1955.

[16] Masters and Johnson, *Human Sexual Inadequacy*, propose the following classification which seems likely to be accepted as authoritative:

Principal masculine 'dysfunctions' treated: (1) Premature ejaculation – the man ejaculates too quickly, and in more than 50 per cent of cases withdraws, leaving his partner unsatisfied; (2) Failure to ejaculate (a relatively rare affliction); (3) Primary impotence: erection absent or too brief, so that the patient has never in his life achieved coition with man or woman; (4) Secondary impotence: failure in 25 per cent of attempts of coition; (5) Masculine dyspareunia.

Principal female dysfunctions treated: (1) Primary orgasmic dysfunctioning – a woman who has never experienced orgasm; (2) Contingent orgasmic dysfunctioning, whether or not connected with any specific sexual practice; (3) Vaginismus; (4) Female dyspareunia.

Note that the two American orgasmologists have replaced the current terms 'essential' and 'circumstantial frigidity' (see J. Wolpe, *Practice of Behaviour Therapy*, Oxford, 1982) with 'primary' or 'contingent orgasmic dysfunction'. For the sake of propriety? If so, why not another name for 'impotence'?

ments envisaged, the amount being 'freely arranged' between the therapists and their patients.[17] The therapists are usually but not necessarily doctors. Freud, after saying that 'four-fifths of his pupils were doctors' stated that 'it is no longer possible to keep the practice of psycho-analysis a monopoly of doctors, and to keep out those who are not doctors.'[18] Masters and Johnson recommend that every (mixed) team of 'co-therapists' claiming to follow their methods should consist of a doctor and a psychologist. 'The presence of a doctor makes it possible to undertake very necessary physiological examinations and laboratory analyses without having to drag in a third person. The presence of a psychologist encourages an awareness of the importance of psycho-social factors.'[19] These therapists, psycho-analysts and sexologists are, in principle, freely chosen by patients, strictly bound to professional secrecy, and controlled more or less effectively by their respective associations. Not all would-be patients are accepted: they have to conform with certain conditions which vary according to the therapy required. Circumstances of age, 'intelligence', 'moral development', the seriousness of the illness, motivation, likelihood of a cure, were some of Freud's requirements.[20] For Masters and Johnson the seriousness of the illness is particularly important, as is the solvency of their patients and their motivation; they further insist that couples treated by them should have been directed to them by certain competent authorities, e.g. doctors, psycho-

[17] Freud justified charging for his services by reference to surgeons (a comparison which often recurs in his writings). The psycho-analyst gives specialist treatment and renders a valuable service to his patients. But, in particular, he asserts that 'free treatment produces a considerable increase in resistance' by reason of the erotic transference, 'of a revolt against the feeling of an obligatory gratitude', of a weakening of the desire to get the treatment over quickly.

The sexologists take for granted that, in a market society, they get paid for the services they render, Moreover, they stress as an advantage the powerful motivation of those couples who undergo a fortnight's treatment with Masters and Johnson. These people are prepared to pay 2,500 dollars, plus the cost of the hotel and the journey, and the loss of earnings during this period (W. Pasini, in G. Abraham and W. Pasini (eds), *Introduction à la sexologie médicale*, Paris, 1975, p. 369.)

It is hard to collect evidence on this point, but it seems that the proportion of free treatments was between 15 per cent and 20 per cent for Freud, and 20 per cent to 25 per cent for Masters and Johnson.

These 'good deeds' are less 'gratuitous' than they appear. They provide therapists with three interesting possibilites: (1) to try out new modes of treatment; (2) to see unusual and hence scientifically 'interesting' cases; (3) to anticipate the preparation of therapeutic methods applicable to future 'markets' with a less well-to-do and less educated clientele, who one day ought to benefit from the 'democritization' of these treatments.

[18] S. Freud, *An Autobiographical Study*, London, 1959, p. 70.
[19] W.H. Masters and V.E. Johnson, *Human Sexual Inadequacy*, *op. cit.*
[20] S. Freud, *La Technique Psychanalytique*, Paris, 1975.

logists, social workers or spiritual advisers.[21] Once patients are
accepted they are asked to believe in the possibility of their
being cured, to have confidence in their therapists,[22] to be totally
frank with them[23] and to observe any temporary restrictions
imposed on them.[24]

The fact that the two therapies have so much in common
should not blind one to the fact that there are a number of radical
differences between them. In order to make this clear we have set
out in a necessarily rather brief table a list of ten of the chief
characteristics of these treatments. The reader will find, principally
in the writings of the leading proponents of these therapies, much
fuller information than we can provide in this article.[25]

First of all we should make clear what we mean by the expression
'behavioural (sexological) therapies'. In using it we wish to indicate
that we consider sexological therapy to belong to the category
'behaviour therapy'. There is nothing inevitable about such categorization,[26] but it seems to follow from a scrutiny of a number of
methodological considerations. The term 'behaviour therapy' was
introduced in 1954 by Skinner and Lindsley, and gained wide
currency at the start of the sixties thanks to Eysenck. In fact these
methods derive from a whole stream of theories and experimental
work which, going backwards in time, include Skinner's research

[21] Masters and Johnson, *Human Sexual Inadequacy*.

[22] For the importance of hopefulness and faith, confidence, and the recognition of
the analyst's authority, see Freud, *La Technique Psychanalitique*, op. cit.

[23] S. Freud, *Psychoanalysis and Medicine* (1926).

[24] In Freud's view these restrictions should be applied to some of the patient's sexual
satisfactions, which replace his symptoms ('the rule of abstinence'), to certain reading
(for instance, psycho-analytical works) and to certain important professional and family
decisions (S. Freud, *La Technique Psychanalytique*).

In the Masters and Johnson therapy these restrictions apply basically to relations
between the couple in the course of the treatment, but most importantly to a premature
rather than a gradual search for orgasm, for this risks causing a reappearance of the
distress associated with the disorder under treatment. These two orgasmologists talk
about 'a regime of supervised freedom'. Masters and Johnson, *Human Sexual Inadequacy*.

[25] For psycho-analysis, see Freud, *La Technique Psychanalytique*, but also 'Analyse
terminée and analyse interminable', *Revue française de psychanalyse*, XI, 1, 1939. This
article, written by Freud two years before his death, is important, for it displays a dis-
illusionment over the results of analysis that some have interpreted as an admission of
failure. See also E. Glover, *The Technique of Psycho-analysis*. For certain definitions,
for example *attention flottante, perlaboration*, see J. Laplanche and J.-B. Pontalis,
Vocabulaire de la psychanalyse, 3rd edn, Paris, 1971. For behaviour and sexological
therapies, see J. Wolpe, *Practice of Behaviour Therapy*, and the short article, a virulent
synthesis, by H.J. Eysenck, 'La thérapeutique du comportement', *La Recherche*, 48,
September 1974, pp. 745–53.

[26] This relation has not been formally established by Masters and Johnson. Wolpe
has accused them of not being aware of the principles of conditioning that they put
into practice.

	Psycho-analytic therapy	Behaviour and sexological therapy
Objectives	to reshape the personality, reinforce the ego; eliminate *past* repressions by enlarging consciousness	to reshape behaviour patterns; for example, impotence, frigidity; eliminate *present* symptoms by deconditioning and reconditioning the organism
Therapeutic principles	free association with patient, who must talk with absolute frankness uncovering traumas, complexes and repressions abolition of resistance effecting transference interpretation by analysis perlaboration and self-awareness of patient (possibly, release of tension)	bringing up and analysing the pathogenic conditioning that causes the symptoms, then: *either* eliminates the distress associated with the behaviour that is to be learned – brusquely, by the immersion method, gradually, by the desensitization method (Masters and Johnson) *or* render the behaviour to be unlearned distressing: aversion therapy (possibly, release of tension)
Relations with therapist	usually back to back, with analyst seated and patient on couch	*either* one therapist face to face with one or more patients *or* a couple of therapists face to face with a couple of patients *or* group therapy
Personal and professional background of therapists	often, but not necessarily, a doctor should have undergone technical analysis (and often aptitude tests with a psycho-analytical association)	often, but not necessarily, a doctor (Masters and Johnson have two therapists, one doctor and one psychologist, both 'psychologically stable' and 'free of prejudice')
Attitude to be desired of therapist	benevolent 'neutrality' 'loosely attentive' (Freud) generally without guidance (except in 'active techniques' àla Ferenczi)	benevolent and axiological 'neutrality'; fairly close attention; generally speaking with some guidance
Subject matter dealt with	the patient's free associations, symptomatic actions, failures, dreams	replies to thorough biographical enquiry; patient's observable behaviour patterns (especially sexual)
Methods of treatment	essentially by talking and listening	talking and listening, but, of equal importance, visual stimuli (demonstrations, photos, films), olfactory (partner's aroma, scents), tactile (by mutual corporal exploration in Masters and Johnson therapy)

(*continued*)

	Psycho-analytic therapy	Behaviour and sexological therapy
Supplementary aids	patient recumbent, facilitating relaxation analyst seated, well disposed for listening (back turned to patient, according to Freud)	relaxation techniques pharmaceutical aids, psycho-tropic drugs, hormones, etc. possibly acupuncture, yoga, hypnosis, etc.
Organization of treatment	usually in the analyst's consulting room no pre-arranged programme, relatively little standardization of treatment, accommodated to patient's daily life long duration, 5 to 7 years theoretically unlimited regular, planned timekeeping no definite timetable, but some essential stages, e.g. transference	usually in a clinic (the 'orgasm clinic') treatment organized in advance, often standardized, often cutting into the patient's daily life ('therapeutic holiday-cum-retreat') treatment usually short (Masters and Johnson, usually two whole weeks) regular, fixed timetable: phase 1 gathering information, 2 setting up treatment (different ranges of desensitization) and presenting it to patient, 3 gradual reconditioning with relaxation, 4 evaluation
Levels of success of treatment	usually indefinable, most frequently introspective (some relief of distress, increased self-knowledge)	often definable: introspective, but physiological also (e.g. vaginal lubrication) and behavioural (e.g. control of ejaculation)

from the end of the thirties, that of N.V. Kantorovich, M.C. Jones etc. in the twenties, Watson with 'behaviorism' and Pavlov with the 'conditioned reflex' at the beginning of the century, even Leuret in the nineteenth century and Mesmer in the eighteenth.[27] The basic premise of these methods is that the disorders they deal with (especially 'neuroses') consist of learned and conditioned behaviour patterns, in general 'bad habits'. 'Neuroses are character-ised, essentially, by maladjusted emotional reactions, especially anxiety, and by the various forms of action the individual takes in order to allay this anxiety . . . According to behaviourist theory most of these emotional reactions come from a conditioning process.'[28] 'The discovery that neurotic behaviour is learned has, among other consequences, the advantage that it places responsi-bility for affecting a cure quite firmly on the shoulders of the

[27] This adventurous summary comes from Wolpe, op. cit.
[28] H.J. Eysenck, op. cit. p. 745.

therapist — contrary to the idea, born of the mystique of psycho-analysis, that the patient is responsible for any setback in his treatment (the therapist's failure being thus presumed to be due to the obnoxious resistance of the patient!).[29]

Consequently it is important for these therapists to eliminate the *present* symptoms (and not *past* repressions) by deconditioning and reconditioning the patient's *organism*. There are two possible ways of dealing with the problem:[30]

1 to eradicate the discomfort associated with a behaviour pattern that needs to be learned, by the method known as 'flooding', or gradually by the technique of 'desensitization',[31]
2 to render disagreeable a behaviour pattern that needs to be unlearned, by means of 'aversion' therapy.[32]

The therapy of Masters and Johnson

Both these approaches figure in contemporary sexological therapy. A small minority employ the aversion method in cases of sexual deviance (homosexuality, paedophilia, fetishism, transvestism, exhibitionism, voyeurism . . .[33]). These belong to the 'protosexological' tradition and are not representative of present day sexological practice. The remainder, the majority, have full recourse to modern orgasmology. Their aim is to reduce sexual 'dysfunctions' and they most commonly employ desensitization or kindred methods. Such is the Masters and Johnson therapy which today is regarded as a model of this type of orgasmotherapy. The following are its principal characteristics:

[29] J. Wolpe, *op. cit.*

[30] I have slightly altered the classifications set out by the behaviour therapists themselves so as to clarify the logic of their methods. Note that actual therapies often use a mixture of the methods here shown separately.

[31] Flooding consists of brusquely applying to the patient anxiogenic stimuli in either natural or artificial surroundings and by means of verbal or visual evocations. See J. Wolpe, *op. cit.*
H.J. Eysenck, *op. cit.*, p. 746.
In the desensitization method the therapist first builds up a series of stimuli which induce a feeling of growing anxiety in the patient; then he explains them to him, in the same order, attempting to impart a state of satisfying relaxation.

[32] This therapy consists of systematically associating painful stimuli (e.g. electric shocks and emetics) with certain responses, the commonest being alcoholism, drug addiction, homosexuality, transvestism, fetishism, in such a way that these 'responses', previously productive of anxiety, are weakened and finally disappear.

[33] See J. Wolpe, *op. cit.*, H.J. Eysenck, *op. cit.*, pp. 747–8.

1 For patients who do not live in the St Louis area the treatment, which is intensive and continuous, lasts for two weeks. They stay at an hotel and have to go daily to the Masters and Johnson 'orgasm clinic'. For the patients this is partly a 'retreat' (in the religious sense) and partly a therapeutic holiday.

2 The dysfunctions treated are difficulties in personal relationships, not individual disturbances; hence the treatment is almost exclusively for couples only.

3 In order to limit the chances of transference and countertransference, to encourage communication between patients and therapists (allegedly easier between members of the same sex) and perhaps to lead to more definite identifications, the couple are treated not by one person but by a team of two 'co-therapists' (a man and a woman). Masters and Johnson recommend, as we have mentioned above, that this team should consist of a doctor and a psychologist.

4 The cure has two main stages. The first is of four days during which the therapists begin to gather and impart the information they need to build up their treatment, and also proceed to a first sensory 're-education' of the patients' who are asked mutually to explore each other's bodies, possibly using a scented lubricant lotion. This is followed by a second stage of ten days, in the course of which, by moving gradually from non-genital caressing to genital contacts (masturbation, then coition) the anxiety associated with coition should be eradicated and orgasmic capacity fully restored.

5 The patients have to observe two temporary restrictions essential to the success of the cure (see note 24). Firstly, they must not tell each other what was said during the interviews of the first two days. Secondly, they are forbidden to attempt prematurely, rather than gradually, to achieve orgasm.

6 The organization of the session is as follows:
1st day Interview of each patient with the therapist of the same sex lasting two hours, in the course of which the following points are gone into: description of troubles, assessment of state of marriage; childhood happenings, adolescence, adulthood (particularly any possible traumatic events: incest, illegitimate pregnancies, abortion, rape . . .), the substance of desires, dreams, fantasies; the extent of self-awareness (do you consider yourself desirable?); a review of the patient's sensory equipment − touch, sight, olfaction, hearing.

2nd day Interview of each patient with a therapist of the opposite sex, lasting one and a half hours. This gives a chance of clarifying and verifying some of the points raised the previous day.

3rd day Questions about medical antecedents, physiological assessments, laboratory tests; a 'round-table' get-together of both patients and the two co-therapists; a start on sensory 're-education'.

4th day Discussions of results; further information on the anatomy and physiology of the sexual organs; further sensory 're-education'.

5th day Daily discussions of about an hour at a time during which the therapists comment on the results of the 'practical work' done by the students and teach them certain techniques calculated to help in their particular difficulties (e.g. 'penis compression', vaginal massage, 'favourable' coital positions, learning to control orgasm by attempting a succession of stops 'in extremis', followed by renewed stimulation.)

7 Patients whose treatment ends in what is called an 'immediate' failure (dysfunction persisting after two weeks of treatment) are not kept on. Supervision of this kind could damage further efforts at curing themselves made by the patients, according to Masters and Johnson. On the other hand, all patients whose troubles have disappeared in the course of treatment are subject to a regular 'post-cure surveillance' by telephone. This is so as to assess any relapses, and possibly to encourage patients, who are having difficulties, to start a new treatment. This surveillance goes on for five years, at the end of which a final assessment of the cure's effects is provided, either face to face or by telephone. The figures for 'immediate' (after a fortnight) failures and successes, 'general' (after five years) relapses, failures and successes are recorded and, if necessary, published for every type of dysfunction treated.[34]

So we see that Masters and Johnson used various weapons from the arsenal of behavioural therapy, teaching self-assertion, the correction of erroneous beliefs (for instance, about the effects of self-abuse or female masturbation) and, above all, desensitization (for the gradual re-conditioning of the orgasm). More fundamentally, this orgasmotherapy is based on an unambiguously

[34] See the statistics, but also the self-criticism, relating to the rate of relapses in cases of 'secondary impotence' in Masters and Johnson, *Human Sexual Inadequacy*. Does anyone ever read anything similar in the works of well-known psycho-analysts?

behaviourist conception of sexual dysfunction as being the result of faulty initiation. This is the fundamental conceptual principle that we now propose to examine, in order to demonstrate the basic reasons for the limitations of psycho-analytic therapy as compared with Masters and Johnson's methods and with behaviourist techniques in general.

The therapeutic limitations of psycho-analysis

Behaviour therapy is, in the first place, based on a more 'continuist' picture of the learning and initiation process. It maintains that this process develops from gradual, recurrent, interacting conditioning phenomena. Psycho-analysis, on the other hand, seems to be based on a more 'discontinuist' concept, in the sense that it attaches special importance to aberrations and disjunctive traumas, for example some episode from the distant past, a child seeing its parents making love, the discovery of sex differences, seduction by an adult, the death of someone dear, some accidental occurrence, etc. Hence there is an immediate handicap: the psycho-analyst is more inclined to look for an origin, by encouraging recall, than to change a process by deconditioning.

In the second place the psycho-analysts are less and less interested in affects, particularly anxiety, in order to concentrate their attention on what patients say. They thus deprive themselves of the undeniably effective techniques of 'relaxation' (to use a behaviourist expression)[35] and of breaking down 'muscular rigidity' (in the Reichian sense).[36]

Thirdly, the psycho-analysts claim that they are acting on 'deep causes' by 'restructuring the personality', as the heavyweights among them say, including Freud himself; 'loosening the tongue' say others, jokingly. The lowly task of symptomatotherapy they leave to 'those philistines', the behaviourists. In doing so they fail to realize the autonomy of 'symptoms' in relation to 'causes' a connection, nevertheless, which was stressed by Freud himself.[37] Besides, what grounds have they for announcing that the afflictions eliminated by behaviour therapy are 'only symptoms'? If such

---

[35] See J. Wolpe, op. cit.

[36] It was Reich's opinion that stiffness of musculature was the somatic side of repression and the cause of its continuance.

[37] 'The cathartic method is not to be regarded as worthless because it is a symptomatic and not a causal one'. S. Freud, Studies on Hysteria, London, 1955, p. 262.

[38] H.J. Eysenck, op. cit., p. 751.

were really the case, one would see numerous 'relapses' or 'substituted symptoms' after such therapy, which is not usually the case. In short, one must agree with Eysenck that 'this allegation that behaviour therapists only treat symptoms . . . comes ill from people who never get as far as even treating symptoms.'[38]

Finally, the psycho-analysts, unlike their rivals, have for the most part proved to be totally unable to rationalize their techniques or to formulate and standardize their therapeutic methods. One wonders if they even want to rationalize them. Many analysts seem to want to make their method look like aesthetic activity, pure and uncontaminated by any vulgar considerations of therapeutic efficiency. It started with Freud, who said that an analyst should be, not a technician, but a divinely inspired artist. He should be 'perceptive', he should have 'taste', 'a fine ear', 'tact' and a 'delicate touch',[39] he should have been 'initiated' and 'inspired'. Only then can he be admitted to the mysteries of psycho-analytical practice; for, thus equipped, he need not be regarded as an outsider or a layman, even if he has had no medical training. One can well imagine that compared with this 'sacred art' behavioural therapy can look very prosaic with its cut-and-dried methods and 'petty' calculations of success rates and relapses. The results of this view of psycho-analysis are well known. Analytical treatment, in principle, goes on for ever and the results, which are imperceptible, are uncontrolled. An esoteric aesthetic activity shrouded in an autistic haze, it rejects any measured criticism of its efficacity that may come from the outside world. In the words of Reich and Freud: 'Round about 1920 it was believed that one could "cure" an average neurosis within three to six months at most. Freud sent me several patients with a note saying "For psycho-analysis. Impotence. Three months." . . . In 1923 a year's treatment was considered a minimum. Soon it came to be thought that two or three years might be better.'[40] 'We ought to aim, not at shortening but at deepening analysis . . . Didactic analysis, like the analysis of a sick person, has no fixed limit, is endless . . . At the end of the day the difference between the non-analysed and the analysed from the point of view of the subsequent behaviour of the latter is not so obvious as we might wish, expect or claim . . . But this hardly matters, since if it does not always work out in practice analysis is always right in theory . . .'[41]

[39] S. Freud, *Psycho-analysis and medicine.*
[40] W. Reich, *The Function of the Orgasm.*
[41] S. Freud, 'Analyse terminée et analyse interminable', pp. 14, 16, 32, 35.

Such are the insurmountable therapeutic limitations of psycho-analysis. It may well be that these limitations derive from the fact that in many ways analytical treatment is a second-rate version of behavioural treatment. Thus analysis often comes close to an unsystematic and clumsy 'desensitization' and surreptiously makes use of the phenomena of 'spontaneous remission'.[42] The psycho-analyst also, occasionally, resorts to 'aversion' techniques; for example, when he denies a patient the satisfaction of his desire for transference, he is only adding an 'aversion' stimulus to a response that the patient wishes to dispose of. Finally 'brutal analysis', the undeniable therapeutic effects[43] of which had been emphasized by Freud, resembles the 'immersion' method in as much as it consists of forcibly applying to the patient stimuli that arouse anxiety and resistance.

To sum up, therapeutically more effective and closely linked with advanced experimental research (in sexual physiology and the curative procedures of behaviourism), sexological practice enjoys a higher scientific legitimacy than psycho-analysis. We should now look at some of the wider aspects of the apparently powerful effect of this legitimacy. Let us compare the strength of contemporary sexologists with the influence of sexology in the past and then with rival forces today.

The way the new sexology developed out of the old is character-ized by the interaction of three processes: the strict definition of their sphere of action with a corresponding increase in potential clients; a modification in ways of producing sexual knowledge; and a move from an overall repressive form of supervision to an essentially educational one.

'Sexual dysfunction'

'Protosexology' was basically concerned with the various obstacles that beset the effective functioning of reproductive sex: venereal disease, 'sexual aberrations' and contraceptive methods (closely tied up with these same obstacles). These aims meant that this first sexology was not very different from psychiatry, forensic medicine, urology, etc. Present day sexology, on the other hand, makes strenuous efforts to maintain its separate identity in the face of contemporary disciplines such as psychiatry, forensic

---

[42] On this point see Eysenck, *op. cit.*, pp. 749, 753.

[43] 'To tell the truth, "wild" analysts do more harm to psycho-analysis than to patients'. S. Freud, *La technique psychanalytique*, p. 42.

medicine, neurology, urology, dermato-venereology, endocrinology, gynaecology, psycho-somatic medicine, etc., even if it borrows something from them all. The reason is that this modern sexology has been able to define its main object — the orgasm — and its fundamental norm — 'the ideal orgasm' — in a positive and detailed manner. Protosexology claimed to study, and often to fight against, abnormalities while it could only cast a faint light on what it put forward as the norm — essentially, heterosexual reproductive coition. 'Orgasmology' has a very different approach: it begins with a definition of its norm and from it 'deduces' the abnormalities it proposes to cure. Since the norm, the 'ideal orgasm' of Masters and Johnson's 'Constitution', is an objective that is often empirically unattainable, there are plenty of such abnormalities. Note that modern sexologists do not regard these 'abnormalities' as 'aberrations'. The sharp distinction between normality and abnormality is replaced by a continuum of dysfunction. In the light of the 'heavenly orgasm' we are all suffering from 'sexual dysfunctions'. All this indicates an enormous extension of the sexologists' potential clientele, which formerly consisted of perverts and sufferers from venereal disease. The actual clientele does seem to be steadily coinciding with the potential clientele. The troubles that interested the proto-sexologists are relatively incidental for the orgasmotherapists: venereal diseases are diverted to the dermato-venereologists; the major 'aberrations' are dealt with by the psychiatrists, the psycho-surgeons and, to a lesser extent, by the psycho-analysts and the behavioural therapists. On the other hand, the 'needs' for sexual therapy that are often voiced during consultations with general practitioners, gynaecologists, marriage counsellors, even sometimes ministers of religion,[44] more and more frequently become 'demands' addressed directly to 'sexologists' with special training and with access to such specialist institutions as the orgasm clinic.

Orgasm laboratories

Although empirical and theoretical knowledge of sex continues to be gathered and preserved in the consulting rooms of doctors and gynaecologists, in hospitals and prisons, the real centres for

---

[44] W. Pasini gives the following particulars, which are difficult to verify: 'The RFA doctors consider that 25% of their patients suffer from some kind of sexual trouble. In the United States it is the religious authorities, not the doctors, to whom people go first with their sexual problems' Pasini, *op. cit.*, pp. 97, 101.

our growing knowledge of sex are the orgasm clinics and labora-
tories. These specialized centres have at their disposal very refined
research techniques employing sophisticated equipment (e.g.
telemeasuring and phallometry).[45] In a more specialist environment it is much easier to exercise systematic control on experimental variables, and hence make statements with scientific
validity and produce more detailed and reliable statistics. The
division of labour is much the same as in other fields of knowledge
and is itself accompanied by functional specializations. The centres
of 'basic research' tend to concentrate on scientific innovation
and advanced therapy, leaving standard therapies and the work of
spreading scientific knowledge to less specialized organizations.
Kinsey, some of whose research anticipated the work of Masters
and Johnson, had sensed the coming of these developments. He
would like to have continued his research on the orgasm in the
laboratory, so as to construct a solid experimental basis and
gain scientific respectability for medical sexology and for even
the sociography of sex.[46] On their side, Masters and Johnson
were completely aware of the decisive character and the prior
necessity of fundamental research; so they began their enquiry
into the physiology of the orgasm in 1954, five years before
starting their clinical orgasmotherapy.

The orgasmologist as programmer

Protosexology had developed its own system of classification. Its
aetiology, for example 'sexual aberrations', was brief. As a result
it only allowed for an essentially repressive a posteriori control,
in close relations with institutions such as prisons and asylums.
Orgasmology is a good deal more refined. It continuously improves
its nosography and its aetiology. But it has especially developed

---

[45] Masters and Johnson, in their first book, describe the implement used for artificial
coition as having been created by radiologists. The penis is made of plastic and has the
same optical qualities as a test-tube. The use of white light gives undistorted vision.
Having doubtless found this description rather flat, the French editor added some
enthusiastic notes. 'For certain lonely women M. and J. have provided plastic organs for
insertion in the vagina. Thanks to the magnification of a colposcope they have been able
to follow the change of colour of the mucous membrane and the movement of the
secretions.' And on the cover: 'Dr Masters' establishment has ultra-modern equipment.
For his experiments he uses some of the techniques of telemetry used to monitor the
health of astronauts far away in space.' Unexpected fall-out of the space programmes!
W.H. Masters and V.E. Johnson, *Human Sexual Response*, London, 1966.

[46] On this question, see W.B. Pomeroy, *Dr Kinsey and the Institute for Sex Research*,
New York, 1973, pp. 16, 176—85.

methods of control both a priori and a posteriori that answer to a basically educational aim: such are orgasmotherapy and the prophylaxis of sexual dysfunctions.[47] The prime aim of modern sexology is to remove and prevent the difficulties affecting orgasmic capacity. As this capacity consists of a corporal equipment, and above all a series of programmes in a logic circuit (to borrow a computer expression) for sexual climax, the orgasmologist plays the part of a programmer — on two levels. On the ethical level he lays down a simple norm, the *orgasmic imperative* (not only the right, but also the duty, to have an orgasm) plus the conditions for achieving this norm, which consist in a respect for the principles of 'sexual democracy' (a social contract with climaxes on a fifty-fifty basis).[48]

On the technical level he teaches his patients *orgasmic self-discipline* (i.e. the best manipulatory tactics for achieving the supreme aim, simultaneous orgasm), and this has to be tried out under a regime of 'supervised freedom' according to Masters and Johnson (see note 24). The development of this kind of control with its educational aims is likely to enhance the influence of sexology. Its time-scale is expanding: isolated therapeutic and/or repressive treatments cannot be enough; it is necessary to guard against disorders by prolonged sexual education and to limit the number of relapses by systematic post-cure supervision. It is expanding spatially: orgasmology claims to be able to put an end not only to personal disorders, but also to polymorphous interpersonal ones; it is thus obliged to treat social groups (couples, etc.) and not just individuals, building up, if need be, multidisciplinary teams of therapists so organized as to cope with this change of objective and enlargement of scale.[49]

Without laying too much stress on the distinction, one may

[47] Some therapists of the pre-orgasmological period were already conscious of the pedagogic effectiveness of the treatments they advocated. Thus Albert Moll for the treatment of 'sexual perversions' had perfected a 'therapy of association', which 'bore a close resemblance to pedagogy'. In naming this method, which resorted rather unsystematically to the various techniques of behaviour therapy, Moll had pondered over such expressions as 'pedagogic therapy' and 'psychic orthopaedics'. See A. Moll in Krafft-Ebing, *Psychopathia Sexualis*, pp. 763–81.

[48] For the principles of 'sexual democracy' and particularly on the numerous applications of 'the rule of fifty-fifty enjoyment of climax', see Béjin and Pollak, 'La Rationalisation de la sexualité', pp. 116–25.

[49] In the long run this could lead to a regional policy. A community of 'regional sexology' might have these features: it might use orgasmic productivity as an additional social indicator; it might keep collective records of orgasms; members of the community might be paid for sexual re-education; people could insure against impotence and frigidity . . .

say that sexological control acts less and less by forceful means
(e.g. pressure and repression) and more and more through *information* (e.g. educational indoctrination and ethico-technical
programming). This is deployed as much for pleasure as for
pain.[50] To be more precise, it tends to disregard 'perverted
pleasures' and concentrate on 'unsatisfied desire' and 'aborted
pleasure'. Such a change could have far-reaching and revolutionary
effects as yet unrealized. Without going into detail we may mention
two. The first consists of an extraordinary scientific 'rehabilitation'
of prostitution, which under proper sexological control could
serve to prevent or treat some individuals' sexual disorders.[51] The
other is even more remarkable and consists of a break in the
tradition of treating onanism as a pathological condition, a tradition
enthusiastically supported by Tissot in the eighteenth century.
Reich's attitude, like that of so many others, was still ambivalent:
'None of my patients could claim to be cured unless he was capable
of masturbating without feeling guilty about it . . . I hope it is
understood that this has nothing to do with the superficial "masturbation therapy" practised by many "brutal analysts".'[52] Cooper
is rather definite, if slightly grandiloquent: 'We cannot love another
unless we totally love ourselves to the extent of really masturbating,
to the point of orgasm. We have to masturbate at least once with
full enjoyment . . . we will move towards others when we are
ready.'[53] Contemporary orgasmologists treat this subject in an
unemotional way: they describe masturbation as a source of
orgasmic pleasure which is a priori normal and which can complete,
stimulate, catalyse and supplement other sexual activities: it can,
moreover, be used to cure certain disorders, and even prevent
them — especially frigidity;[54]

[50] Medical science has traditionally seen illness and pain as its *raison d'être*, death
as the enigmatic symbol of its limits, pleasure as a sphere in which it has no control.
The situation has changed in the course of this century. Death and sexual enjoyment
have been progressively drawn into the field of medical skill, with a status approaching
that of sickness and pain. Death is often seen as a major dysfunction whose negative
effects can be limited and perhaps one day 'cured'. Deficiency in pleasure is also classed
as a dysfunction which has to be treated medically. It is interesting to note that the
medicalization of death by the thanatologists and of sexual enjoyment by the orgasmologists seem to proceed side by side.

[51] For the therapeutic advantages of deputy wives, see Masters and Johnson, *Human
Sexual Inadequacy*, and Pasini, *op. cit.*, p. 367.

'Perhaps one day there will be a pool of approved women who will sell their services
to men burdened with sexual problems. At the moment the only way is to find a professional prostitute . . .' J. Wolpe, *op. cit.*

[52] W. Reich, *The Function of the Orgasm.*

The 'therapy market'

So far we have looked at the means by which the sexologist has strengthened his hold on his patients in a way that is increasingly firm, flexible and all-pervading. There remains the question of how he defends his exalted position against the possible encroachments of his rivals, old and new. Generally speaking, it is by means of the segmentation of functions that different groups of specialists manage to maintain their ascendancy. As we have seen, the sexologists succeeded in dominating the *sexual therapy market*. Today they are consolidating their position by weaving a double web, expository and institutional. They have a foot in secondary and even primary schools, where they push 'sex education' which often consists in nothing more than teaching the sexological creed of the moment. They pervade the world of publishing, and the mass media in general, helping to make the public aware of minor dysfunctions and causing sexological jargon to become the basis of idiomatic talk about sex. They even run phone-in radio programmes for sexual confessions which sometimes lead to self-critical sessions, giving much joy to the austerer groups. Finally, they form associations and tirelessly set up orgasm clinics to fight what Masters and Johnson call 'this scourge of society — sexual incapacity'.[55] One day perhaps the community will bear the cost of these efforts.

---

[53] D. Cooper, *The Death of the Family*, Harmondsworth, 1972.

[54] See among others J. Wolpe, *op. cit*. and W. Pasini, *op. cit.*

G. Tordjman, in *Le Dialogue sexuel*, Paris, 1976, pp. 40, 71–7, has given a clear explanation of recent ideas on the subject. In it he shows masturbation as an excellent stage on the way to maturity. It is quite possible that masturbation may be increasingly resorted to and even be seen as the foundation, the infrastructure of all sexual activity. The latter has all the more prospect of being satisfactory if its foundation is solid. Various pieces of socio-graphical research have given prominence to the widespread usefulness of this kind of support (particularly striking where women are concerned, men having already gone further ahead in this field). Such a development would be entirely in keeping with our self-service civilization.

[55] Masters and Johnson in *Human Sexual Inadequacy*, talk of a 'misery' that has to be helped out, a 'scourge' that must be fought, and this recurs in the writings of the other therapy promoters. Freud talks about 'the great wretchedness spread across the earth.' *La Technique Psychanalytique*, p. 140.

According to Reich this sort of categorization has often been used in the past (e.g. under the guise of traditional 'philanthropy') to justify policies of assistance that have been transformed into welfare state administration of different sorts of 'poverty' — material and psychological. What will be done about this new kind of 'poverty', this long unsuspected 'scourge' — sexual inadequacy? (*Character Analysis*).

With an ever-diminishing share of the 'sexual therapy market', psycho-analysis finds itself forced to concentrate on what P.L. Berger has called the 'identity market', or more exactly, as I would put it, the 'identity therapy market'.[56] It seems, in fact, that the only possible 'specific' contribution that psycho-analysts can make, in their consulting rooms, or in the mental health services, or in medico-psychological teaching, is to help their patients to 'know themselves better' and 'achieve self-realization'. One has to admit that this can sometimes be very helpful. Yet, well-established as they are in this market, they are not without competition. For, as in contemporary society physical ease, the ability to integrate painlessly in a group, to 'communicate' readily are becoming vital aspects of personal identity, so new kinds of specialists have appeared who claim to be able to strengthen their patients' identity by means that are not strictly 'logotherapeutic'. These specialists belong to what is called today 'the human potential movement'. The movement, which originated in the United States at the beginning of the sixties, has perfected a whole battery of techniques such as 'encounter groups', 'bio-energy', '*Gestalt*-therapy', etc. One thing they have in common is the stress they lay on non-verbal corporal communication and on group communication. In all this the 'potentialists' seem to be aiming not so much at the 'identity therapy market' as at a newly emerging market that one may call the 'communication and body consciousness market'.[57]

This specialization of functions, which seems to be getting established in the therapy market, does not mean that interdependence between sexologists, psycho-analysts and potentialists cannot develop. To take one example, some orgasmotherapists are now trying to incorporate in their treatments methods borrowed from potentialists and even psycho-analysts.[58] Various combinations of orgasmotherapeutic methods with certain techniques developed by the potentialists may prove profitable by enabling quicker joint treatments (e.g. several couples at a time) to achieve economies of scale and provide a chance of therapy for the ever-growing demand. The 'wild sexologists' and other 'bare-footed healers', who have learnt their job in the field, seem very keen on this sort of collaboration.

[56] P.L. Berger, 'Towards a sociological understanding of psycho-analysis', *Social Research*, 32, 1, Spring 1965.

[57] On all these points see Béjin, 'Les thérapies de l'identité, de la sexualité, de la communication et de la conscience corporelle', *Cahiers internationaux de sociologie*, LVIII, 1977, pp. 363—70.

[58] See Pasini, *op. cit.*, pp. 373—9.

16

The influence of the sexologists and sexual democracy

André Béjin

The scientific authority of contemporary sexologists comes from the fact that they have managed to agree on an empirical, relatively precise definition of 'sexual well-being', a definition arising out of methodical laboratory research. All individuals capable of achieving at will (many sexologists, we shall see, would add 'but without violent effort') that acme of sexual enjoyment that today is called 'orgasm', may be considered to be in good sexual health. One might add, moreover, that an individual's sexual health is reckoned all the more perfect when his satisfactions approximate most closely to the 'ideal orgasm', that is to say the normative model of perfect sexual enjoyment as defined by such sexologists as are, at a given moment, considered to be the most 'competent'. This 'ideal orgasm' can be considered under two complementary aspects: on the one hand by a standard of *measure*, with which one can add up the number of satisfactions,[1] and on the other as the paradigm of a *quality* and *process* of sexual enjoyment, in relation to which one may say of an orgasm that it was 'complete', 'incomplete', or more or less 'intense'.

On the basis of this definition of sexual good health there has been elaborated:

---

[1] I have analysed the circumstances and effects of systematically recording orgasms in articles to which I may venture to refer the reader: 'Crises des valeurs, crises des mesures', *Communications*, 25 June 1976 (especially pp. 53–6 and 64); 'La rationalisation de la sexualité', *Cahiers internationaux de sociologie*, LXII, 1977, pp. 105–25 (in collaboration with Michael Pollak); 'The decline of the psycho-analyst and the rise of the sexologist', ch. 15 above.

1 a formal classification of the different types of orgasmic dysfunction: roughly, premature ejaculation, lack of ejaculation, forms of impotence and frigidity;
2 an etiology of orgasmic troubles, arising mostly from faulty initiation and bad habits;
3 sexotherapies, or more exactly 'orgasmotherapies', which aim at re-establishing orgasmic capacity by means of conditioning techniques derived, in general, from the principles of behaviour therapy;
4 but equally by recommendations of a prophylactic character.

The undeniable fact that their theories and their treatments[2] actually work has contributed to the confidence on which the influence of the sexologists is based. But a lack of initial confidence (or 'motivation', to use Masters and Johnson's expression) diminishes the prospect of a successful result. Today a growing number of people, even though most of them are quite ignorant of the success or failure rate of orgasmotherapy, approach the sexologists in total confidence with requests for help over troubles that earlier were unnoticed, tolerated or submitted to other kinds of treatment; and this because people with this sort of problem find themselves on the same wavelength as the sexologists. So strong is this sympathy that the singular associations of ideas that I am about to describe have occurred widely.

The orgasmic imperative

As we have seen, the orgasm is held up as a measure of good health, and therefore an essential component of 'happiness'. Now, in societies that pride themselves on looking after the well-being of all their members, the individual is supposed to have 'a right to happiness'. It would be absurd in democratic countries living under the benevolent protection of a welfare state not to take full advantage of one's acknowledged rights. There are so many con-

---

[2] Since I have been mainly concerned in this chapter with the theories and methods of the two leaders of contemporary sexology, William H. Masters and Virginia E. Johnson, I shall refer chiefly to their writings, especially the following: *Human Sexual Inadequacy, The Pleasure Bond* and *Sexuality in Perspective*. Also to the French sexologist Gilbert Tordjman's book, which is aimed at a wider public, *Le Dialogue Sexuel, Questions de Madeleine Chapsal*, Paris, Pauvert, 1976. In referring to these works I use the following abbreviations: *Inadequacy, Bond, Perspective* and *Dialogue*.

straints on individual initiative in this kind of society, imposed in the name of 'fairness' or 'equality', that it would seem irrational or merely stupid not to make unrestricted use of all the rights to which we are entitled. Under a system whereby the powers that be are given the responsibility for devising and providing the institutional machinery for the ration of 'mandatory altruism' without which the social bond would cease to exist, it is not surprising that, having paid in full the price demanded for collective altruism — taxes, military service, obedience to the law, etc. — people should be tempted to make full use of all the benefits the state allows them. Not to make use of them is to make a present — invisible, and so no one will thank you for it — to the masses; the masses being seen by a lot of people as a crowd of swindlers and parasites. The collectivization of altruism is bringing about an outbreak of urges; and the absorption by the state of most of these urges has released in its citizens a sort of bad-tempered egocentricity, verging on irresponsibility, which almost amounts to a hatred of their fellow men. The destruction of state property and the abuse of social security are two of the forms taken by this anti-social egocentricity that has been fostered by the collectivization of altruism. In a wider sense, this helps to explain the growing desire to maximize the benefits to be gained from all these rights the state has not taken over, and to transform these rights somehow into 'duties'.

The right to be happy, that is, among other things, the right to an orgasm, is by this same logic transformed into the 'duty of having an orgasm'; and since the authorities who watch over us recognize a right to sexual enjoyment, it would be foolish not to use it as much as possible. It is always something gained — gained from death, from the state, but equally from our fellow beings. Shared orgasm, much more than 'egoism for two', constitutes very often a momentary rejection of social restrictions, a way of cocking a snook at society.

So we are ordered to have orgasms, generally 'break out', become stakhanovites of hedonism. But take care! Don't be loutish and rough! Be nice to your partners and help them to function too!

Before the various waves of sexual liberalization in the twentieth century this orgasmic imperative applied above all to the lawful copulations of married heterosexual men. The most serious dysfunction was the married man's impotence during his repro-ductive years. For women sterility was far more worrying than frigidity. But now, within a few decades, we have seen a vast enlargement of the field in which the orgasmic imperative may be applied, and hence an extension of the sexologist's scope for intervention.

An extension first for woman, whatever her matrimonial status or sexual orientation; for existing norms differ from earlier apparently analogous ones, in that a whole series of constraints which limited the field in which they were valid have been abandoned. This seems quite natural in the perspective of a 'humanism' that tends to scrap certain differences between not only the sexes but equally between ages, classes, nations, races, and to lump the entire race into a mass of 'sexual partners', whose only distinguishing marks are that some function better and more often than others! Dr Masters, during his course of 'preventive action', in addressing five couples who had been married for two years or less, remarked 'men and women are unbelievably and eternally alike. Oh, of course there are some fundamental . . . and fortunate differences, which give us all enormous pleasure (laughter).'[3]

The orgasmic imperative now applies to nearly all periods of life. One must no more delay one's arrival at genital sexuality than one should let one's sexual career come prematurely to an end. Special therapies have been devised for elderly folk who want to go on 'functioning normally'. So far sexologists have kept fairly quiet on the subject of sex in children; this is no doubt because, largely for legal reasons, they have been unable to carry out any experimental work in that field. But they maintain a tolerant attitude towards childish masturbation. They do not approve of paedophilia, which they consider 'asymmetrical' and 'unegalitarian', children seeming incapable of the 'freely given consent' they prize so much.

One must be prepared to have orgasms with partners to whom one is not necessarily married. Sexologists do, on the whole, believe in peaceful domesticity, but it need not be legally connubial. Most of them seem to prefer a rather elastic form of monogamy, or possibly a succession of stable relationships in the course of a lifetime, interspersed with passing affairs. This model has the advantage of providing a settled way of life with emotional security and a deeper relationship, harmoniously combined with the pleasures of variety and novelty.

There are many routes ('positions', 'techniques') to orgasms, and, say the sexologists, we must be ready to use them all. To limit oneself to particular techniques, to use only certain positions is to lose the chance of all manner of interesting possibilities out

[3] *Bond.*

of a craven fear of the unknown. Quite logically, Masters and Johnson point out to their patients that dysfunctions at the time of copulation are not the only ones they have to worry about; there are others too, affecting masturbation, fellatio and cunnilingus.

Finally, orgasms with partners of the same sex are no less legitimate than those with the opposite sex. Homosexuals have the same orgasmic obligations as heterosexuals. If they suffer from dysfunctions they 'ought' to undergo treatment. 'Therapists' write Masters and Johnson, 'will have to admit that homosexuality is not an ailment ... homosexuals have to be treated with the same psychotherapeutic methods, the same medical care, and the same psychosexual objectivity as we apply to the problems of heterosexuals.'[4] The clinic run by these two American orgasmologists actually offers two kinds of 'treatment': one helps to restore normal homosexual functioning for people who have no desire to change their habits, the other helps disgruntled homosexuals to be changed or returned to heterosexuality, with, in the second case, rather more uncertain results.

The whole concept of 'perversion' has been changed. The words 'illegitimate' and 'perverted' now apply to orgasms obtained by an individual in an 'inegalitarian' relationship, particularly if achieved by force. For Gilbert Tordjman 'the only definition of perversion is when there is no emotional feeling between two people copulating, when one uses the other without letting him or her derive any benefit.'[5] As 'normality' means regarding one's body as a property of which one can 'dispose freely', henceforward the standard form of perversion is rape, i.e. grabbing one's pleasure and breaking the rule of fair exchange.

What were formerly called 'perversions' are now viewed as 'variations' indulged in by 'minorities', of whom one should be tolerant. What is all important is to establish fair and equitable relationships and avoid that form of sexual inadequacy — not 'perversion' — that constitutes sexual 'dysfunction'. This has brought about a change in possible reasons for having feelings of guilt: it has become easier, possibly even a cause for pride, to belong to a sexual minority. On the other hand sexual inadequacy may cause guilt. This is all the more frequent now that there are plenty of research results, and especially statistics, on sexual behaviour readily available. 'We give people' writes Gilbert Tordjman 'norms, figures, comparative standards, which start them asking

[4] *Perspective.*
[5] *Dialogue*, 123.

themselves questions . . . Once you start informing people they want to know it all. This is why they increasingly feel the need for professional advice. The mass media have awakened an enormous demand for information in all spheres, particularly the sexual. They are the cause of the sexual "grievance".[6]

Masters and Johnson point out in this connection that in the fifties worry about sexual inadequacy was predominantly a male preoccupation, but research carried out in the sixties showed that women were beginning to show just as much concern about their own performance. Talking freely about sex, which had been a masculine preserve, became a female habit as well, a habit that, unfortunately, was accompanied by the worst of all forms of sexual anxiety — that of being physiologically incapable of functioning.[7] Sexologists are not blind. They are well aware that to some extent their very existence helps to cause the afflictions it is their business to eliminate; but they firmly believe that they are meeting a social need, which always existed and which they have merely uncovered. An analysis ought to be undertaken of the communal ethical presuppositions which have made possible the existence of this pre-adaptation of sexological supply to meet the social demand. The dominance of the sexologist can be studied from the point of view of the experts or of the public. It is probably useful to combine the two methods of approach. Beginning with a study of the supply has the advantage that, as the experts are under much great pressure to explain their assumptions, the enquiry can get more swiftly to the heart of the problem.

Let us take the orgasmic obligation as the central assumption. According to the sexologists it means that every individual should exploit his or her sexual capacities to the full, taking care to keep them in good shape and not letting them lie fallow too long; something which implies a permanent re-education of the faculties and a remodelling of failing capabilities. For individuals to be able to define the 'problems' that face them and overcome them with the help of carefully chosen therapists, they must be able to express themselves adequately by speech or bodily action.

The sexologist as teacher

All patients, whether actual or potential, must be taught to communicate with their partners in total frankness, with no guilt

[6] *Dialogue*, 8 and 40.
[7] *Perspective.*

feelings, ignoring all taboos, in such a way that they can talk about their most secret fantasies, recall in their company, if not practise in front of them, their masturbations, and confess their infidelities without embarrassment. Even that is not enough. W.H. Masters, at the end of the session I mentioned earlier, said to the five young couples: 'From now on there are no taboo subjects. Ask any question you like and we will answer as best we can. Who's going to start?' After a moment of silence he smiles and says: 'So you are all experts?' For the sexologist the answer is obvious:[8] pillow talk, like free association on the couch, can often prove useful, but it is no substitute for interviews carried out by 'real experts' — themselves in fact.

Such interviews will be all the more helpful if the patient has managed to develop his or her own capacity for self-analysis and an unembarrassed use of language about sexuality. He should be able to describe his difficulties in totally unambiguous terms, so colourless that they do not arouse any over-affective reactions. This is the sort of vocabulary provided by a sexual education (especially in school) that is inspired by sexology, and it is deemed the most effective way of satisfying the need for affective neutrality and scientific precision. Sexologists attach very great importance to linguistic usage. Gilbert Tordjman notes that:

'Very often people use childish or slang expressions when talking about sexual organs and functions; this is because they are shy of using the proper words . . . Today children call a penis a penis, if they know the word. If not, as soon as they know it, they use it at once without any embarrassment, which is not always the case with their parents . . . Patients . . . must know . . . the correct scientific terms, otherwise they will have a feeling of inferiority'.

It may be interesting to compare these lines with another passage from the same work. 'A sexual relationship should be spontaneous and playful. One should be able to recover the language of childhood, of the child who is within us all, spontaneous and creative.'[10] What the sexologist is proposing is not a total uniformity of linguistic usage, but a complete separation between an 'up to date', more 'lofty, exact and scientific' vocabulary, sexologically inspired, for use in public, and an 'old-fashioned, childish and

[8] Bond.
[9] Dialogue, 148–50.
[10] Dialogue, 216.

slangy' language to be kept for moments of total intimacy. This dissociation will emphasize the idea that private life is a world of freedom, a haven of legitimate self-indulgence, the domain where speaks the 'real ego', which has to be protected against the encroachment of the outside world, of faceless authorities and compulsory altruism.

Alongside this linguistic education the orgasmologist also finds that he has even to teach anatomy. Tordjman uses strong language about this: 'Every day in my sexological consulting room I find that cultured people of high intelligence are ignorant of the most elementary facts. CNRS research staff, physicists, engineers are all too often quite ignorant of where a woman's clitoris is to be found, including of course their wife's.'[11] Teaching people to know the strategic points, and a correct vocabulary, is only a beginning. The sexologist's ultimate aim is to work upon sexual behaviour itself, to inculcate the best ways of arriving at an orgasm. Among other things this means that patients have to be introduced to various 'sexual aids', contraceptive methods, implements and products designed to stimulate and enhance sensory reaction and, above all, they must be persuaded to use physical techniques that yield the best orgasmic results, particularly masturbation, fellatio and cunnilingus. Some of the better known sexologists have worked out 'sexual career programmes' based on the following theory: any individual who does not masturbate 'sufficiently' during adolescence, or who hesitates to try out varieties of sexual satisfaction that used to be considered 'perverted', such as oral and anal connections, bears greater risk of dysfunction. We have come a long way from the Old Testament condemnation of the crime of Onan. Of course sexologists do not generally see successful autoerotism as the supreme end. All they have done is to turn this former poison, masturbation, taken in small doses at the right moment, into a homoeopathic remedy against copulatory dysfunction in heterosexuals and even homosexuals. Above all, as we shall see, they have attached a quite exceptional importance to masturbation.

Sexologists and sexual democracy

The strength of the sexologists springs from the fact that they have won acceptance of their definition of the common aim of

[11] *Dialogue*, 164.

every sex act, i.e. the orgasm, and of the legitimate ways of achieving this goal. They have also gained recognition of their ability to define, correct and prevent sexual failure, understood as the combination of behaviour patterns which is unable to bring on this orgasm, however hard they try, or which achieves it by illegitimate means.

One might suppose that, with the advance of what I shall call 'sexual democracy', the ordinary man and woman will manage to organize their own sexual lives without difficulty and the power of the experts will melt away. But is this so certain? First of all, what exactly do we mean by the expression 'sexual democracy'? It could signify a state of society characterized by − among others − the following traits:

1 *The rule of reason*: mental attitudes and habits should be controlled by reason. Sexual relations should be 'thought out', even 'calculated' or 'programmed'. Cost and gain should be carefully calculated, with the implication that procreation should be controlled with deliberation, instead of being left to be decided by instinct, habit or the unconscious.

2 *The submission of 'private life' to the control of public opinion*, which should itself be the product of a rational system of education forming part of a 'policy for sex': the 'private life' of individuals would thus be at the same time *more private and more public*, or again more subjected to the control of enlightened public opinion as it gains in privacy. Exposure to the pressures exerted by one's nearest and dearest, relations, parents, children, neighbours, would by this process of privatization be replaced by the obviously more distant, more anonymous, less restrictive influence of the various 'experts', but also by the many professional givers of 'sexual second opinions', all those 'revolutionaries' and 'reformists' who think that 'what is private should be politicized'.

3 *Equality of rights* for partners: that is to say, applying article 1 of the Declaration of the Rights of Man, 'men are born and remain free and equal in rights' to the 'natural, inalienable and sacred rights' of *Homo sexualis*, with the aim of 'sexual happiness for all'.

4 *The greatest possible freedom of expression* in sexual questions, which, in the words of article 11 of the Declaration, can be stated as 'Freedom to exchange (sexual) thoughts and opinions is one of man's most precious rights.'

5 Within any limits imposed by the above rules, the *greatest possible freedom* in all that concerns sexual behaviour consistent with article 4, which allows 'any action that does not harm another'.
6 *Toleration*, namely total acceptance of the idea that others should be free to exercise the freedom allowed them in sexual thought and action.

A society that lived by these rules ought not to be under the thumb of the sexologists. But the fact that the principle of equality of sexual rights is not respected increases their power. Hence individuals who are indifferent to their partner's pleasure can help to cause dysfunctions, thus giving the sexologists reason to intervene. Is not their sway also reinforced by the darkness in which this subject is shrouded, by intolerance, and by the unwarranted restrictions on sexual thought and practice – from which spring ignorance, pathogenic prejudices, inhibitions and guilt feelings? In actual fact, far from the power of the sexologists being threatened by the advance of sexual democracy, it is actually boosted by it. 'Sexual technocracy' like other technocracies, develops, not in spite of democracy, but because of it.

Sexual theories and therapies have been developed since the end of the last century, and particularly since the Second World War, essentially in the west, that is in a period and a region where the ideals of sexual democracy are most widely diffused. So obviously sexological power and sexual democracy are far from incompatible. On the contrary they are closely interlinked. Primarily this is because the diffusion of information, whether descriptive, by which one 'places' oneself, or explicitly normative, with its guide to the orgasm, contributes to make people increasingly intolerant of dysfunction and more and more ambitious in the matter of sexual performance; more sensitive to failures and more dissatisfied at not at once arriving at perfection.

Above all, the demands of sexual democracy impose their own strains on individuals and place them in mutually conflicting difficulties apparently insoluble without the help of a therapist. Borrowing the language of communication theory we might say that they are submitted to an excess of contradictory stimuli, and have to withstand the 'complexification' of sexuality. In order to clarify this point we propose to consider in turn the contradictory injunctions concerning the roles assigned respectively to the *body* and *brain* on the one hand, and to *egoism* and *altruism* on the other.

Programmed spontaneity

Present-day norms tend to provoke a conflict between immediate surrender to the demands of the senses and an increased conscious mastery of the organic processes. This is the outcome of a monist definition of the orgasm combined with a dualistic interpretation of 'sexual rights'. In effect one must be at one with the body, or rather even *be* one's body, so as to allow the pleasure to come of its own accord without the inhibiting control of consciousness, but equally to distance oneself from one's body the better to master what happens to it, both for one's own and one's partner's satisfaction. One must, in other words, abandon oneself to sensation without ceasing to submit one's actions to a rational calculation of 'sexual expedience'. The pleasure should be at one and the same time an absolutely spontaneous happening and a theatrical performance stage-managed by the brain. At the very moment of consummation one has to be both angel and animal, to obey the regulations of sexual democracy while abandoning oneself to the transports of ecstasy roused by the instincts.

It would be wrong to conclude that the body today is more suppressed than ever before, or on the contrary that it has never been so favoured. It is experiencing both treatments at the same time, but at different levels. The fundamental level remains the one defined by the dualist opposition of body and mind. It is hard, even for the most radical monists, to deny the surreptitious re-entry of this antithesis and all that flows from it, chiefly asceticism and intellectualism. Meanwhile, at another level, a monist vision of sexual satisfaction prevails, enshrined today in orgasmological behaviourism, a vision which seems to favour hedonism and sensualism.

So one finds onself instructed to distance oneself from one's body by means of the mind, the better to coincide with the sensations that arise spontaneously in it, to be a spectator of the sexual act without ceasing to take part in it, to be overwhelmed by stimuli while at the same time activating them through the fantasies one has evoked oneself and mastered, expressing oneself 'spontaneously' in the course of actions which have to be programmed and controlled yet in the grip of external forces. To be ascetically hedonistic, sensual in a super-intellectual way, to be both performer and spectator, to be spontaneous while never ceasing to programme each step in one's behaviour, to be independent yet conform with other people's norms, and, we may add, to wish to feel different while all the time subscribing to the ideal of conformism, to yearn for permanence, yet long to drown oneself in the moment, to feel frustrated in satisfaction, insecure in security; these contradictory imperatives, consubstantial with the ethical foundations of contemporary democracy, also prevail in the sphere of sexuality. Yet still another paradoxical injunction calls for our attention, the prescription of egoistic altruism.

A new addition to the rule book: masturbation

Masters and Johnson's treatment is mainly for couples, not individuals. They maintain that orgasmic dysfunctions are basically caused by interpersonal difficulties. However Masters also makes the following remark: 'A moment's reflection is enough to convince one that for the male, no less the female, orgasm is an entirely egocentric affair.'[12] Given this theory, should it be necessary to involve in this 'entirely egocentric' act a partner whose desires have to be given consideration? For Masters the answer is clear: one has to think of every sexual act as a way of giving oneself so as to get something in exchange from one's partner.[13] But does one's partner 'produce' this egocentric orgasm? No, it is not possible for he/she to produce it, since it is an innate act:[14] he/she can aid its coming. If he/she is incapable, fantasies can be provided or substituted. So what is this partner who is at once present (in the preliminaries) and absent (at the moment of consummation), whose place can sometimes be taken by fantasies,[15] and to whom one gives in order to receive? The only definition I can offer is that the partner is the helpful parasite in a fundamentally autoerotic act. The more mindful he is of the other's pleasure, the more you can ignore him and vice versa.

Looked at in this way coition is not a 'communion' but a series of acts of 'communication' between two quasi-monads leading to two moments of pleasure, isolated, but if possible simultaneous so as to 'cancel each other out'. It is neither a pair of egoisms or a pair of narcissisms, but a combination of two egoisms in one climax. According to this eminently humanistic and egalitarian theory, one's partner in love is no more than the catalyst in a masturbatory event, stimulating a sexual reaction at the end of

---

[12] Bond.
[13] Bond.
[14] Inadequacy.
[15] Bond.

which the partner remains almost unaffected. One might say that coition constitutes a sort of autocatalyst in that it creates the very fantasies and stimuli that will act as catalysts.

Such then is the situation in which the ideals of our sexual democrats leave us: in a libidinous quasi-solipsist world of calculating onanists. Such is the result of destroying human relationships, degrees of affection and natural feelings in the world of sexuality; at the end is the idea that every act of sex is nothing but a manifestation or variation of that sole orthodox form — masturbation. Wet dreams, heterosexual, homosexual and bestial copulation, are all varieties of *masturbation catalysed* by a dream, the company of a partner of the opposite sex, the same sex, or an animal. There is no great gulf fixed between these different relationships — particularly between heterosexual and homosexual: they all spring from the same thing — autosexuality.

After this one is obliged to admit that there is a certain 'functional equivalence' between these various forms of sexual catalysts (i.e. men, women, animals, fantasies, aphrodisiacs, 'orgasmogenic implements', etc.) and, at a pinch, they are virtually interchangeable. Here one sees very clearly where egalitarian individualism is leading us, in the world of sexuality as elsewhere — namely to its self-destruction as a form of 'humanism'. For genuine interchangeability cannot be limited to human beings only. We have for some time been invited to treat our fantasies and desires as realities. Fetishes and aphrodisiacs abound in the haunts of avant-garde sexuality. Animals have rights, and so, of course, sexual rights. Perhaps this principle, so dear to the hearts of the egalitarians and the engineers of 'mechanical' sex, that everything is equivalent (a voice is a voice, a hole is a hole), had first to take on the forms already known to us before the dangers that lurk in them could come to light.

It has to be made clear that most sexologists do not subscribe to the extreme conclusions that I have hastily sketched above. Generally speaking they do not claim to be 'liberators', but rather 'liberalizers' or 'liberals'. All the same their ethical presuppositions and their therapeutic methods are not far removed from the ideals I have depicted. Thus, according to Gilbert Tjordman, 'Masturbation provides easy access to a first step in the process of sexual and psychological masturbation which makes it possible to have satisfactory sexual relationships later on. It provides an apprenticeship that logically precedes the training for the real relationship.'[16] This kind of 'logic' is simply a form of behaviourist reductionism.

[16] *Dialogue*, 71.

Moreoever, one is not surprised to find that the same sexologist, in describing the pleasures of copulation, uses the word 'request', whereas another kind of 'logic' might say 'transmutation', for example 'The moment the penis is inserted the physical presence of the partner is felt in its entirety, which ends in what one may call the "request", and which depends on the build-up of a great many sensations.'[17] But perhaps it is a question of 'requesting an orgasm'.

Tordjman goes so far as to suggest a sort of 'sexological crusoeism'. It is well known that infants born on desert islands, growing up in isolation and with identical behaviour patterns, discover their sexuality through masturbation. 'All children, of both sexes, masturbate very early on, in the first months of life.'[18] After this good start they must take care not to slip back, especially at puberty, for 'adolescents who have not been through this stage on the road to maturity suffer much more from sexual difficulties on growing up than do others.'[19] Then comes the time when masturbations are 'requested', and when things go wrong here the sexologist is summoned.

So we are back in the orgasm clinic. It is only a seeming paradox that we have come full circle. Generally speaking there are two stages in the cure. The first lasts several days (four with Masters and Johnson) during which the therapists collect and impart the essential information, and start on the sensory 're-education' of their patients, asking them (they are couples, remember) to explore each others' bodies, but forbidding them any 'premature' orgasm. This is followed by a second, longer stage (ten days with Masters and Johnson) during which the patients should gradually recover their full orgasmic capacity, moving from non-genital to genital contacts (masturbation, then various forms of coition).

As we have seen, orgasmic dysfunctions are helped by the contradictory instructions inherent in the principles of sexual democracy. Individuals are required to have programmed spontaneity and uncontrolled self-control. They are asked to be altruists through egoism and egoists through altruism, to be whole-hearted actors without ever ceasing to be spectators, etc. One reason for the considerable success achieved by sexologists derives from a judicious use of this self-same system of contradictory instructions (rather like the 'double binds' of Gregory Bateson's theory) —

[17] *Dialogue*, 42.
[18] *Dialogue*, 71.
[19] *Dialogue*, 40.

'Be spontaneous!', 'Find your body again by forgetting about it!' etc. The most paradoxical of all these instructions is, of course, the ban on orgasm. The effect of this is to underline the very aim of the treatment, which one is supposed never to discuss, and even to deny, at least while it has not been attained. The objective is no secret, nor is it out of mind, nor forgotten, nor unconscious, but implicit and yet, inevitably, explicit. At the beginning of the cure orgasm is forbidden, in the middle optional, at the end, and before leaving, obligatory. By banning orgasm for a patient who is unable to achieve one, the sexologist is merely ordaining the status quo ('prescribe the symptom' say some sexologists). For the patient this serves a double purpose. It helps to diminish or eliminate the sense of failure associated with inability; and the sexologist in charge at one stroke changes an involuntary dysfunction into an artifically imposed one. And the veto is such that it invites disobedience. 'It occasionally happens,' says Tordjman, 'that some couples will come back after the first session saying they could not resist it; they had sex, and it went very well. In such cases the veto played the role of stimulant.'[20] This is a well-known ploy for dealing with children: encourage what they are doing so as to stop them, and forbid what you really want them to do and they will do it. The same policy seems to work satisfactorily in the world of sexual democracy, but this time with grown-ups. What the experts are saying is roughly 'If you want to improve sexually, you must submit to educational and therapeutic discipline. You reach maturity through a return to childhood.'

Sexual egalitarianism: A questionable utopia

We have just discussed some of the circumstances that have increased the influence of the sexologists. In conclusion I would like to show how much more marked this influence could become if, among the various aspirations that follow in the wake of democracy, the pressure for more equality were to gain increased support. Methods for adapting the facts of sex to the ideals of equality would doubtless be much the same as in other spheres: they would have names like 'rationing', 'controls', 'programming' and so on. The development of state intervention in the realm of public health — especially over contraception and abortion —

[20] *Dialogue*, 64.

shows what might happen in the realm of sexuality if egalitarian doctrines extended their sway.

Just as it is accepted, in the name of fair shares for all, that the public effort in the matter of contraception and abortion should be concentrated on women of the lower classes, who are more exposed to 'dangers' and 'risks' (i.e. having children unintentionally), so, in the matter of sexual health, it would probably be devoted to 'high risk' groups (i.e. sufferers from sexual dysfunctions). These would undoubtedly be subjected to 'remedial' or 'compensatory' sex education, thus exposing to the supervision of the sexologists groups which at the moment are largely out of reach.

Moreover it might soon be realized that we have for too long tolerated 'disgraceful inequalities' in ability to feel sexual desire or power to seduce. Following this, regulations might have to be drawn up exhorting people not previously interested in the subject to start enjoying sex. They might find it pretty difficult to get out of the clutch of the experts before they had finished their 'compulsory' orgasm course. More and more patent medicines would appear in shops aimed at smoothing out inequalities in libido. The drug firms would make a killing. The unattractive and ugly would claim cosmetic surgery so as to make them equal to those favoured with good looks who only copulate with those similarly well favoured. A whole mass of regulations, quota systems, sexual 'services' of a more or less compulsory kind would be set up so that those 'underprivileged' in this respect could profit from the benefits of the sexual welfare state. All this beneath the benevolent eye of the experts, and . . . of the magistrates.

For state control would involve the increasing use of tribunals to decide cases arising from this insistence on absolute sexual equality. Going to law would probably become the usual way for patients to 'get their own back' on their instructors. Not only might one sue one's partner for not observing the principle of fair sexual exchange (husbands and wives already do this), but one could also prosecute one's sexologist for not turning one into an orgasmic athlete, just as today more and more people sue their doctors for not healing them and their dieticians for failing to make them slim.

The demand for equal rights and equal opportunities is a slope which would inevitably lead to a demand for equal performance. Later people might be surprised to find the 'subject peoples' themselves wanting an extension of the 'benevolent' control under which they live. The quotas, the rationing, the controls might not be enough. A whole programme might be called for to eradicate inequalities, to eliminate as far as possible the effects of chance or the accidents which constantly give rise to further inequalities. One might end up by contemplating, as an ideal, the production of one or several varieties of artificial human beings — clones, in fact.

Perhaps this is all rather overstated. I was only looking at the extreme implications of a theoretical model. What one has to bear in mind is that, far from detracting from the power build up of the 'social controllers' of sexuality, the propagation of ideals of sexual democracy is in danger of reinforcing it. So what is to be done? If we derive pleasure from this more or less gentle supervision, which should one day assure each of us the same advantages as our fellow creatures, we must go further and object to the slightest inequality, eliminate the hazards of life, do away with risk and speed on the politicization of sex, as is the way of the totalitarian states. Or else . . .

Index